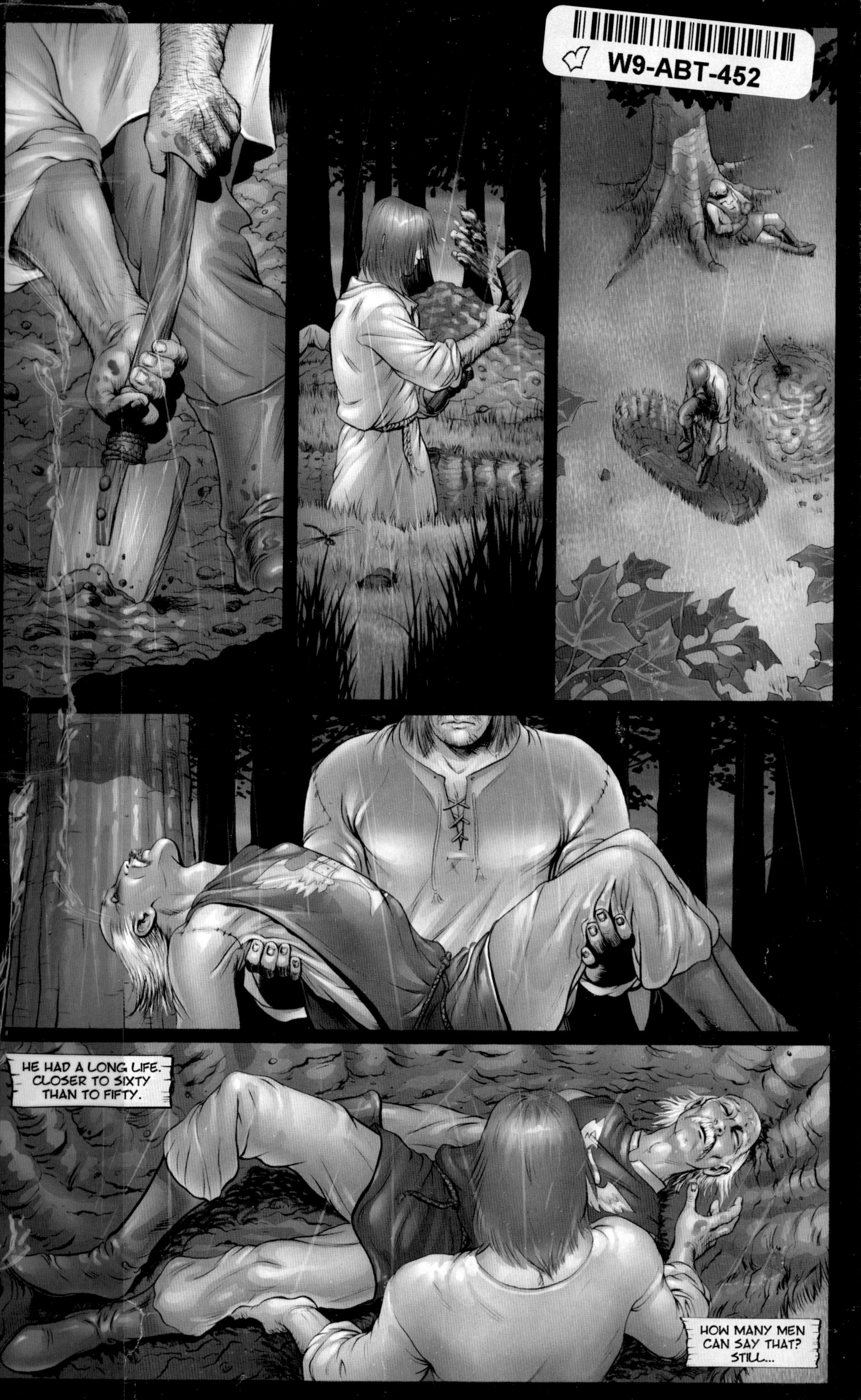
HE HAD A LONG LIFE.
CLOSER TO SIXTY
THAN TO FIFTY.
HOW MANY MEN
CAN SAY THAT?
STILL...

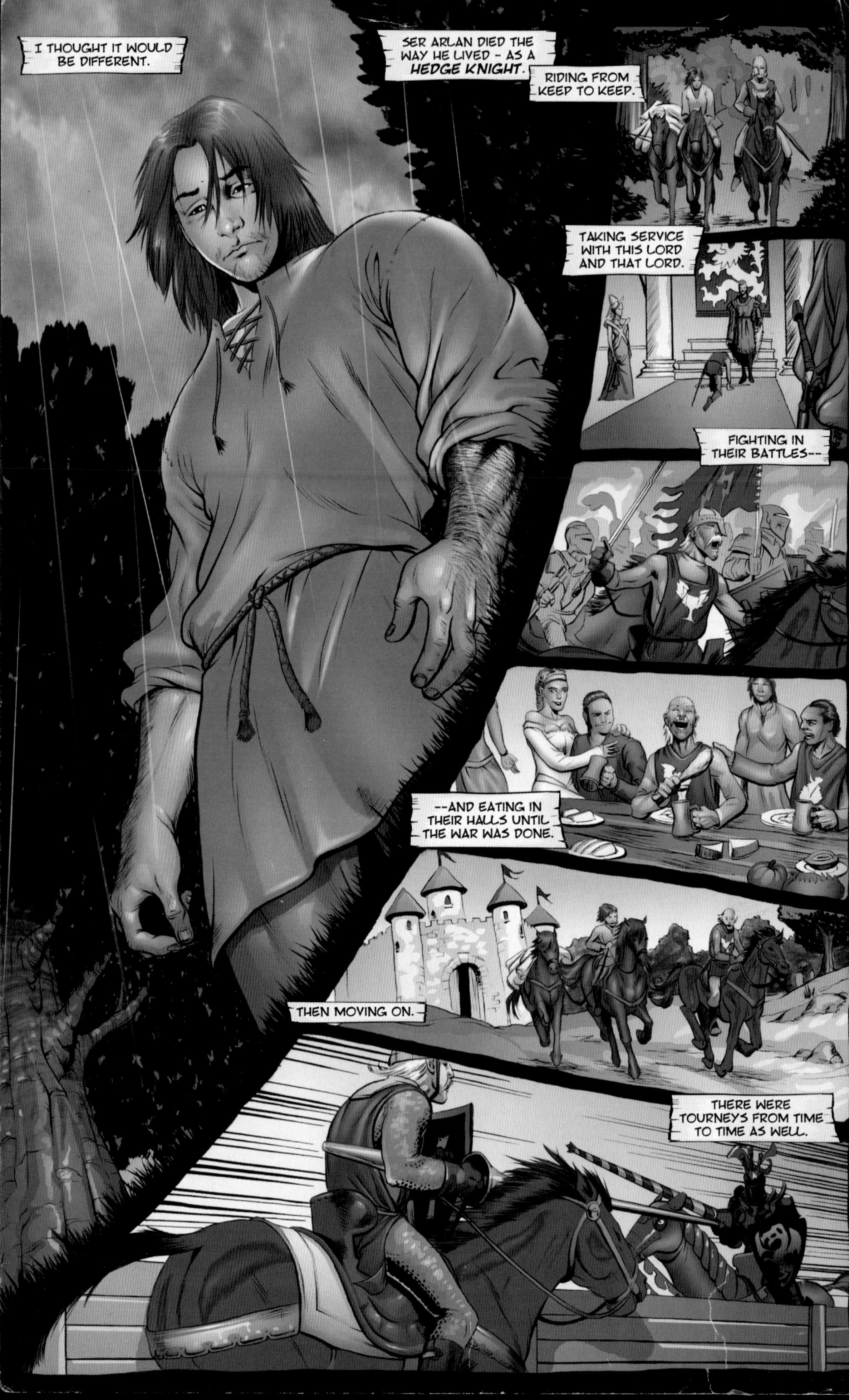
I THOUGHT IT WOULD BE DIFFERENT.
SER ARLAN DIED THE WAY HE LIVED - AS A HEDGE KNIGHT.
RIDING FROM KEEP TO KEEP.
TAKING SERVICE WITH THIS LORD AND THAT LORD.
FIGHTING IN THEIR BATTLES--
--AND EATING IN THEIR HALLS UNTIL THE WAR WAS DONE.
THEN MOVING ON.
THERE WERE TOURNEYS FROM TIME TO TIME AS WELL.

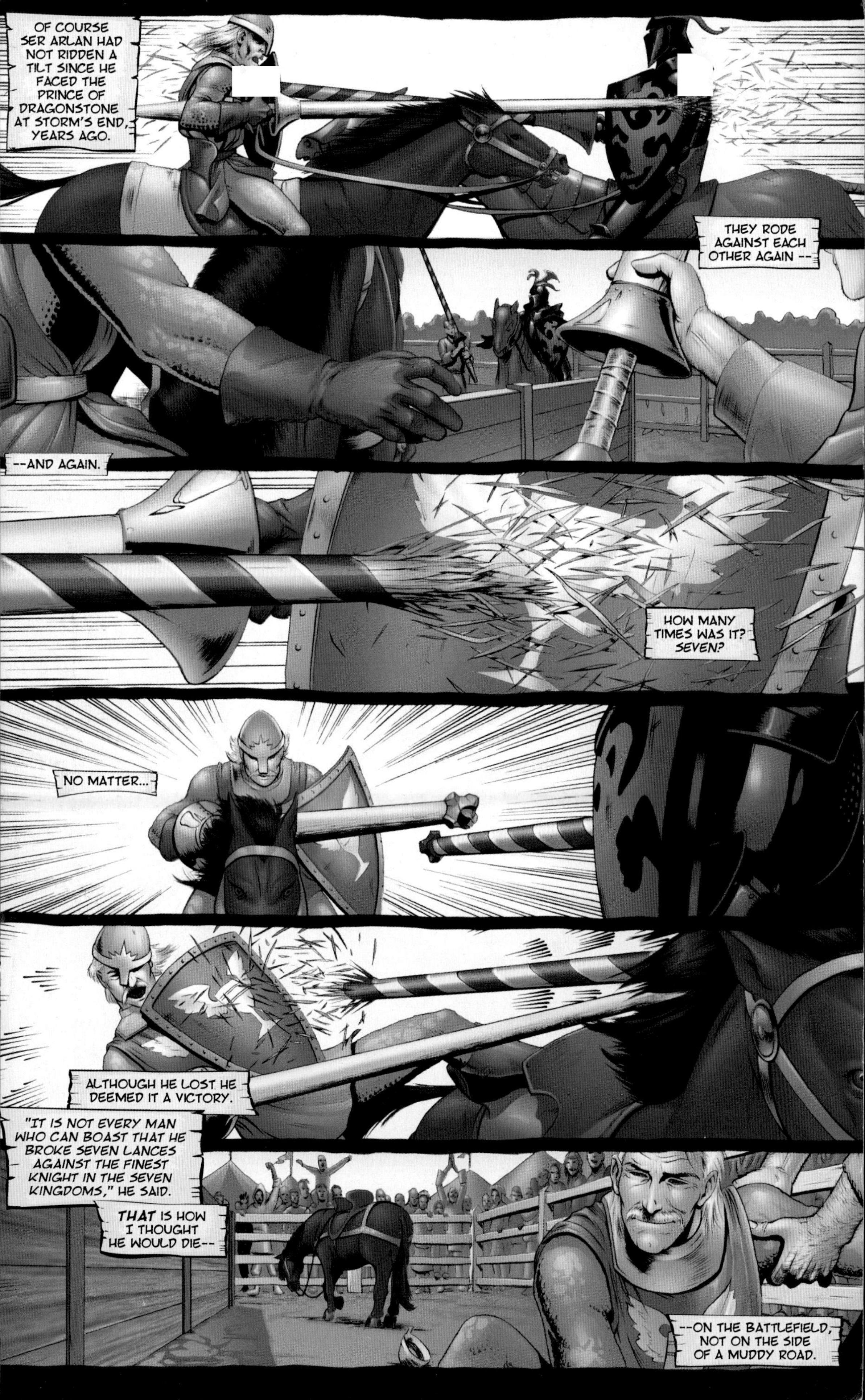
OF COURSE SER ARLAN HAD NOT RIDDEN A TILT SINCE HE FACED THE PRINCE OF DRAGONSTONE AT STORM'S END, YEARS AGO.
THEY RODE AGAINST EACH OTHER AGAIN --
--AND AGAIN.
HOW MANY TIMES WAS IT? SEVEN?
NO MATTER...
ALTHOUGH HE LOST HE DEEMED IT A VICTORY.
"IT IS NOT EVERY MAN WHO CAN BOAST THAT HE BROKE SEVEN LANCES AGAINST THE FINEST KNIGHT IN THE SEVEN KINGDOMS," HE SAID.
THAT IS HOW I THOUGHT HE WOULD DIE--
--ON THE BATTLEFIELD, NOT ON THE SIDE OF A MUDDY ROAD.

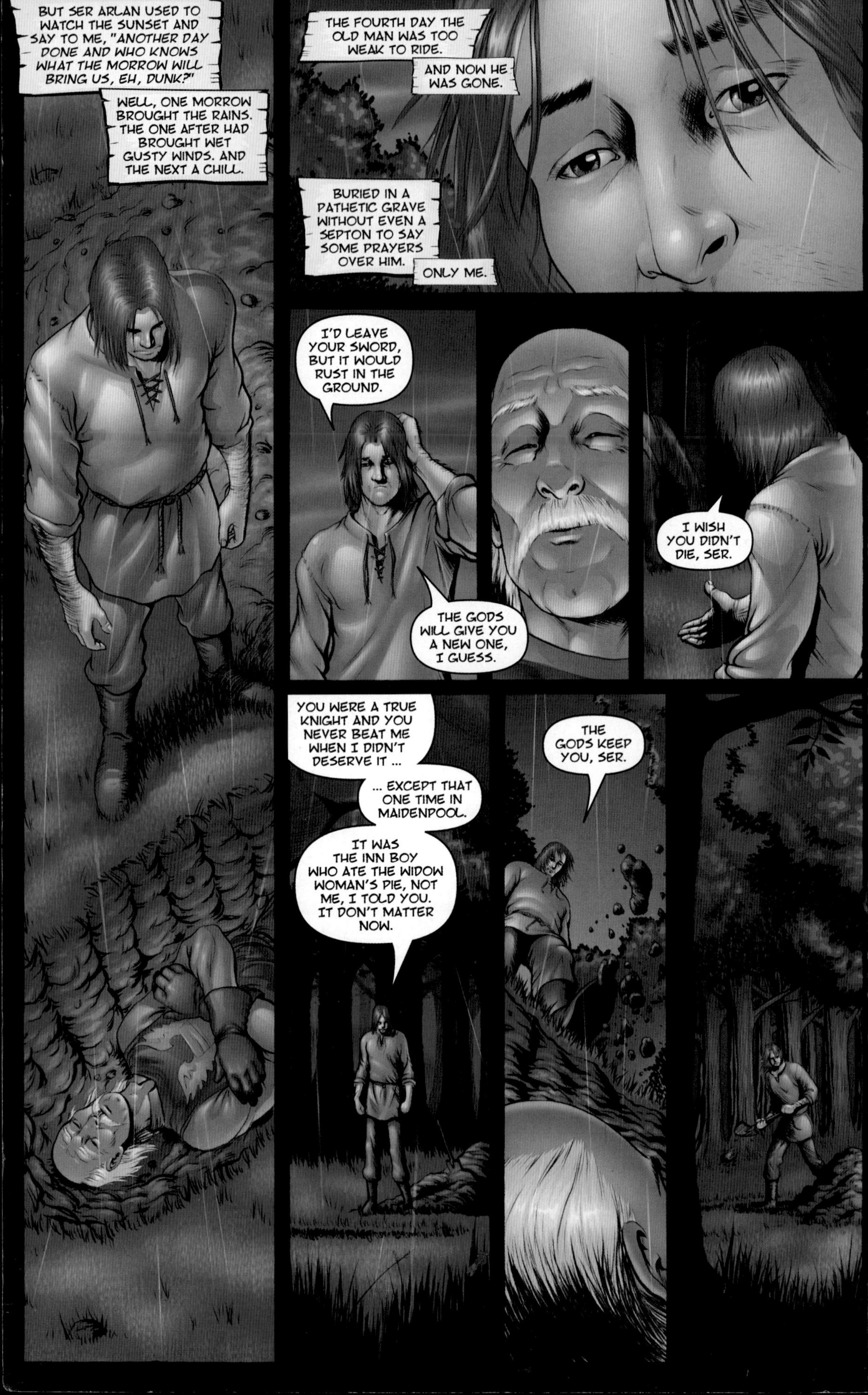
BUT SER ARLAN USED TO WATCH THE SUNSET AND SAY TO ME, "ANOTHER DAY DONE AND WHO KNOWS WHAT THE MORROW WILL BRING US, EH, DUNK?"
WELL, ONE MORROW BROUGHT THE RAINS. THE ONE AFTER HAD BROUGHT WET GUSTY WINDS. AND THE NEXT A CHILL.
THE FOURTH DAY THE OLD MAN WAS TOO WEAK TO RIDE.
AND NOW HE WAS GONE.
BURIED IN A PATHETIC GRAVE WITHOUT EVEN A SEPTON TO SAY SOME PRAYERS OVER HIM.
ONLY ME.
I'D LEAVE YOUR SWORD, BUT IT WOULD RUST IN THE GROUND.
THE GODS WILL GIVE YOU A NEW ONE, I GUESS.
I WISH YOU DIDN'T DIE, SER.
YOU WERE A TRUE KNIGHT AND YOU NEVER BEAT ME WHEN I DIDN'T DESERVE IT ...
... EXCEPT THAT ONE TIME IN MAIDENPOOL.
IT WAS THE INN BOY WHO ATE THE WIDOW WOMAN'S PIE, NOT ME, I TOLD YOU. IT DON'T MATTER NOW.
THE GODS KEEP YOU, SER.

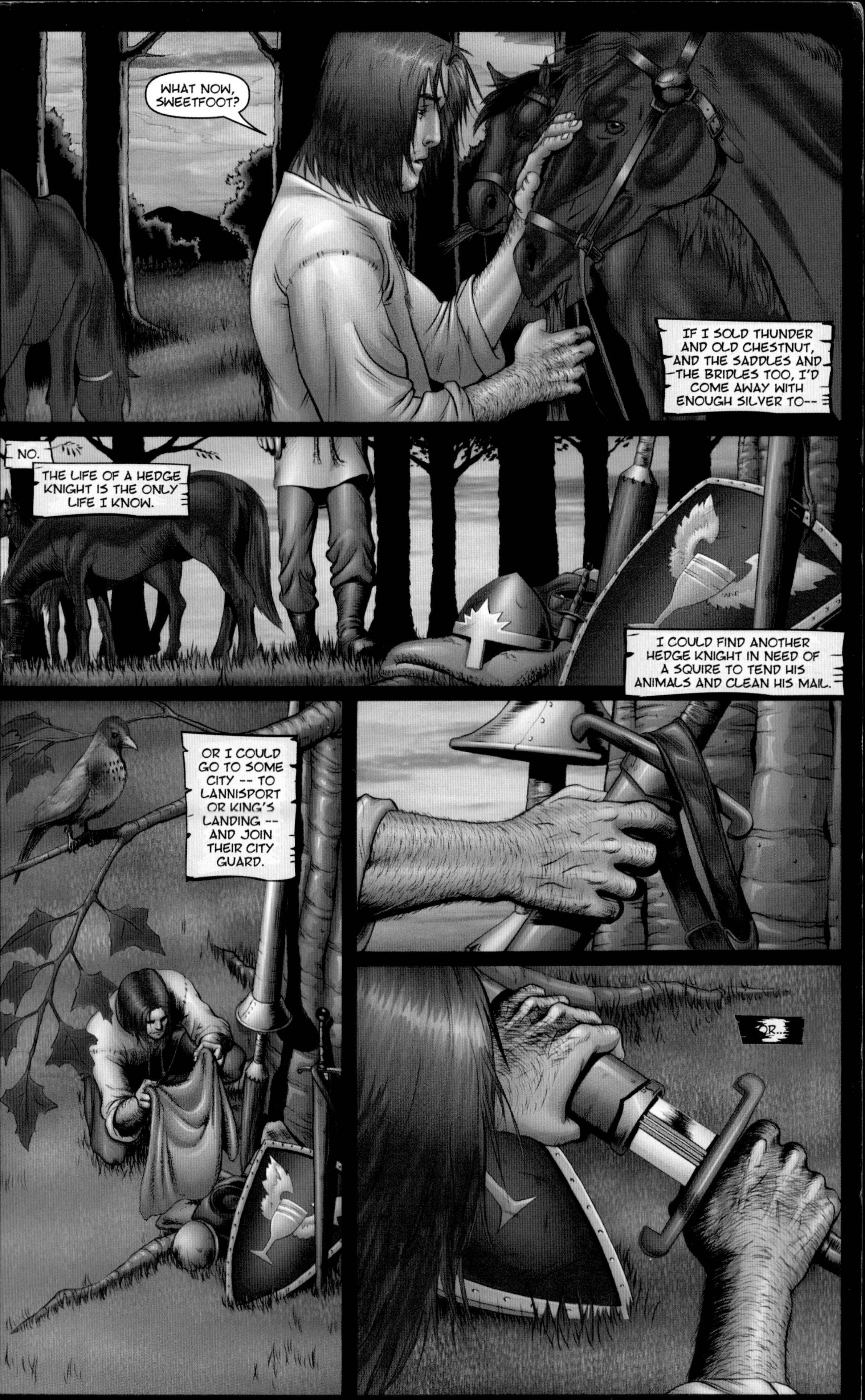
WHAT NOW, SWEETFOOT?
IF I SOLD THUNDER AND OLD CHESTNUT, AND THE SADDLES AND THE BRIDLES TOO, I'D COME AWAY WITH ENOUGH SILVER TO--
NO.
THE LIFE OF A HEDGE KNIGHT IS THE ONLY LIFE I KNOW.
I COULD FIND ANOTHER HEDGE KNIGHT IN NEED OF A SQUIRE TO TEND HIS ANIMALS AND CLEAN HIS MAIL.
OR I COULD GO TO SOME CITY -- TO LANNISPORT OR KING'S LANDING -- AND JOIN THEIR CITY GUARD.
OR...

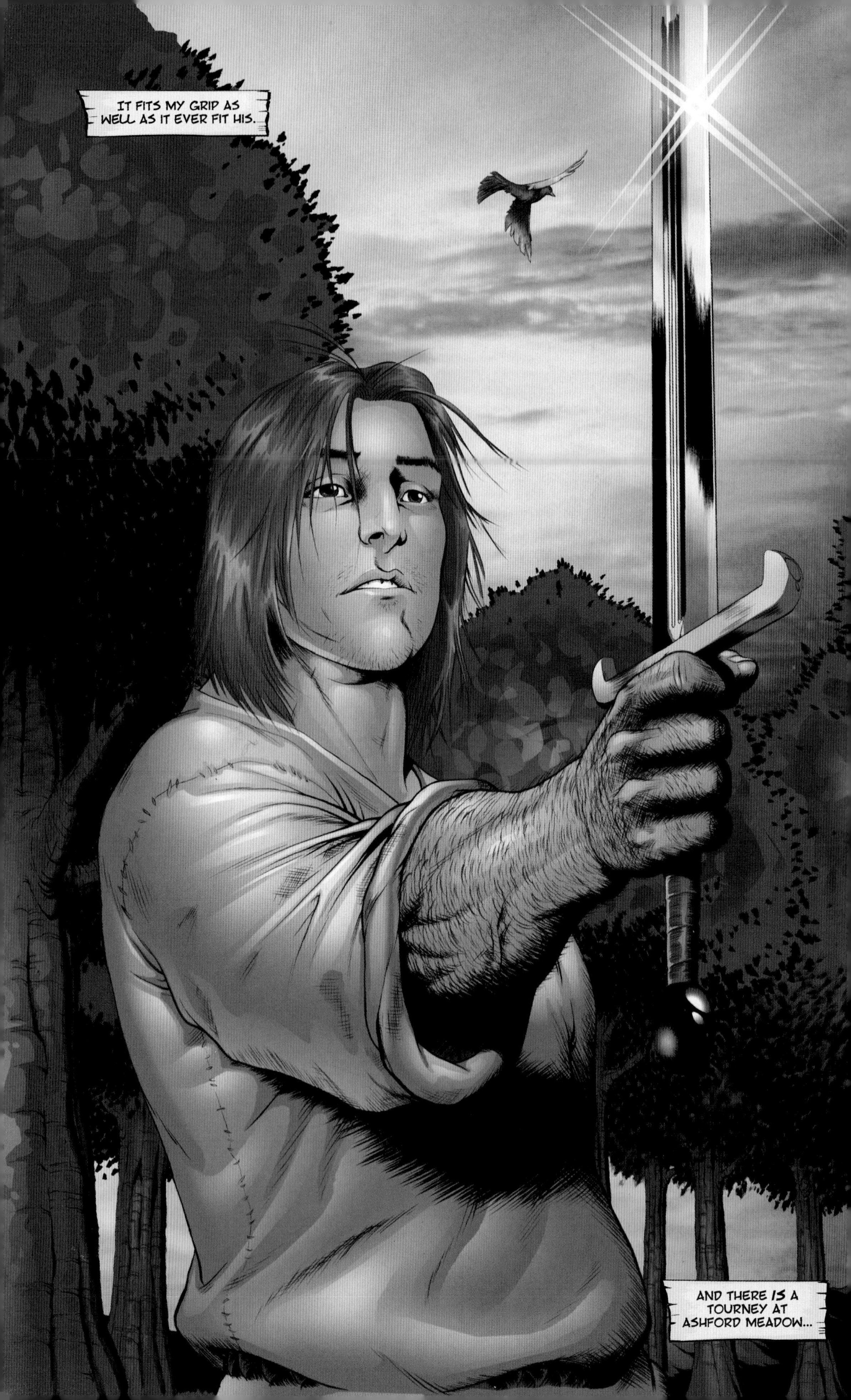
IT FITS MY GRIP AS WELL AS IT EVER FIT HIS.
AND THERE IS A TOURNEY AT ASHFORD MEADOW...

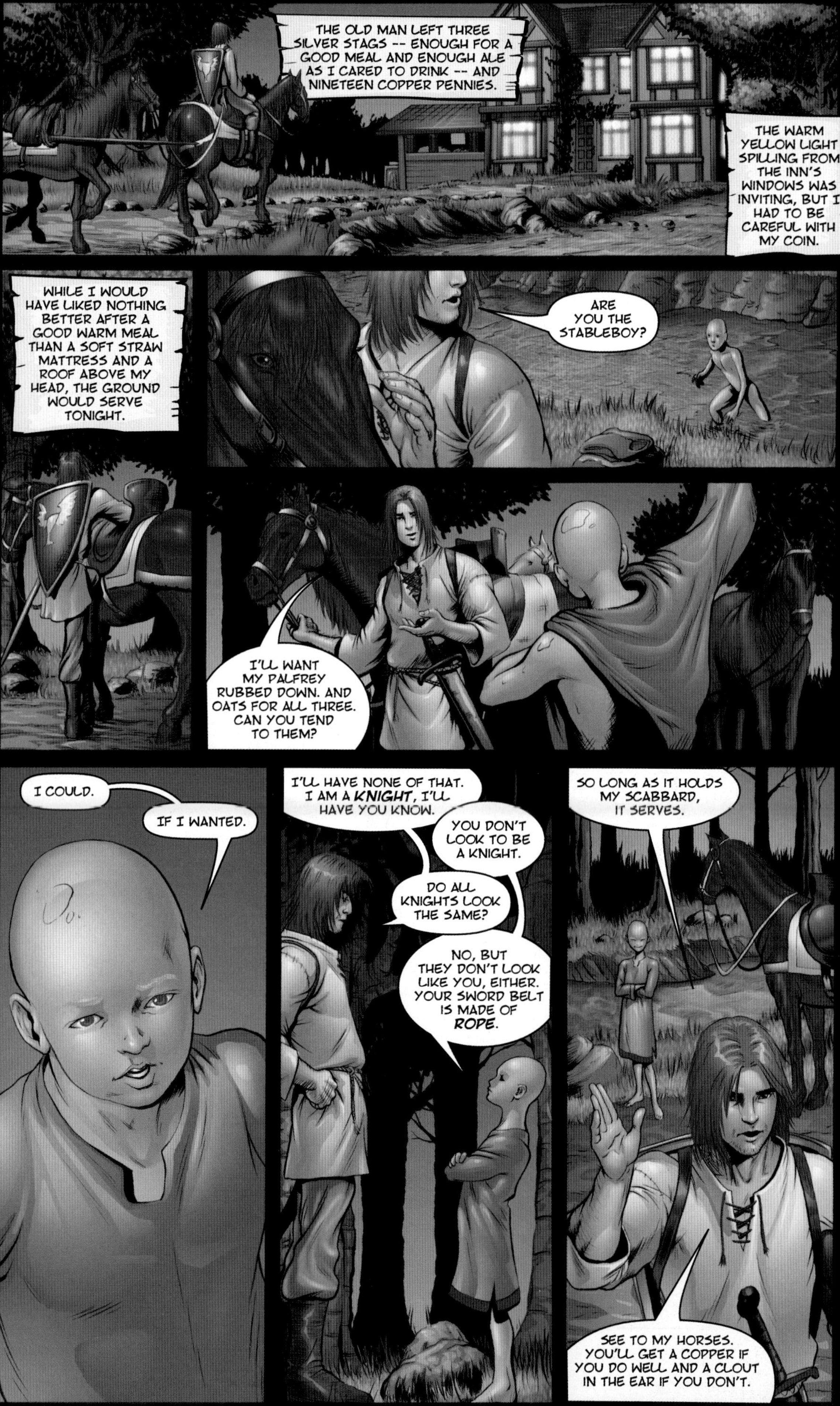
THE OLD MAN LEFT THREE SILVER STAGS -- ENOUGH FOR A GOOD MEAL AND ENOUGH ALE AS I CARED TO DRINK -- AND NINETEEN COPPER PENNIES.
THE WARM YELLOW LIGHT SPILLING FROM THE INN'S WINDOWS WAS INVITING, BUT I HAD TO BE CAREFUL WITH MY COIN.
WHILE I WOULD HAVE LIKED NOTHING BETTER AFTER A GOOD WARM MEAL THAN A SOFT STRAW MATTRESS AND A ROOF ABOVE MY HEAD, THE GROUND WOULD SERVE TONIGHT.
ARE YOU THE STABLEBOY?
I'LL WANT MY PALFREY RUBBED DOWN. AND OATS FOR ALL THREE. CAN YOU TEND TO THEM?
I COULD.
IF I WANTED.
I'LL HAVE NONE OF THAT. I AM A ***KNIGHT***, I'LL HAVE YOU KNOW.
YOU DON'T LOOK TO BE A KNIGHT.
DO ALL KNIGHTS LOOK THE SAME?
NO, BUT THEY DON'T LOOK LIKE YOU, EITHER. YOUR SWORD BELT IS MADE OF ***ROPE***.
SO LONG AS IT HOLDS MY SCABBARD, IT SERVES.
SEE TO MY HORSES. YOU'LL GET A COPPER IF YOU DO WELL AND A CLOUT IN THE EAR IF YOU DON'T.

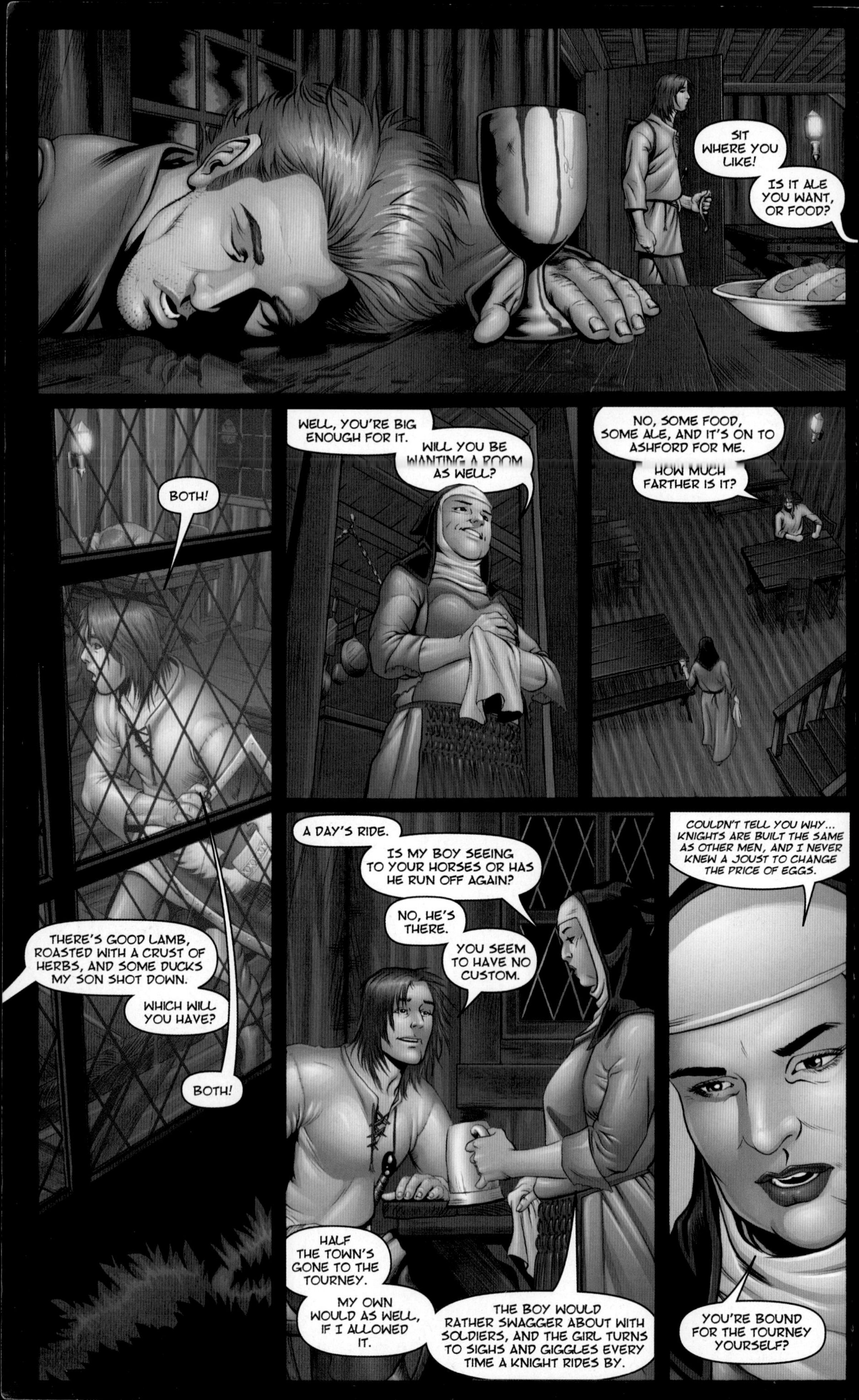

SIT WHERE YOU LIKE!
IS IT ALE YOU WANT, OR FOOD?
BOTH!
WELL, YOU'RE BIG ENOUGH FOR IT.
WILL YOU BE WANTING A ROOM AS WELL?
NO, SOME FOOD, SOME ALE, AND IT'S ON TO ASHFORD FOR ME.
HOW MUCH FARTHER IS IT?
THERE'S GOOD LAMB, ROASTED WITH A CRUST OF HERBS, AND SOME DUCKS MY SON SHOT DOWN.
WHICH WILL YOU HAVE?
BOTH!
A DAY'S RIDE.
IS MY BOY SEEING TO YOUR HORSES OR HAS HE RUN OFF AGAIN?
NO, HE'S THERE.
YOU SEEM TO HAVE NO CUSTOM.
HALF THE TOWN'S GONE TO THE TOURNEY.
MY OWN WOULD AS WELL, IF I ALLOWED IT.
THE BOY WOULD RATHER SWAGGER ABOUT WITH SOLDIERS, AND THE GIRL TURNS TO SIGHS AND GIGGLES EVERY TIME A KNIGHT RIDES BY.
COULDN'T TELL YOU WHY... KNIGHTS ARE BUILT THE SAME AS OTHER MEN, AND I NEVER KNEW A JOUST TO CHANGE THE PRICE OF EGGS.
YOU'RE BOUND FOR THE TOURNEY YOURSELF?

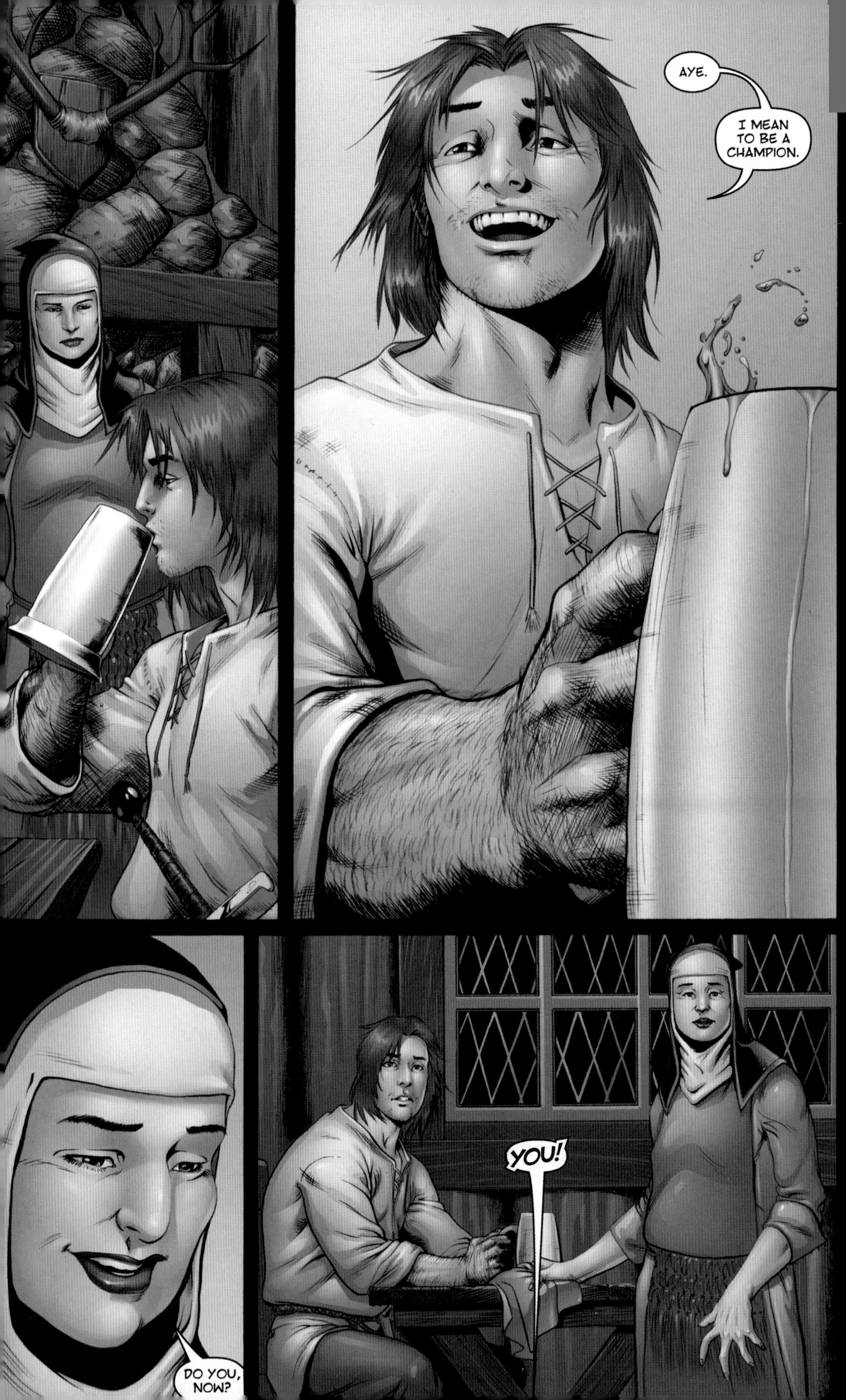
AYE.
I MEAN TO BE A CHAMPION.
DO YOU, NOW?
YOU!

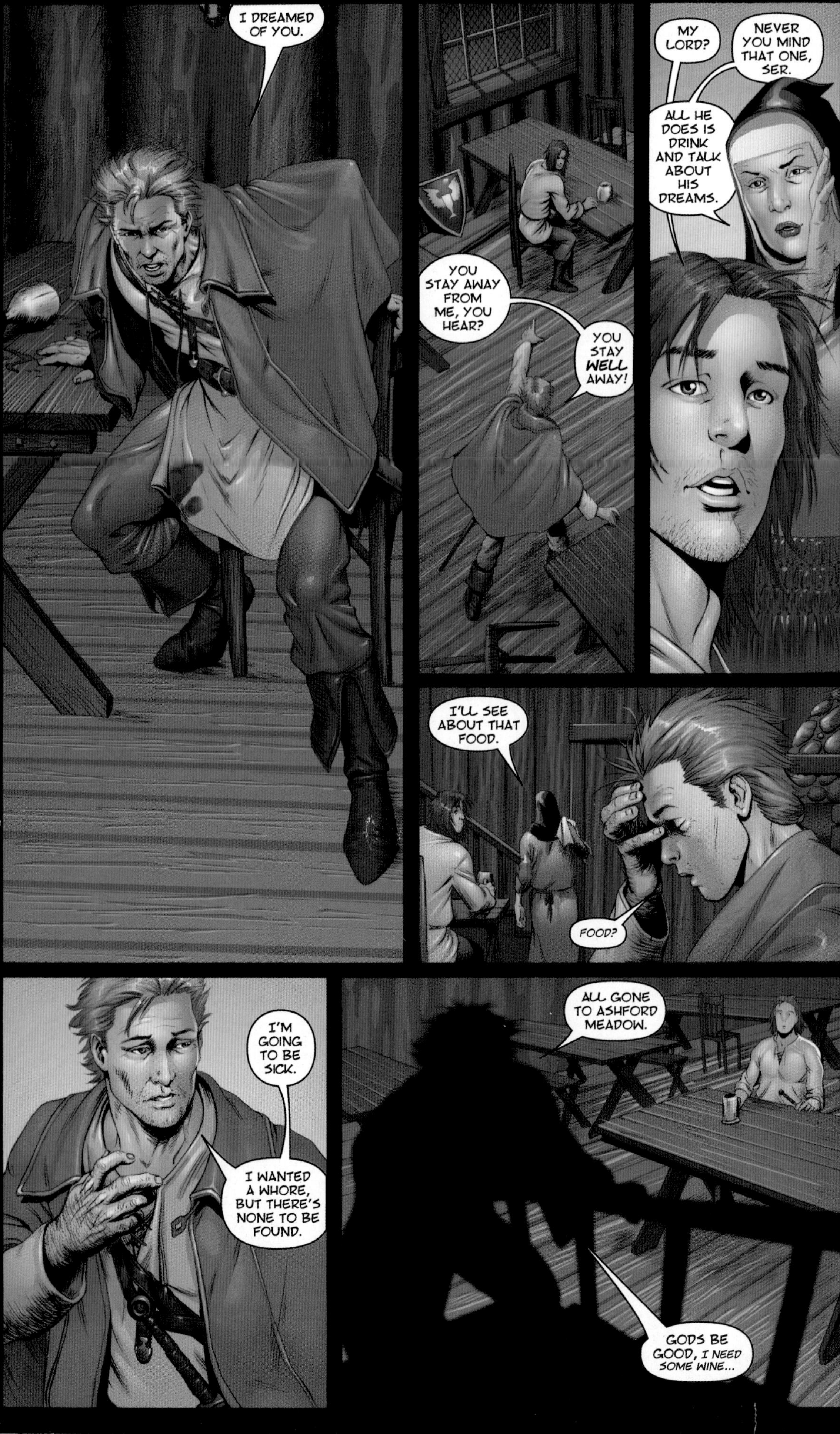
I DREAMED OF YOU.
YOU STAY AWAY FROM ME, YOU HEAR?
YOU STAY **WELL** AWAY!
MY LORD?
NEVER YOU MIND THAT ONE, SER.
ALL HE DOES IS DRINK AND TALK ABOUT HIS DREAMS.
I'LL SEE ABOUT THAT FOOD.
*FOOD?*
I'M GOING TO BE SICK.
I WANTED A WHORE, BUT THERE'S NONE TO BE FOUND.
ALL GONE TO ASHFORD MEADOW.
GODS BE GOOD, I NEED SOME WINE...

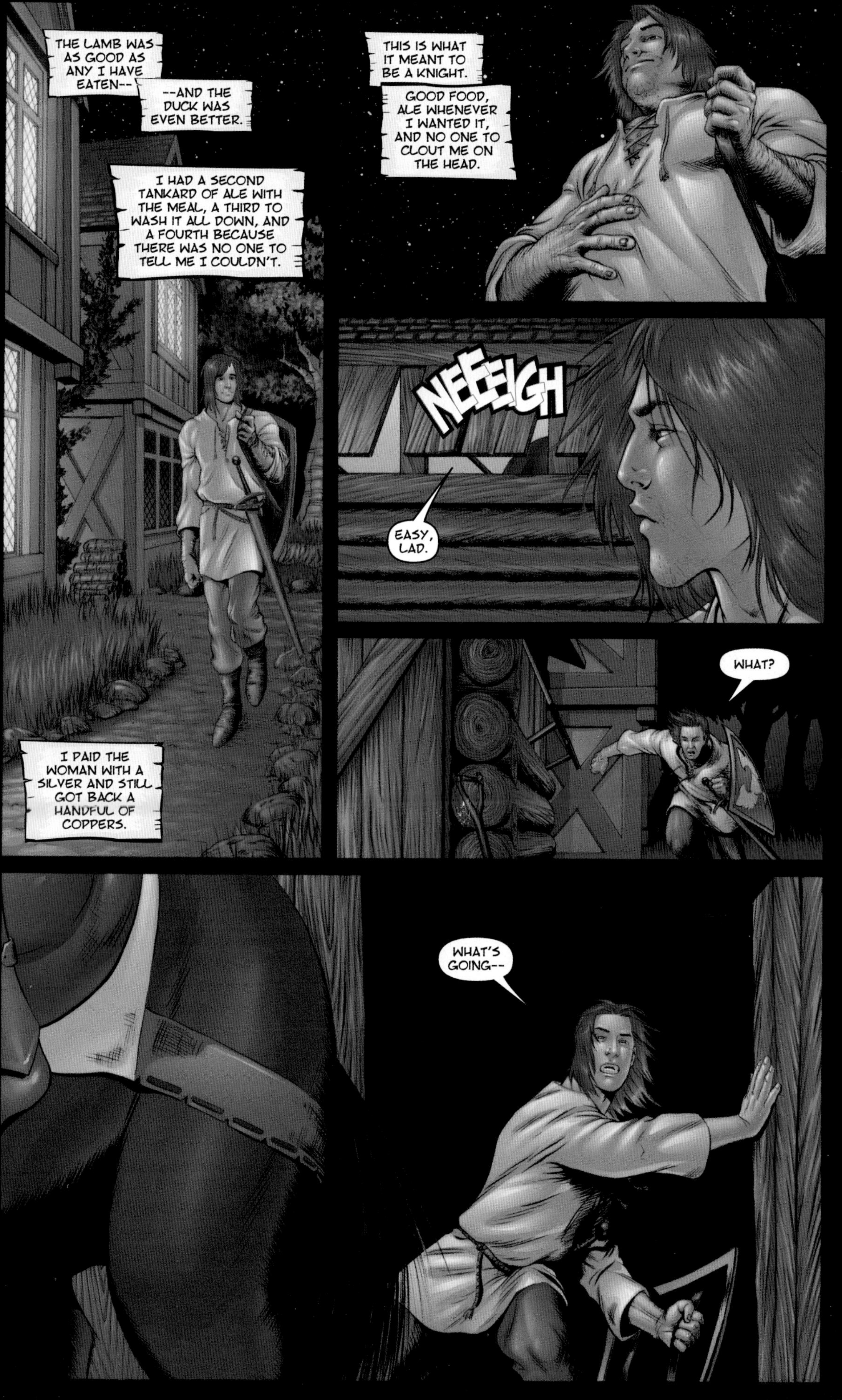
THE LAMB WAS AS GOOD AS ANY I HAVE EATEN--
--AND THE DUCK WAS EVEN BETTER.
I HAD A SECOND TANKARD OF ALE WITH THE MEAL, A THIRD TO WASH IT ALL DOWN, AND A FOURTH BECAUSE THERE WAS NO ONE TO TELL ME I COULDN'T.
I PAID THE WOMAN WITH A SILVER AND STILL GOT BACK A HANDFUL OF COPPERS.
THIS IS WHAT IT MEANT TO BE A KNIGHT.
GOOD FOOD, ALE WHENEVER I WANTED IT, AND NO ONE TO CLOUT ME ON THE HEAD.
NEEEIGH
EASY, LAD.
WHAT?
WHAT'S GOING--

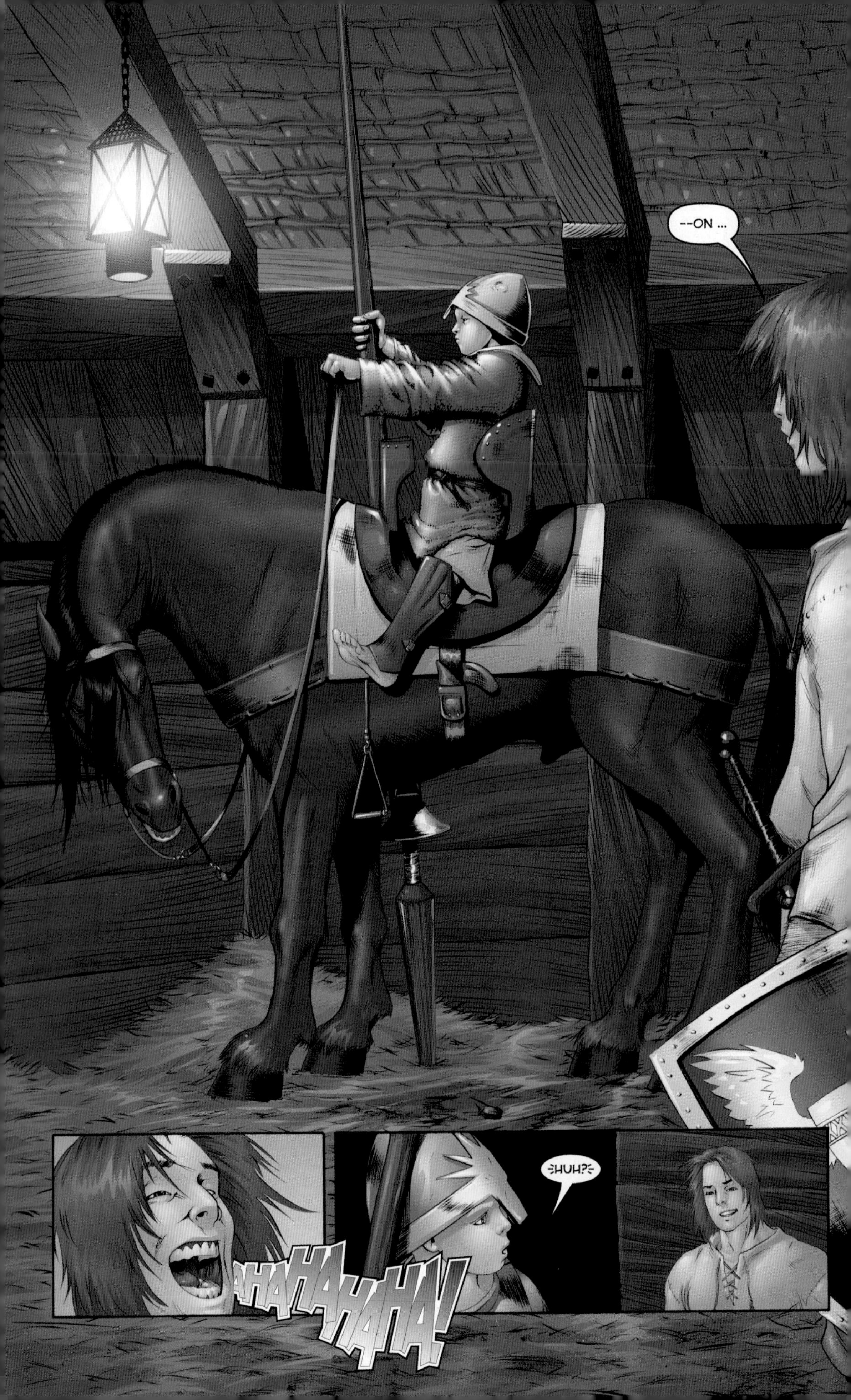
--ON ...
HAHAHAHAHA!
HUH?

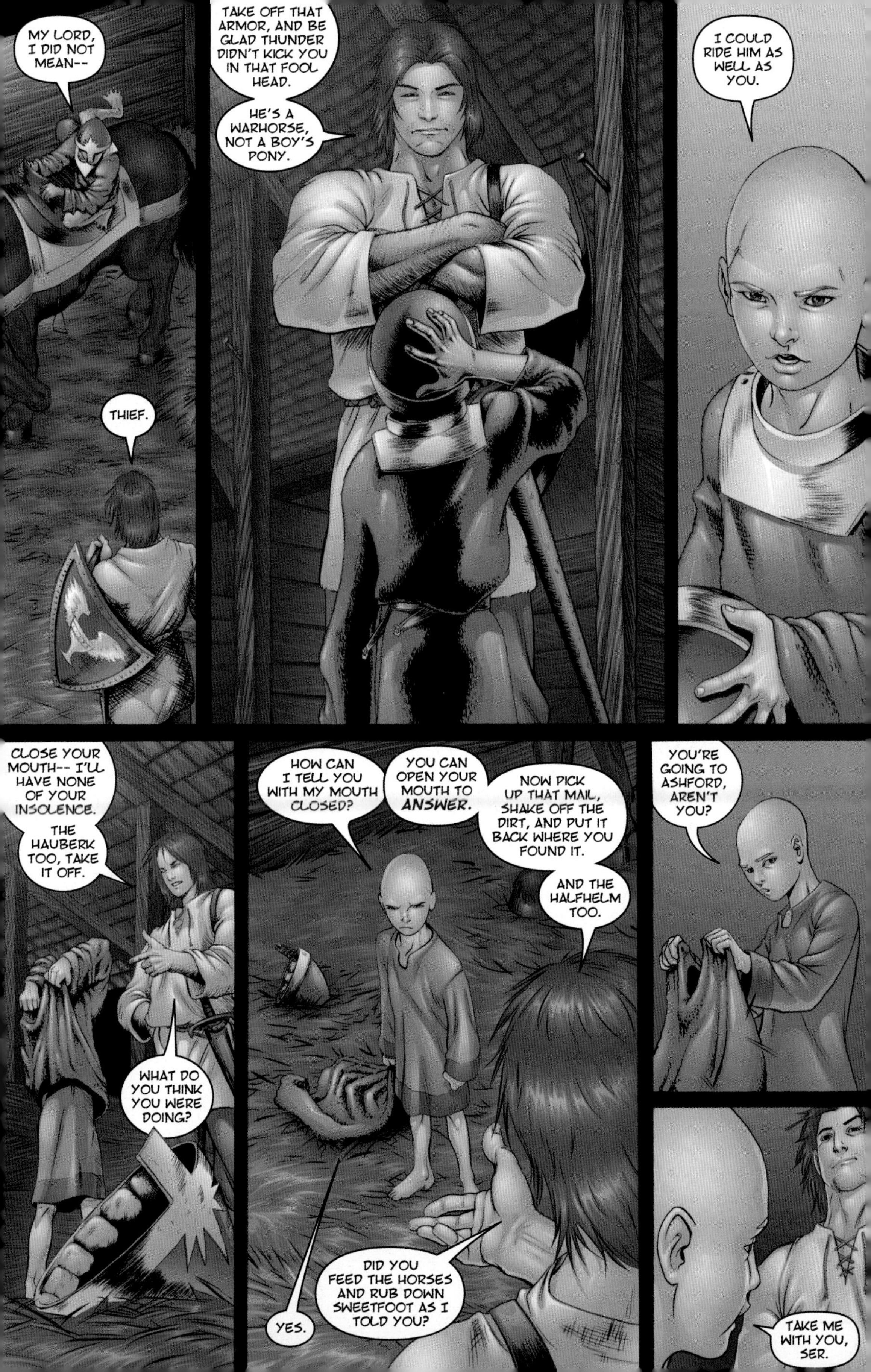
MY LORD, I DID NOT MEAN--
THIEF.
TAKE OFF THAT ARMOR, AND BE GLAD THUNDER DIDN'T KICK YOU IN THAT FOOL HEAD.
HE'S A WARHORSE, NOT A BOY'S PONY.
I COULD RIDE HIM AS WELL AS YOU.
CLOSE YOUR MOUTH-- I'LL HAVE NONE OF YOUR INSOLENCE.
THE HAUBERK TOO, TAKE IT OFF.
WHAT DO YOU THINK YOU WERE DOING?
HOW CAN I TELL YOU WITH MY MOUTH CLOSED?
YOU CAN OPEN YOUR MOUTH TO ANSWER.
NOW PICK UP THAT MAIL, SHAKE OFF THE DIRT, AND PUT IT BACK WHERE YOU FOUND IT.
AND THE HALFHELM TOO.
DID YOU FEED THE HORSES AND RUB DOWN SWEETFOOT AS I TOLD YOU?
YES.
YOU'RE GOING TO ASHFORD, AREN'T YOU?
TAKE ME WITH YOU, SER.

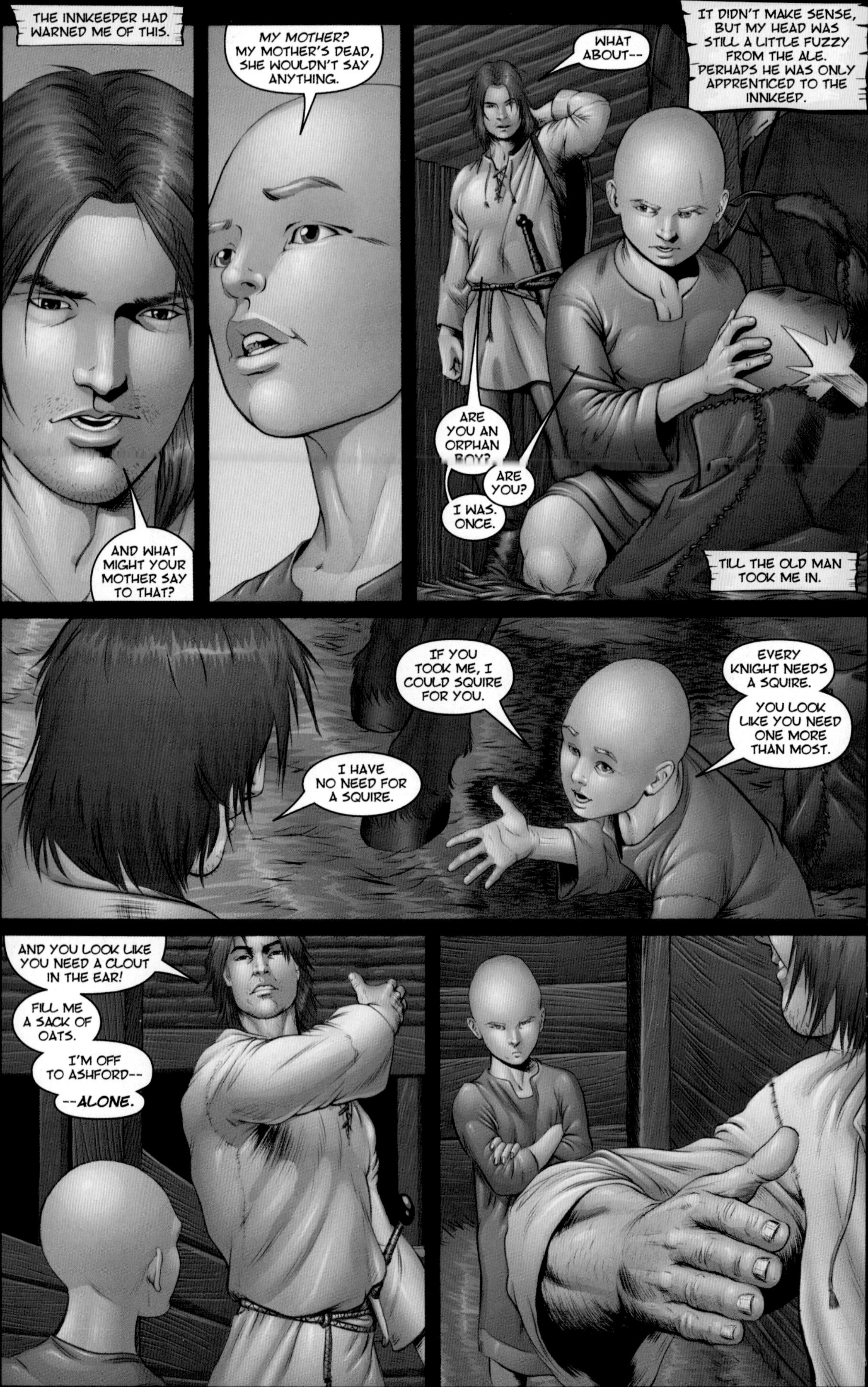
THE INNKEEPER HAD WARNED ME OF THIS.
AND WHAT MIGHT YOUR MOTHER SAY TO THAT?
MY MOTHER? MY MOTHER'S DEAD, SHE WOULDN'T SAY ANYTHING.
IT DIDN'T MAKE SENSE, BUT MY HEAD WAS STILL A LITTLE FUZZY FROM THE ALE. PERHAPS HE WAS ONLY APPRENTICED TO THE INNKEEP.
WHAT ABOUT--
ARE YOU AN ORPHAN BOY?
ARE YOU?
I WAS. ONCE.
TILL THE OLD MAN TOOK ME IN.
IF YOU TOOK ME, I COULD SQUIRE FOR YOU.
I HAVE NO NEED FOR A SQUIRE.
EVERY KNIGHT NEEDS A SQUIRE.
YOU LOOK LIKE YOU NEED ONE MORE THAN MOST.
AND YOU LOOK LIKE YOU NEED A CLOUT IN THE EAR!
FILL ME A SACK OF OATS.
I'M OFF TO ASHFORD--
--ALONE.

IT WAS A PITY I
COULDN'T TAKE
HIM WITH ME--

--BUT HE HAD A GOOD
LIFE THERE AT THE INN,
A BETTER ONE THAN
HE'D HAVE SQUIRING
FOR A HEDGE KNIGHT.

HERE, LAD,
FOR YOUR
HELP.

TAKING HIM
WOULD HAVE
BEEN NO
KINDNESS.

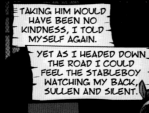

TAKING HIM WOULD
HAVE BEEN NO
KINDNESS, I TOLD
MYSELF AGAIN.

YET AS I HEADED DOWN
THE ROAD I COULD
FEEL THE STABLEBOY
WATCHING MY BACK,
SULLEN AND SILENT.

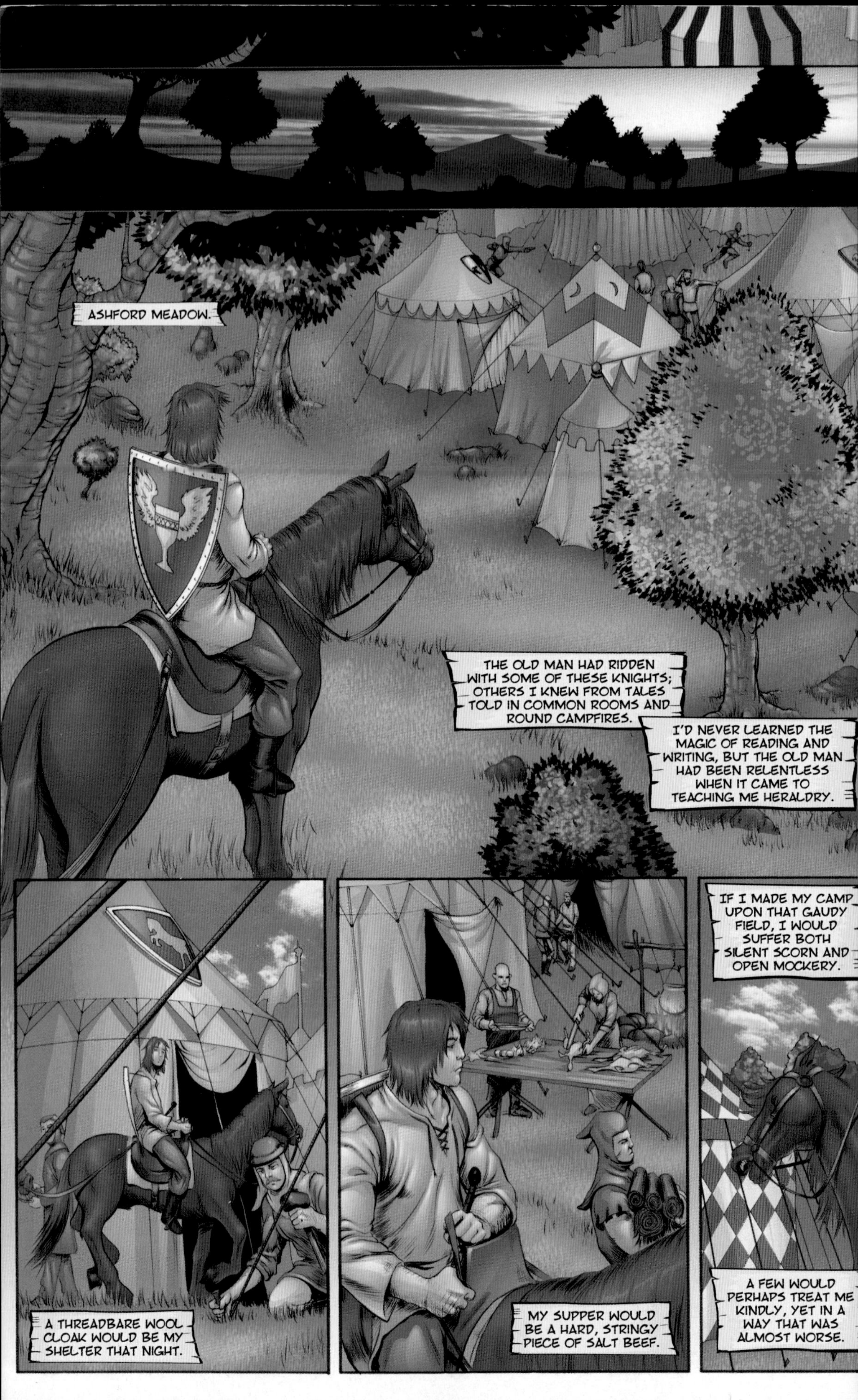
ASHFORD MEADOW.
THE OLD MAN HAD RIDDEN WITH SOME OF THESE KNIGHTS; OTHERS I KNEW FROM TALES TOLD IN COMMON ROOMS AND ROUND CAMPFIRES.
I'D NEVER LEARNED THE MAGIC OF READING AND WRITING, BUT THE OLD MAN HAD BEEN RELENTLESS WHEN IT CAME TO TEACHING ME HERALDRY.
A THREADBARE WOOL CLOAK WOULD BE MY SHELTER THAT NIGHT.
MY SUPPER WOULD BE A HARD, STRINGY PIECE OF SALT BEEF.
IF I MADE MY CAMP UPON THAT GAUDY FIELD, I WOULD SUFFER BOTH SILENT SCORN AND OPEN MOCKERY.
A FEW WOULD PERHAPS TREAT ME KINDLY, YET IN A WAY THAT WAS ALMOST WORSE.

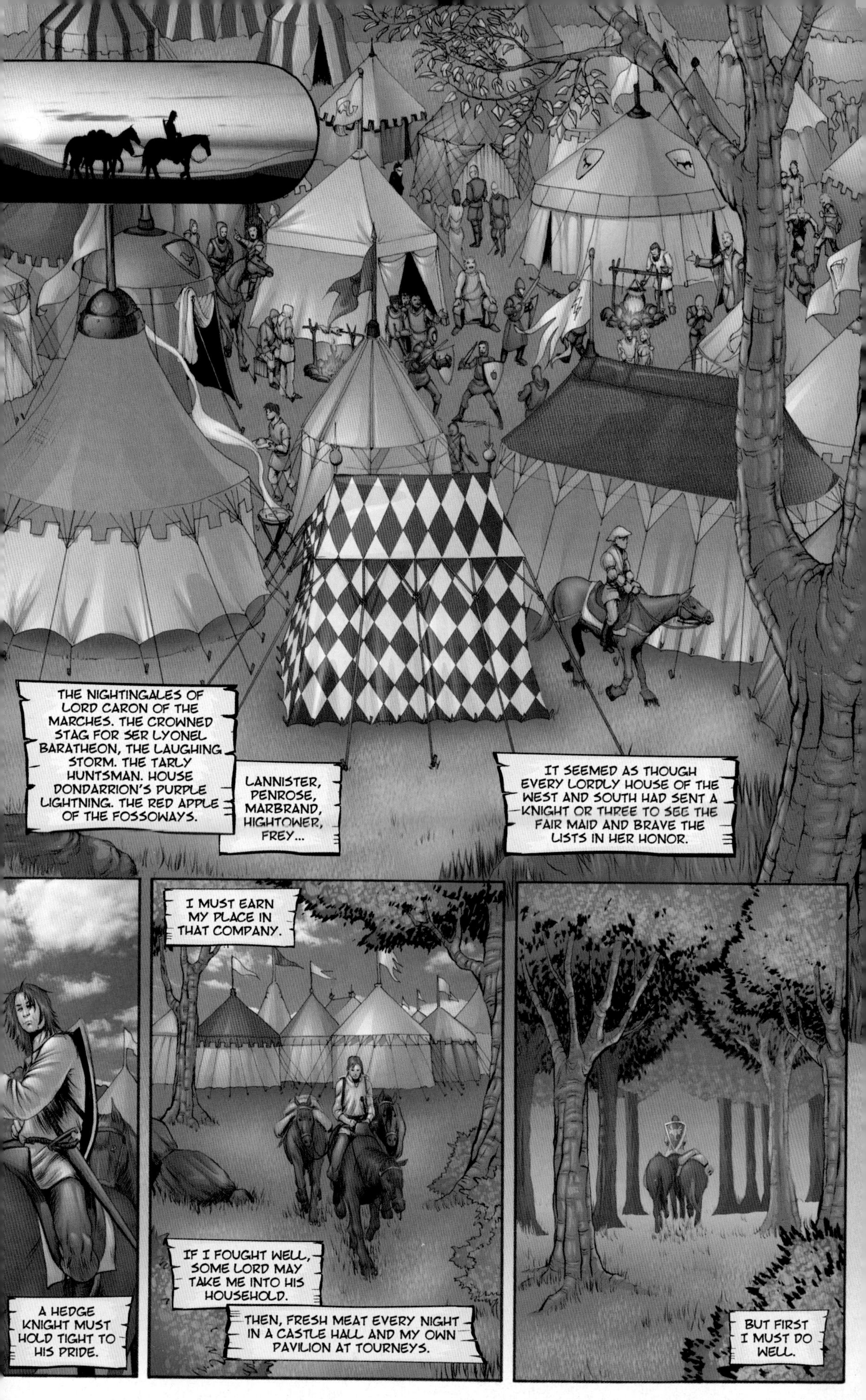
THE NIGHTINGALES OF LORD CARON OF THE MARCHES. THE CROWNED STAG FOR SER LYONEL BARATHEON, THE LAUGHING STORM. THE TARLY HUNTSMAN. HOUSE DONDARRION'S PURPLE LIGHTNING. THE RED APPLE OF THE FOSSOWAYS.
LANNISTER, PENROSE, MARBRAND, HIGHTOWER, FREY...
IT SEEMED AS THOUGH EVERY LORDLY HOUSE OF THE WEST AND SOUTH HAD SENT A KNIGHT OR THREE TO SEE THE FAIR MAID AND BRAVE THE LISTS IN HER HONOR.
A HEDGE KNIGHT MUST HOLD TIGHT TO HIS PRIDE.
I MUST EARN MY PLACE IN THAT COMPANY.
IF I FOUGHT WELL, SOME LORD MAY TAKE ME INTO HIS HOUSEHOLD.
THEN, FRESH MEAT EVERY NIGHT IN A CASTLE HALL AND MY OWN PAVILION AT TOURNEYS.
BUT FIRST I MUST DO WELL.

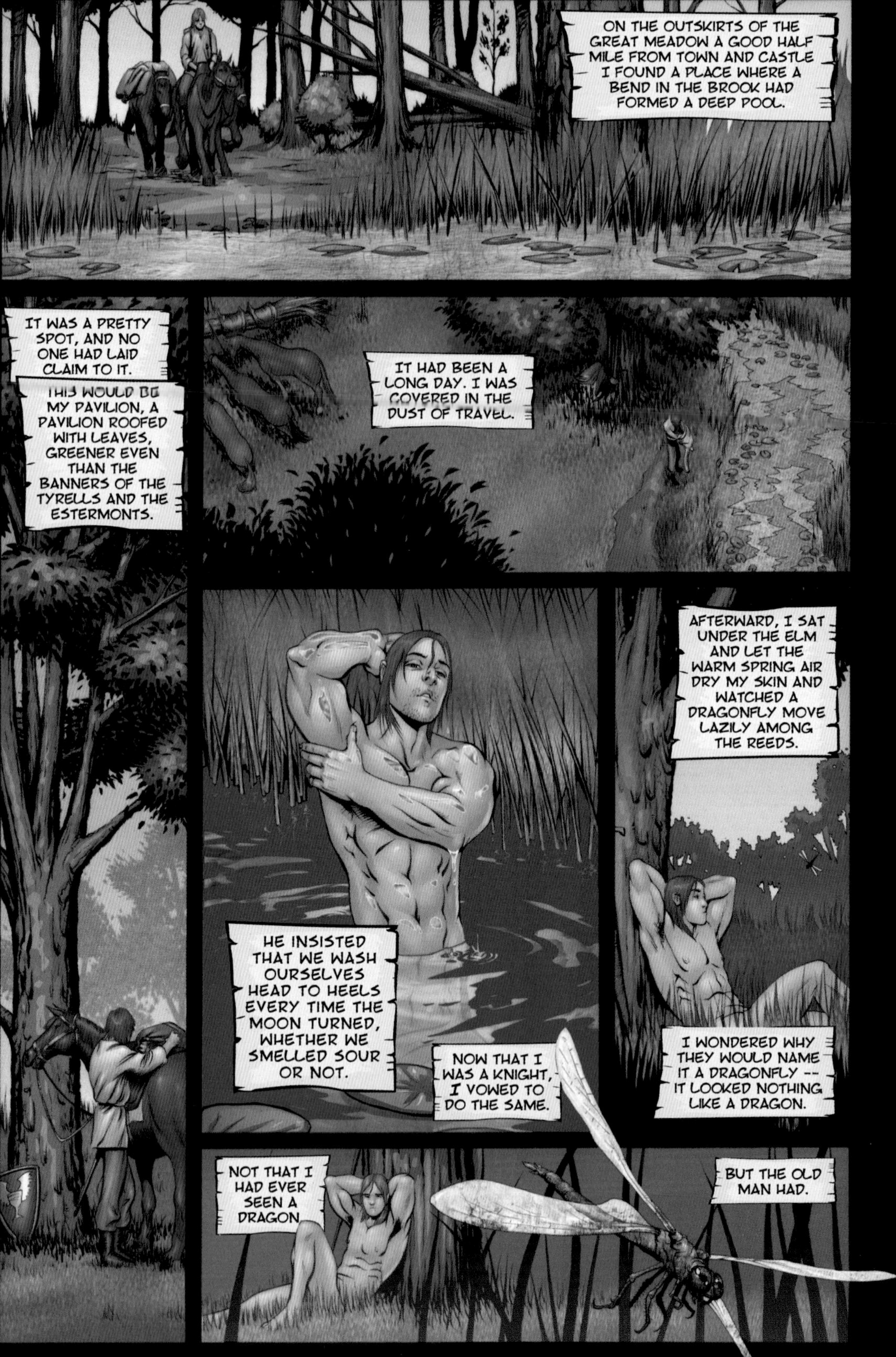
ON THE OUTSKIRTS OF THE GREAT MEADOW A GOOD HALF MILE FROM TOWN AND CASTLE I FOUND A PLACE WHERE A BEND IN THE BROOK HAD FORMED A DEEP POOL.
IT WAS A PRETTY SPOT, AND NO ONE HAD LAID CLAIM TO IT.
THIS WOULD BE MY PAVILION, A PAVILION ROOFED WITH LEAVES, GREENER EVEN THAN THE BANNERS OF THE TYRELLS AND THE ESTERMONTS.
IT HAD BEEN A LONG DAY. I WAS COVERED IN THE DUST OF TRAVEL.
HE INSISTED THAT WE WASH OURSELVES HEAD TO HEELS EVERY TIME THE MOON TURNED, WHETHER WE SMELLED SOUR OR NOT.
NOW THAT I WAS A KNIGHT, *I* VOWED TO DO THE SAME.
AFTERWARD, I SAT UNDER THE ELM AND LET THE WARM SPRING AIR DRY MY SKIN AND WATCHED A DRAGONFLY MOVE LAZILY AMONG THE REEDS.
I WONDERED WHY THEY WOULD NAME IT A DRAGONFLY -- IT LOOKED NOTHING LIKE A DRAGON.
NOT THAT I HAD EVER SEEN A DRAGON
BUT THE OLD MAN HAD.

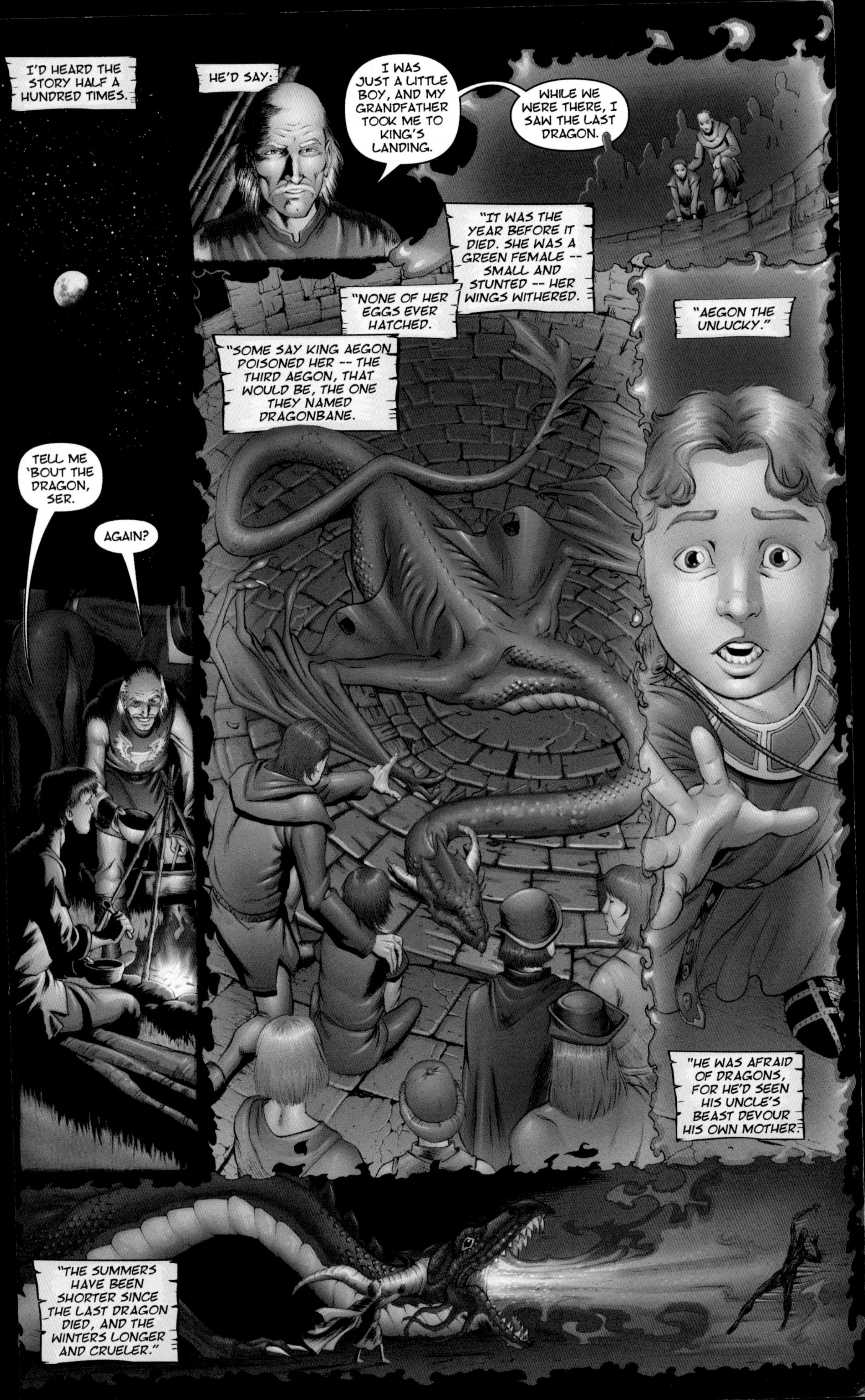
I'D HEARD THE STORY HALF A HUNDRED TIMES.
HE'D SAY:
I WAS JUST A LITTLE BOY, AND MY GRANDFATHER TOOK ME TO KING'S LANDING.
WHILE WE WERE THERE, I SAW THE LAST DRAGON.
"IT WAS THE YEAR BEFORE IT DIED. SHE WAS A GREEN FEMALE -- SMALL AND STUNTED -- HER WINGS WITHERED.
"NONE OF HER EGGS EVER HATCHED.
"SOME SAY KING AEGON POISONED HER -- THE THIRD AEGON, THAT WOULD BE, THE ONE THEY NAMED DRAGONBANE.
"AEGON THE UNLUCKY."
TELL ME 'BOUT THE DRAGON, SER.
AGAIN?
"HE WAS AFRAID OF DRAGONS, FOR HE'D SEEN HIS UNCLE'S BEAST DEVOUR HIS OWN MOTHER.
"THE SUMMERS HAVE BEEN SHORTER SINCE THE LAST DRAGON DIED, AND THE WINTERS LONGER AND CRUELER."

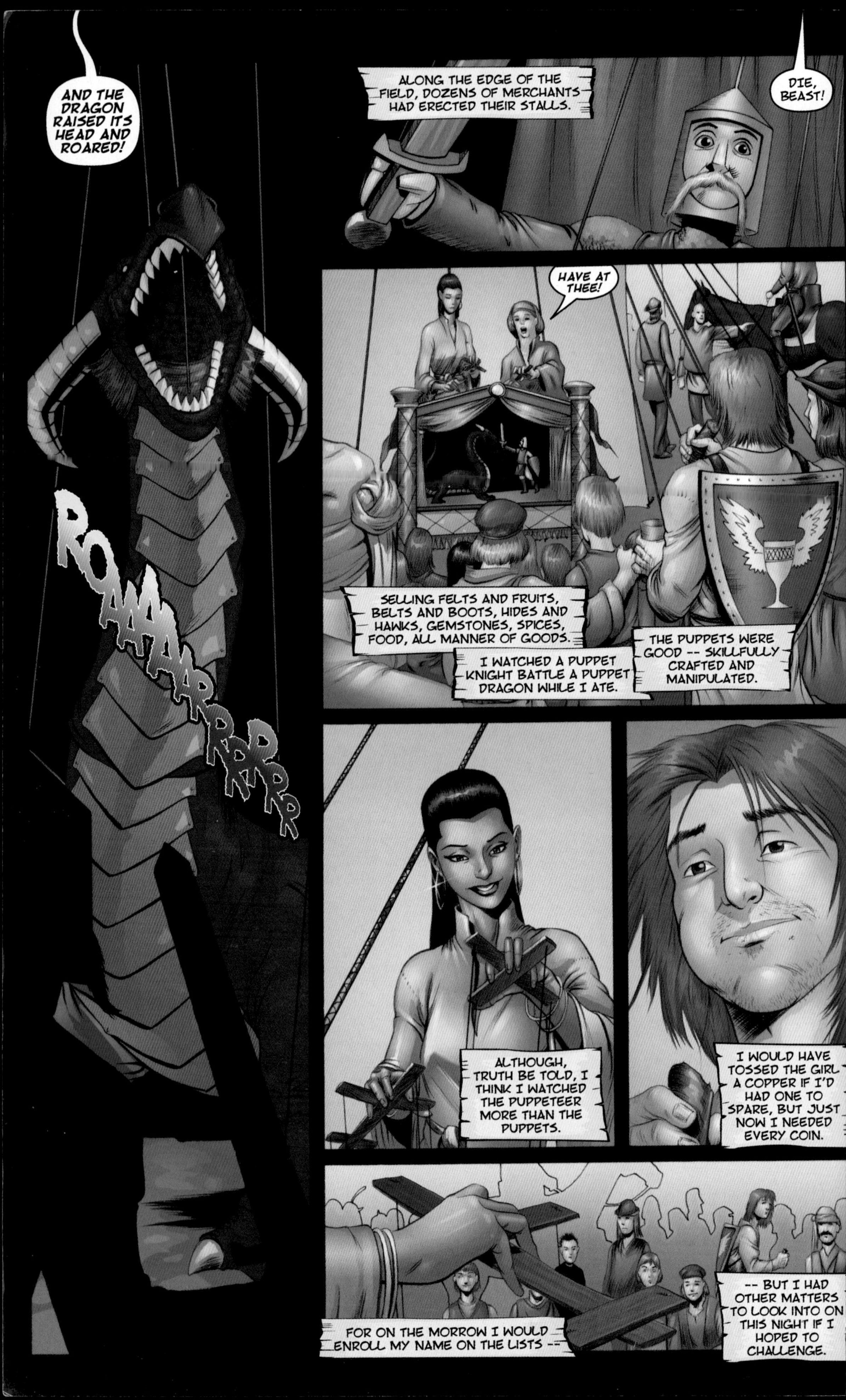
AND THE DRAGON RAISED ITS HEAD AND ROARED!
ROAAAAARRRRR
ALONG THE EDGE OF THE FIELD, DOZENS OF MERCHANTS HAD ERECTED THEIR STALLS.
DIE, BEAST!
HAVE AT THEE!
SELLING FELTS AND FRUITS, BELTS AND BOOTS, HIDES AND HAWKS, GEMSTONES, SPICES, FOOD, ALL MANNER OF GOODS.
I WATCHED A PUPPET KNIGHT BATTLE A PUPPET DRAGON WHILE I ATE.
THE PUPPETS WERE GOOD -- SKILLFULLY CRAFTED AND MANIPULATED.
ALTHOUGH, TRUTH BE TOLD, I THINK I WATCHED THE PUPPETEER MORE THAN THE PUPPETS.
I WOULD HAVE TOSSED THE GIRL A COPPER IF I'D HAD ONE TO SPARE, BUT JUST NOW I NEEDED EVERY COIN.
FOR ON THE MORROW I WOULD ENROLL MY NAME ON THE LISTS --
-- BUT I HAD OTHER MATTERS TO LOOK INTO ON THIS NIGHT IF I HOPED TO CHALLENGE.

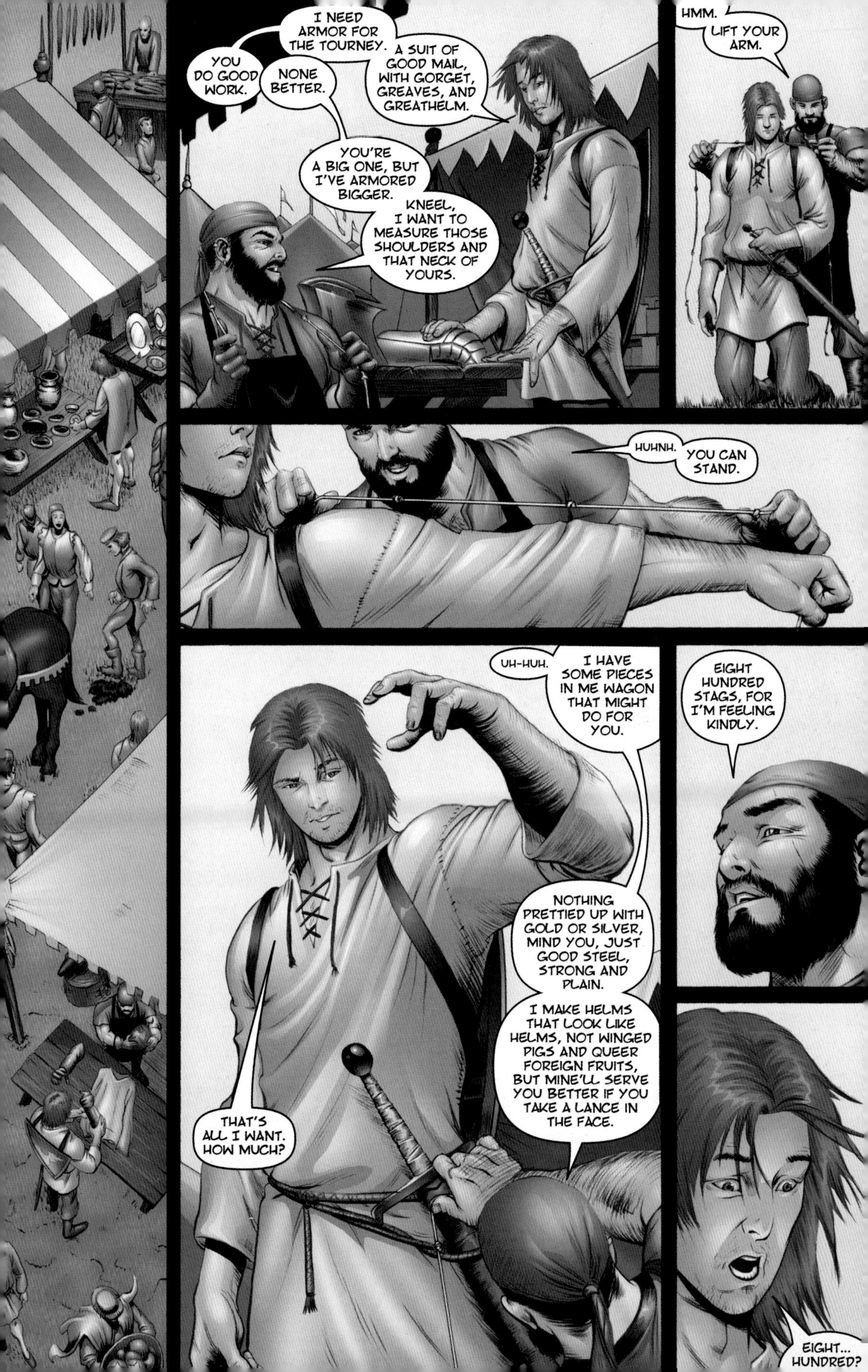
I NEED ARMOR FOR THE TOURNEY.
A SUIT OF GOOD MAIL, WITH GORGET, GREAVES, AND GREATHELM.
YOU DO GOOD WORK.
NONE BETTER.
YOU'RE A BIG ONE, BUT I'VE ARMORED BIGGER.
KNEEL, I WANT TO MEASURE THOSE SHOULDERS AND THAT NECK OF YOURS.
HMM.
LIFT YOUR ARM.
HUHNH.
YOU CAN STAND.
UH-HUH.
I HAVE SOME PIECES IN ME WAGON THAT MIGHT DO FOR YOU.
NOTHING PRETTIED UP WITH GOLD OR SILVER, MIND YOU, JUST GOOD STEEL, STRONG AND PLAIN.
I MAKE HELMS THAT LOOK LIKE HELMS, NOT WINGED PIGS AND QUEER FOREIGN FRUITS, BUT MINE'LL SERVE YOU BETTER IF YOU TAKE A LANCE IN THE FACE.
THAT'S ALL I WANT. HOW MUCH?
EIGHT HUNDRED STAGS, FOR I'M FEELING KINDLY.
EIGHT... HUNDRED?

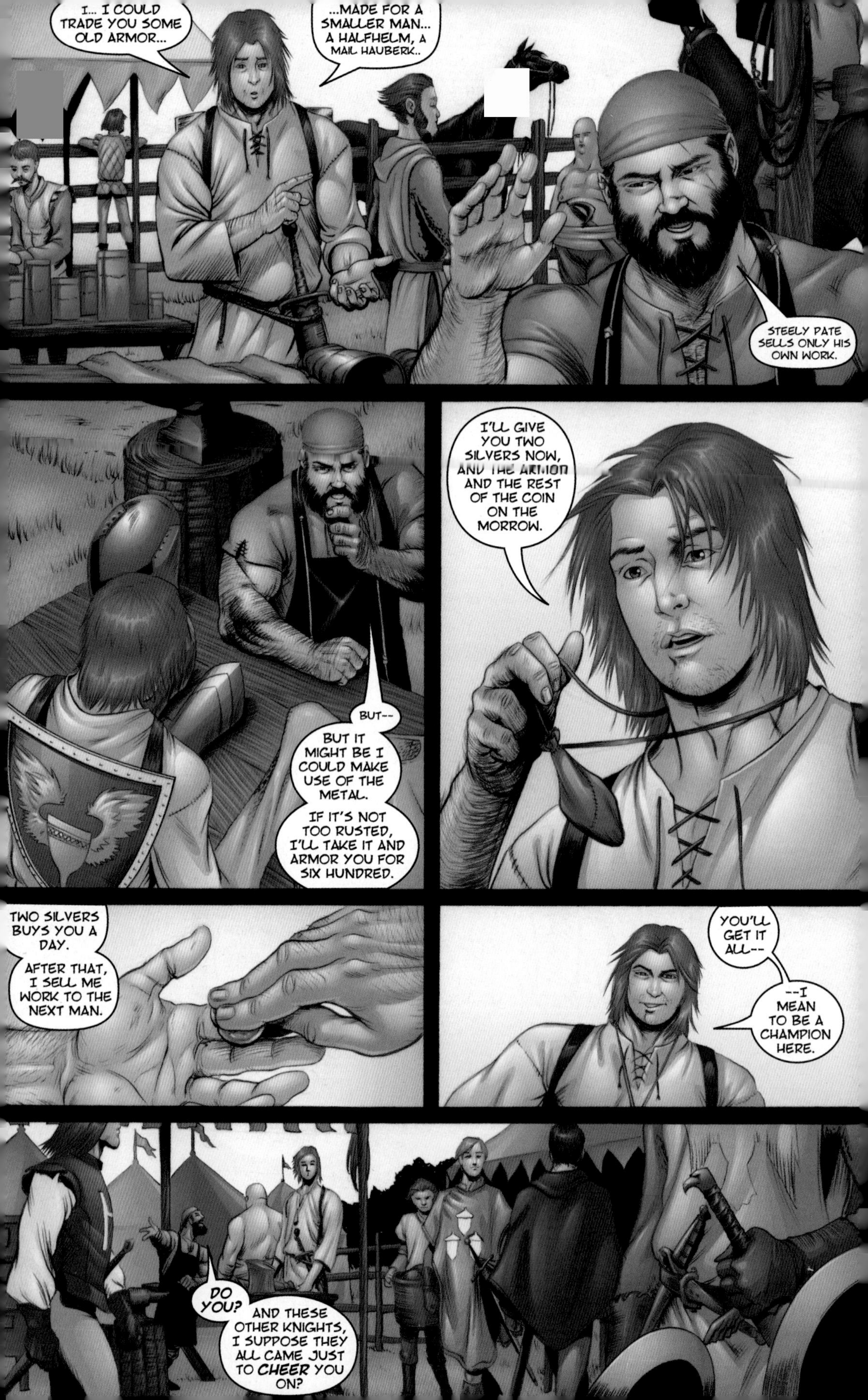
I... I COULD TRADE YOU SOME OLD ARMOR...
...MADE FOR A SMALLER MAN... A HALFHELM, A MAIL HAUBERK..
STEELY PATE SELLS ONLY HIS OWN WORK.
BUT--
BUT IT MIGHT BE I COULD MAKE USE OF THE METAL.
IF IT'S NOT TOO RUSTED, I'LL TAKE IT AND ARMOR YOU FOR SIX HUNDRED.
I'LL GIVE YOU TWO SILVERS NOW, AND THE ARMOR AND THE REST OF THE COIN ON THE MORROW.
TWO SILVERS BUYS YOU A DAY.
AFTER THAT, I SELL ME WORK TO THE NEXT MAN.
YOU'LL GET IT ALL--
--I MEAN TO BE A CHAMPION HERE.
DO YOU?
AND THESE OTHER KNIGHTS, I SUPPOSE THEY ALL CAME JUST TO **CHEER** YOU ON?

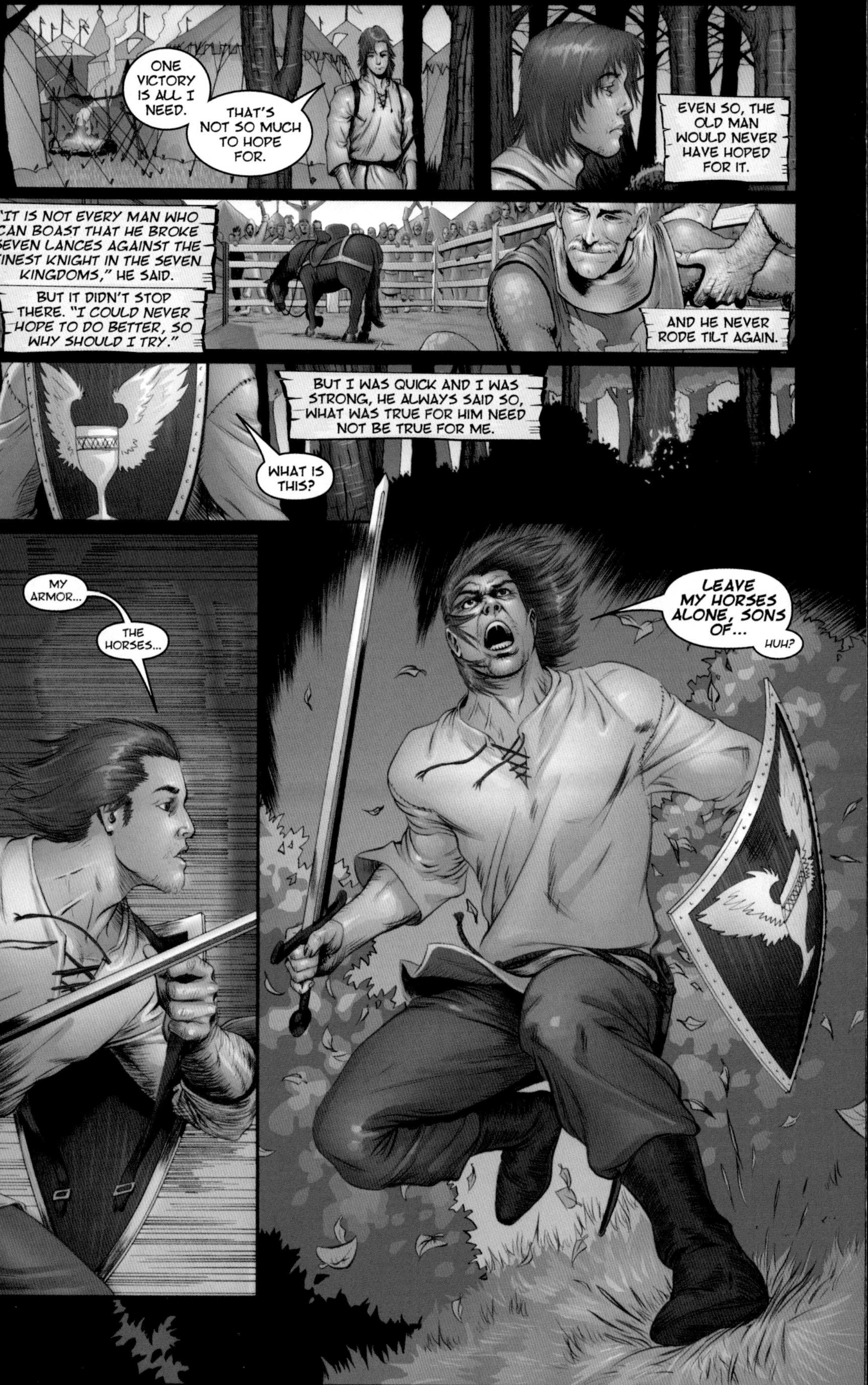
ONE VICTORY IS ALL I NEED.
THAT'S NOT SO MUCH TO HOPE FOR.
EVEN SO, THE OLD MAN WOULD NEVER HAVE HOPED FOR IT.
"IT IS NOT EVERY MAN WHO CAN BOAST THAT HE BROKE SEVEN LANCES AGAINST THE FINEST KNIGHT IN THE SEVEN KINGDOMS," HE SAID.
BUT IT DIDN'T STOP THERE. "I COULD NEVER HOPE TO DO BETTER, SO WHY SHOULD I TRY."
AND HE NEVER RODE TILT AGAIN.
BUT I WAS QUICK AND I WAS STRONG, HE ALWAYS SAID SO, WHAT WAS TRUE FOR HIM NEED NOT BE TRUE FOR ME.
WHAT IS THIS?
MY ARMOR...
THE HORSES...
LEAVE MY HORSES ALONE, SONS OF...
HUH?

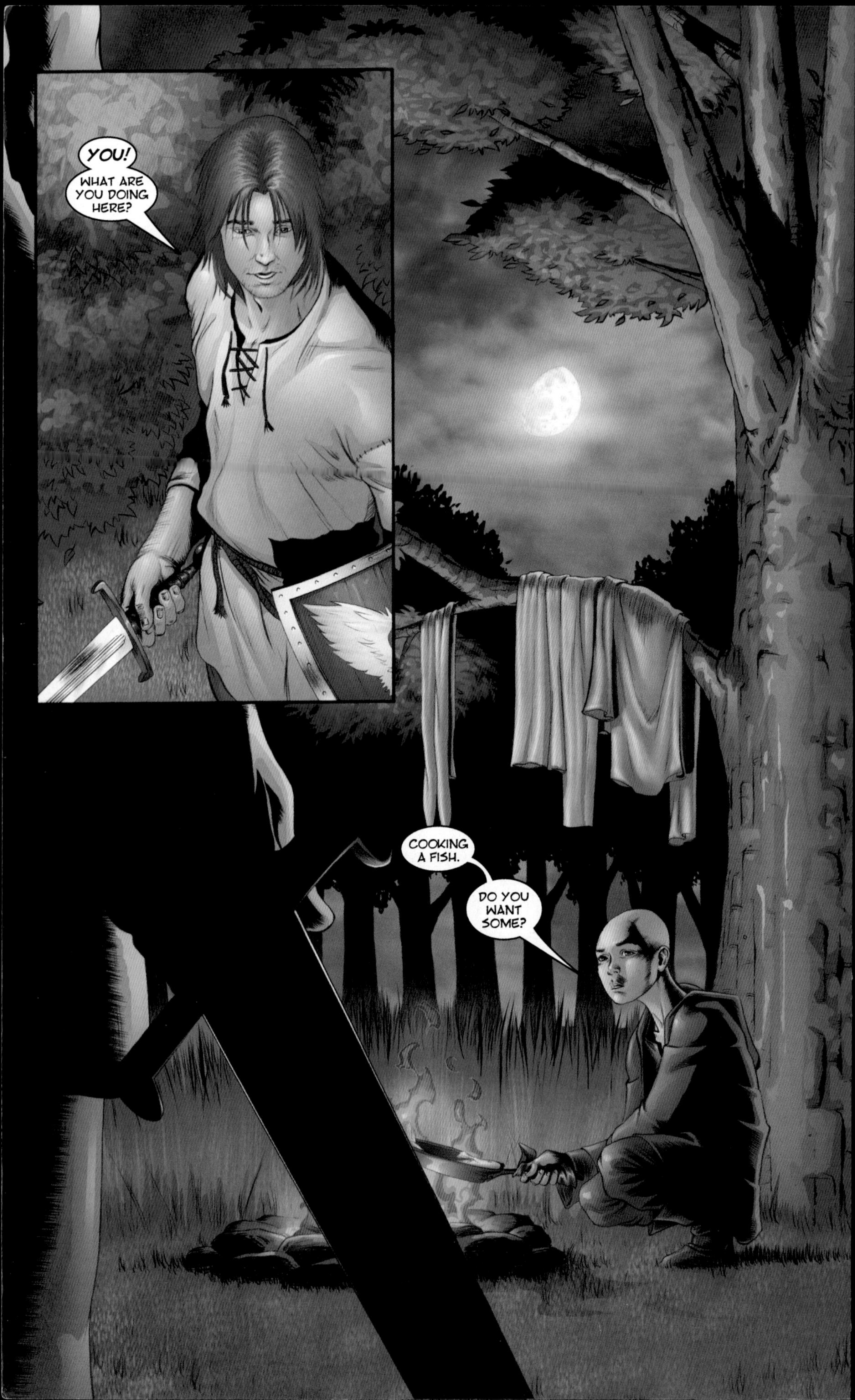
YOU!
WHAT ARE YOU DOING HERE?
COOKING A FISH.
DO YOU WANT SOME?

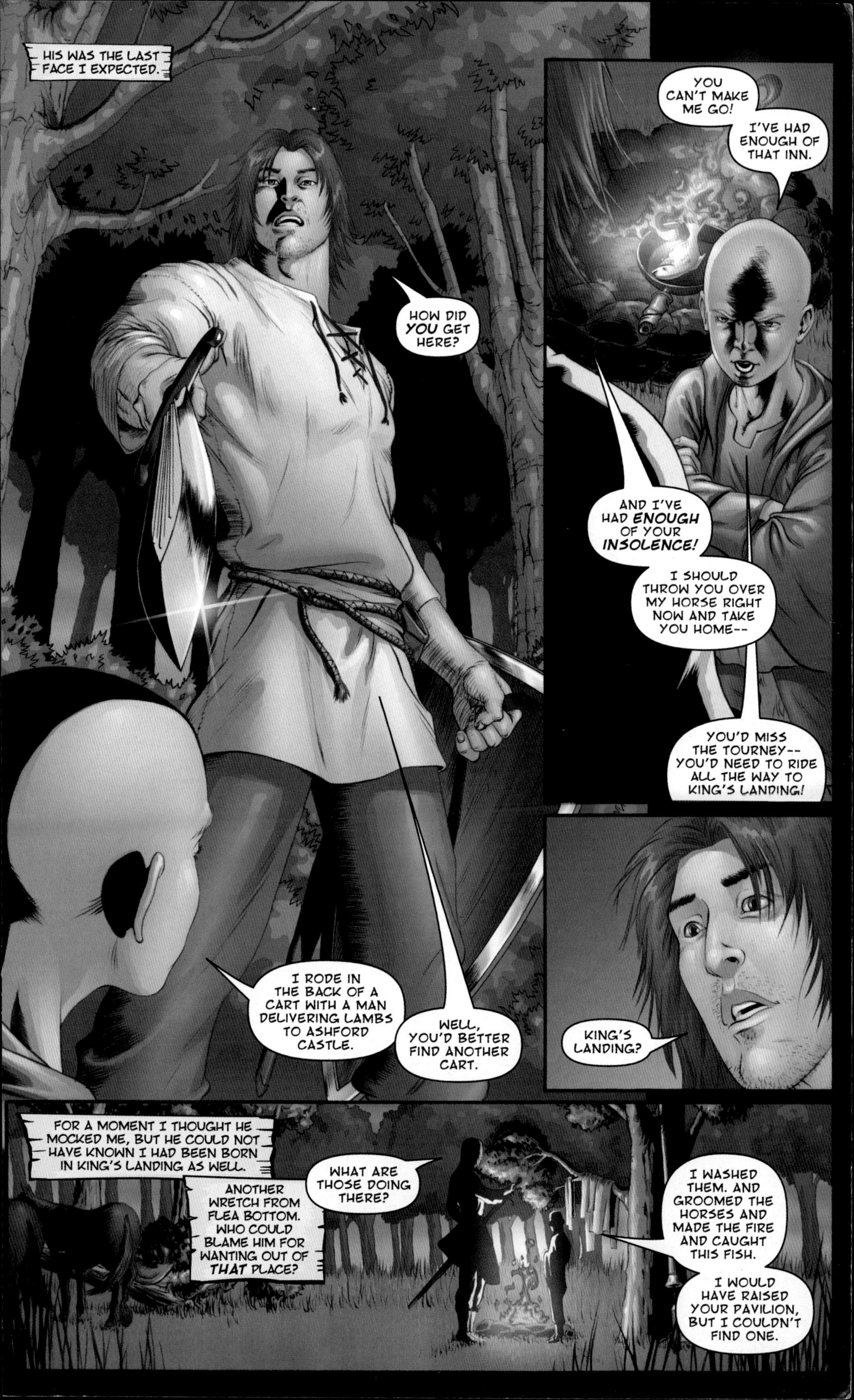
HIS WAS THE LAST FACE I EXPECTED.
HOW DID YOU GET HERE?
I RODE IN THE BACK OF A CART WITH A MAN DELIVERING LAMBS TO ASHFORD CASTLE.
WELL, YOU'D BETTER FIND ANOTHER CART.
YOU CAN'T MAKE ME GO!
I'VE HAD ENOUGH OF THAT INN.
AND I'VE HAD ENOUGH OF YOUR INSOLENCE!
I SHOULD THROW YOU OVER MY HORSE RIGHT NOW AND TAKE YOU HOME--
YOU'D MISS THE TOURNEY-- YOU'D NEED TO RIDE ALL THE WAY TO KING'S LANDING!
KING'S LANDING?
FOR A MOMENT I THOUGHT HE MOCKED ME, BUT HE COULD NOT HAVE KNOWN I HAD BEEN BORN IN KING'S LANDING AS WELL.
ANOTHER WRETCH FROM FLEA BOTTOM. WHO COULD BLAME HIM FOR WANTING OUT OF THAT PLACE?
WHAT ARE THOSE DOING THERE?
I WASHED THEM. AND GROOMED THE HORSES AND MADE THE FIRE AND CAUGHT THIS FISH.
I WOULD HAVE RAISED YOUR PAVILION, BUT I COULDN'T FIND ONE.

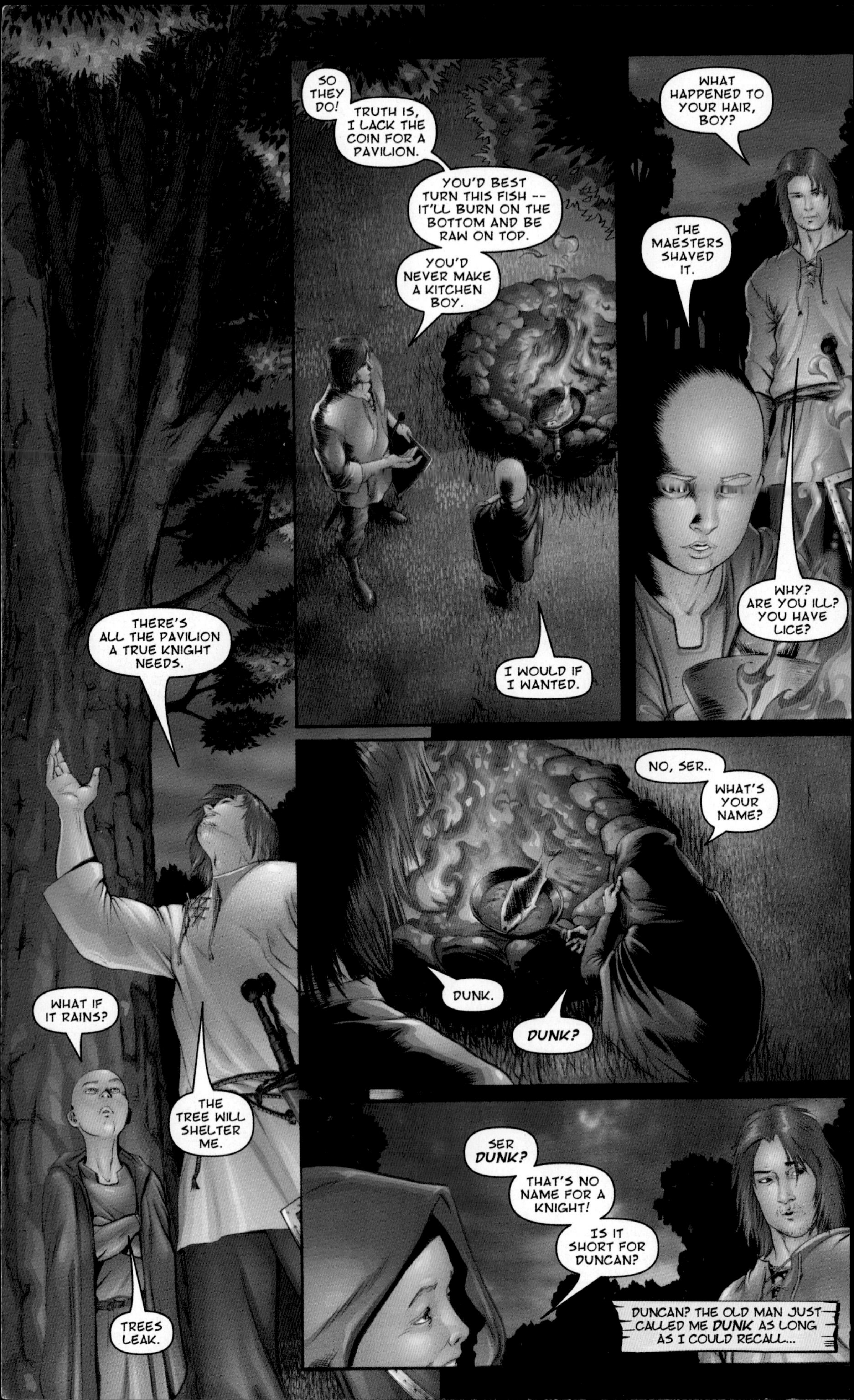

SO THEY DO!
TRUTH IS, I LACK THE COIN FOR A PAVILION.
YOU'D BEST TURN THIS FISH -- IT'LL BURN ON THE BOTTOM AND BE RAW ON TOP.
YOU'D NEVER MAKE A KITCHEN BOY.
I WOULD IF I WANTED.
WHAT HAPPENED TO YOUR HAIR, BOY?
THE MAESTERS SHAVED IT.
WHY? ARE YOU ILL? YOU HAVE LICE?
THERE'S ALL THE PAVILION A TRUE KNIGHT NEEDS.
WHAT IF IT RAINS?
THE TREE WILL SHELTER ME.
TREES LEAK.
NO, SER..
WHAT'S YOUR NAME?
DUNK.
DUNK?
SER DUNK?
THAT'S NO NAME FOR A KNIGHT!
IS IT SHORT FOR DUNCAN?
DUNCAN? THE OLD MAN JUST CALLED ME DUNK AS LONG AS I COULD RECALL...

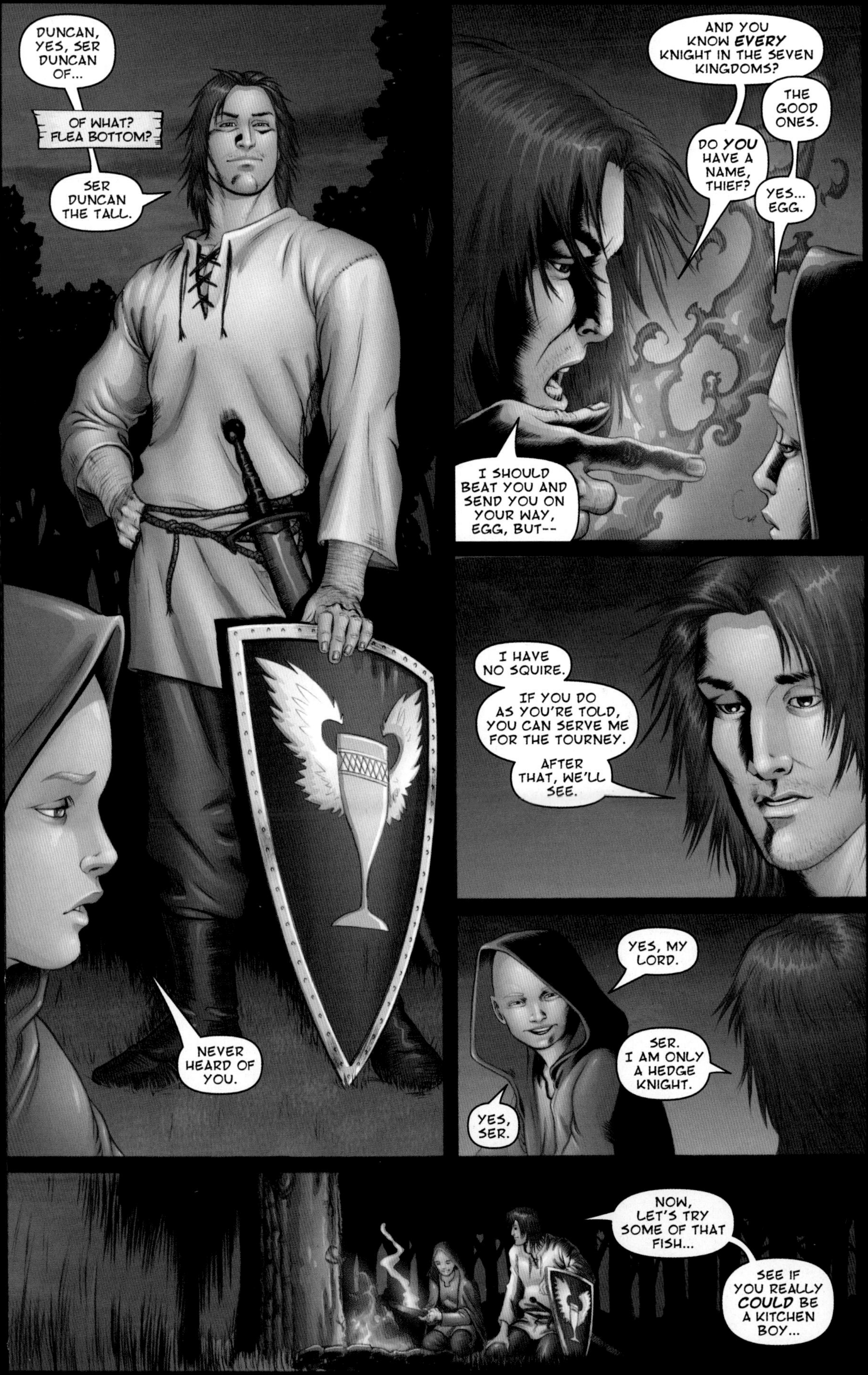
DUNCAN, YES, SER DUNCAN OF...
OF WHAT? FLEA BOTTOM?
SER DUNCAN THE TALL.
NEVER HEARD OF YOU.
AND YOU KNOW EVERY KNIGHT IN THE SEVEN KINGDOMS?
THE GOOD ONES.
DO YOU HAVE A NAME, THIEF?
YES... EGG.
I SHOULD BEAT YOU AND SEND YOU ON YOUR WAY, EGG, BUT--
I HAVE NO SQUIRE.
IF YOU DO AS YOU'RE TOLD, YOU CAN SERVE ME FOR THE TOURNEY.
AFTER THAT, WE'LL SEE.
YES, MY LORD.
SER. I AM ONLY A HEDGE KNIGHT.
YES, SER.
NOW, LET'S TRY SOME OF THAT FISH...
SEE IF YOU REALLY COULD BE A KITCHEN BOY...

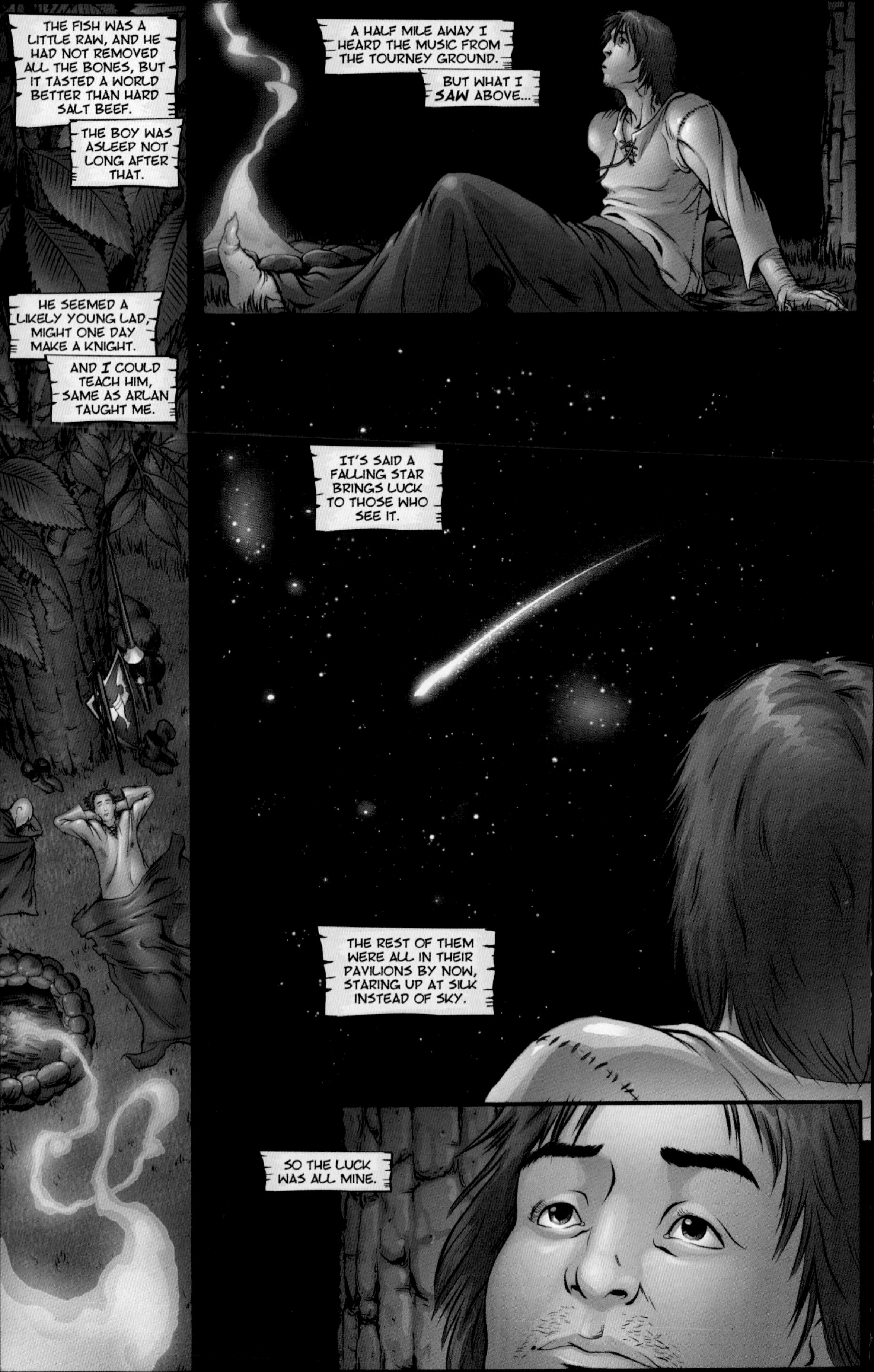
THE FISH WAS A LITTLE RAW, AND HE HAD NOT REMOVED ALL THE BONES, BUT IT TASTED A WORLD BETTER THAN HARD SALT BEEF.
THE BOY WAS ASLEEP NOT LONG AFTER THAT.
A HALF MILE AWAY I HEARD THE MUSIC FROM THE TOURNEY GROUND.
BUT WHAT I SAW ABOVE...
HE SEEMED A LIKELY YOUNG LAD, MIGHT ONE DAY MAKE A KNIGHT.
AND I COULD TEACH HIM, SAME AS ARLAN TAUGHT ME.
IT'S SAID A FALLING STAR BRINGS LUCK TO THOSE WHO SEE IT.
THE REST OF THEM WERE ALL IN THEIR PAVILIONS BY NOW, STARING UP AT SILK INSTEAD OF SKY.
SO THE LUCK WAS ALL MINE.

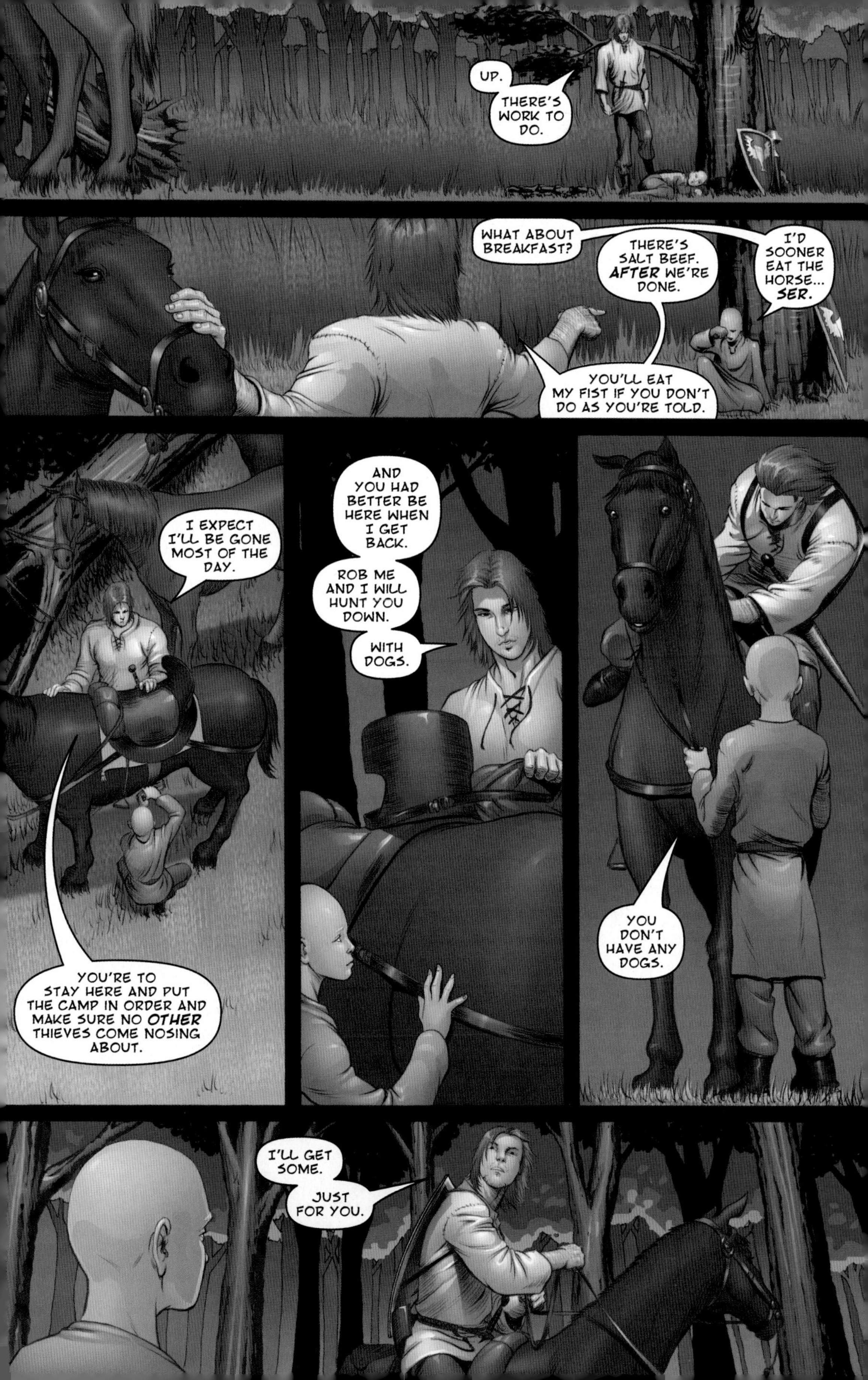
UP.
THERE'S WORK TO DO.
WHAT ABOUT BREAKFAST?
THERE'S SALT BEEF. **AFTER** WE'RE DONE.
I'D SOONER EAT THE HORSE... **SER.**
YOU'LL EAT MY FIST IF YOU DON'T DO AS YOU'RE TOLD.
I EXPECT I'LL BE GONE MOST OF THE DAY.
YOU'RE TO STAY HERE AND PUT THE CAMP IN ORDER AND MAKE SURE NO *OTHER* THIEVES COME NOSING ABOUT.
AND YOU HAD BETTER BE HERE WHEN I GET BACK.
ROB ME AND I WILL HUNT YOU DOWN.
WITH DOGS.
YOU DON'T HAVE ANY DOGS.
I'LL GET SOME.
JUST FOR YOU.

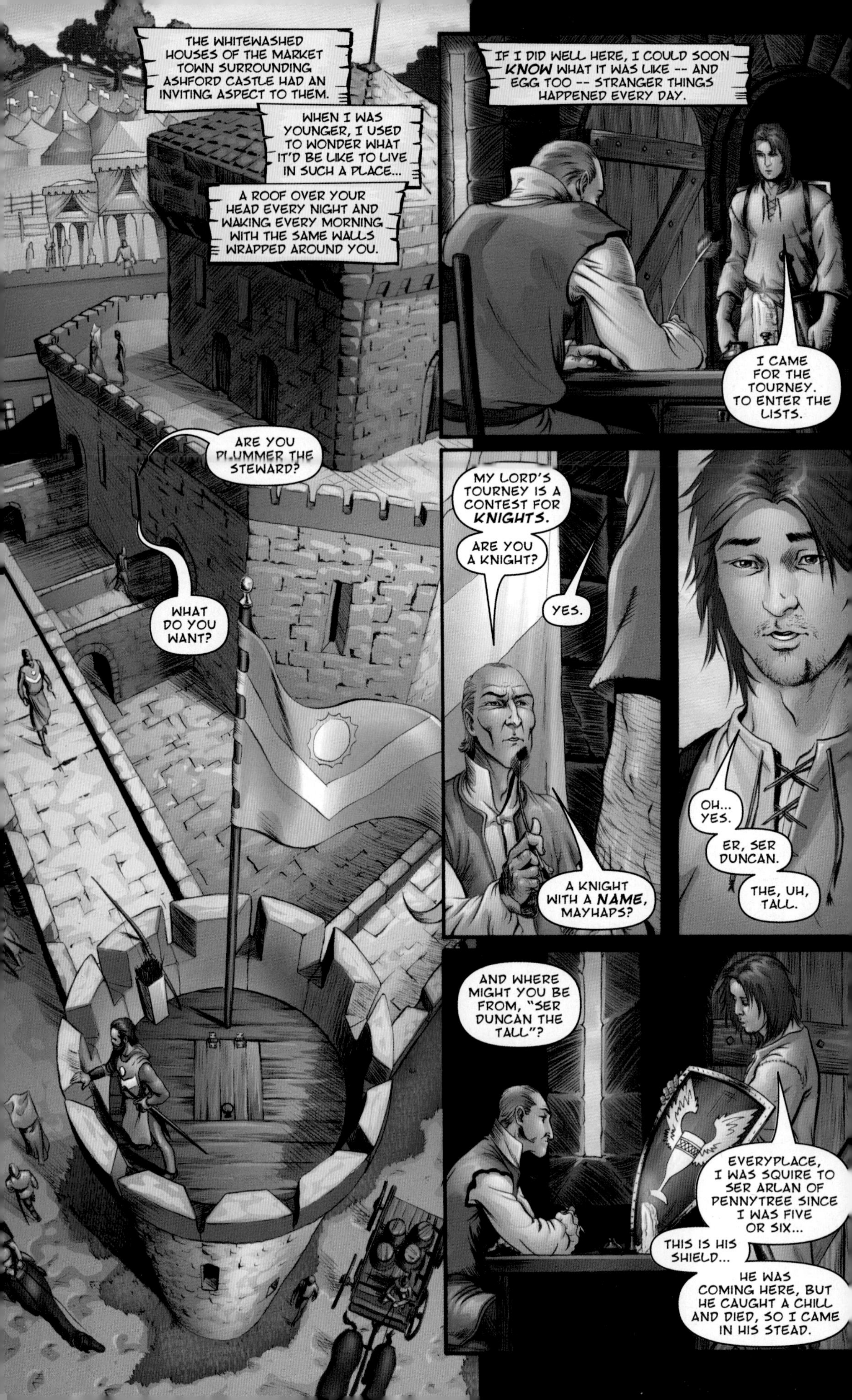
THE WHITEWASHED HOUSES OF THE MARKET TOWN SURROUNDING ASHFORD CASTLE HAD AN INVITING ASPECT TO THEM.
WHEN I WAS YOUNGER, I USED TO WONDER WHAT IT'D BE LIKE TO LIVE IN SUCH A PLACE...
A ROOF OVER YOUR HEAD EVERY NIGHT AND WAKING EVERY MORNING WITH THE SAME WALLS WRAPPED AROUND YOU.
ARE YOU PLUMMER THE STEWARD?
WHAT DO YOU WANT?
IF I DID WELL HERE, I COULD SOON KNOW WHAT IT WAS LIKE -- AND EGG TOO -- STRANGER THINGS HAPPENED EVERY DAY.
I CAME FOR THE TOURNEY. TO ENTER THE LISTS.
MY LORD'S TOURNEY IS A CONTEST FOR KNIGHTS.
ARE YOU A KNIGHT?
YES.
A KNIGHT WITH A NAME, MAYHAPS?
OH... YES.
ER, SER DUNCAN.
THE, UH, TALL.
AND WHERE MIGHT YOU BE FROM, "SER DUNCAN THE TALL"?
EVERYPLACE, I WAS SQUIRE TO SER ARLAN OF PENNYTREE SINCE I WAS FIVE OR SIX...
THIS IS HIS SHIELD...
HE WAS COMING HERE, BUT HE CAUGHT A CHILL AND DIED, SO I CAME IN HIS STEAD.

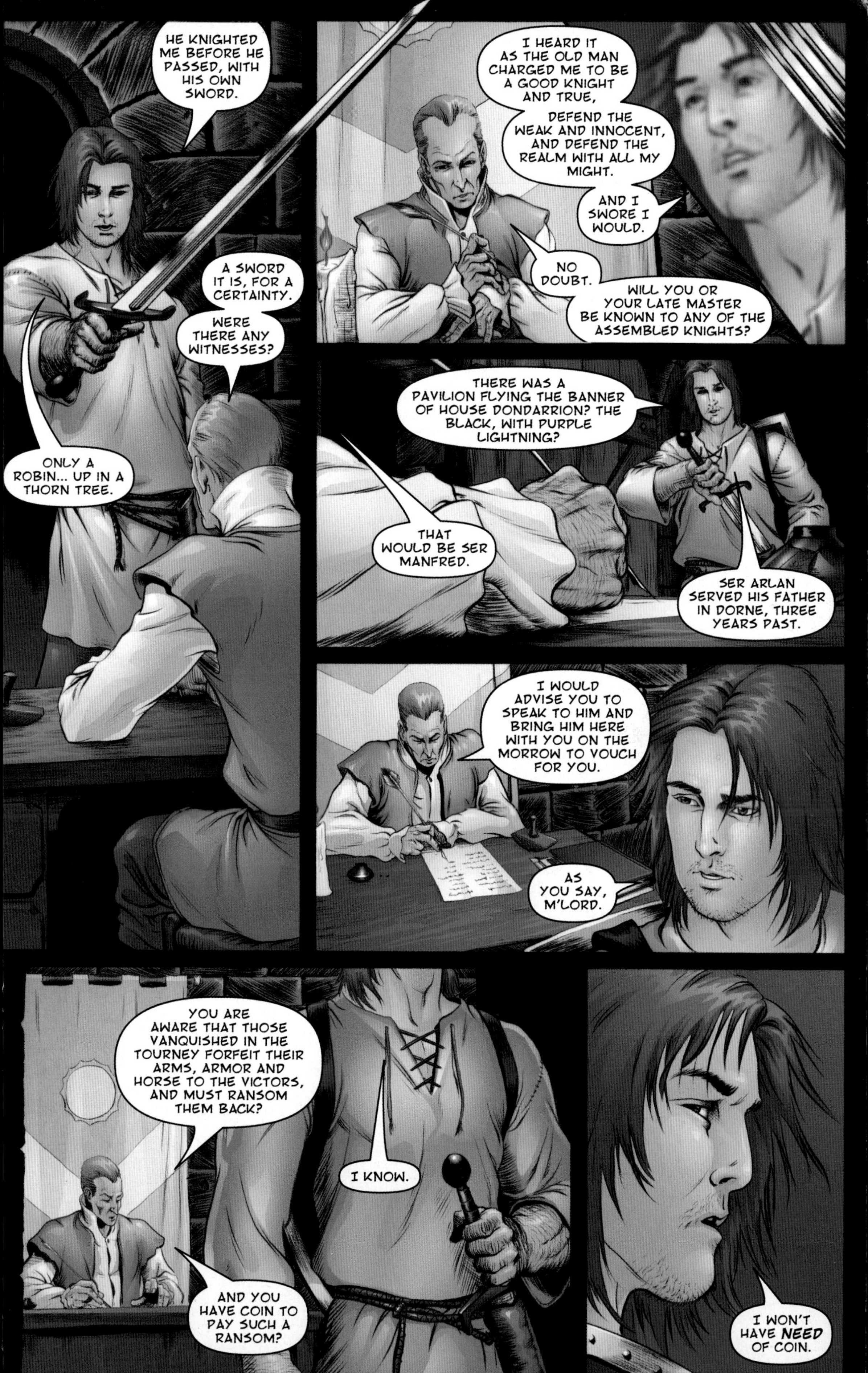
HE KNIGHTED ME BEFORE HE PASSED, WITH HIS OWN SWORD.
A SWORD IT IS, FOR A CERTAINTY.
WERE THERE ANY WITNESSES?
ONLY A ROBIN... UP IN A THORN TREE.
I HEARD IT AS THE OLD MAN CHARGED ME TO BE A GOOD KNIGHT AND TRUE,
DEFEND THE WEAK AND INNOCENT, AND DEFEND THE REALM WITH ALL MY MIGHT.
AND I SWORE I WOULD.
NO DOUBT.
WILL YOU OR YOUR LATE MASTER BE KNOWN TO ANY OF THE ASSEMBLED KNIGHTS?
THERE WAS A PAVILION FLYING THE BANNER OF HOUSE DONDARRION? THE BLACK, WITH PURPLE LIGHTNING?
THAT WOULD BE SER MANFRED.
SER ARLAN SERVED HIS FATHER IN DORNE, THREE YEARS PAST.
I WOULD ADVISE YOU TO SPEAK TO HIM AND BRING HIM HERE WITH YOU ON THE MORROW TO VOUCH FOR YOU.
AS YOU SAY, M'LORD.
YOU ARE AWARE THAT THOSE VANQUISHED IN THE TOURNEY FORFEIT THEIR ARMS, ARMOR AND HORSE TO THE VICTORS, AND MUST RANSOM THEM BACK?
I KNOW.
AND YOU HAVE COIN TO PAY SUCH A RANSOM?
I WON'T HAVE ***NEED*** OF COIN.

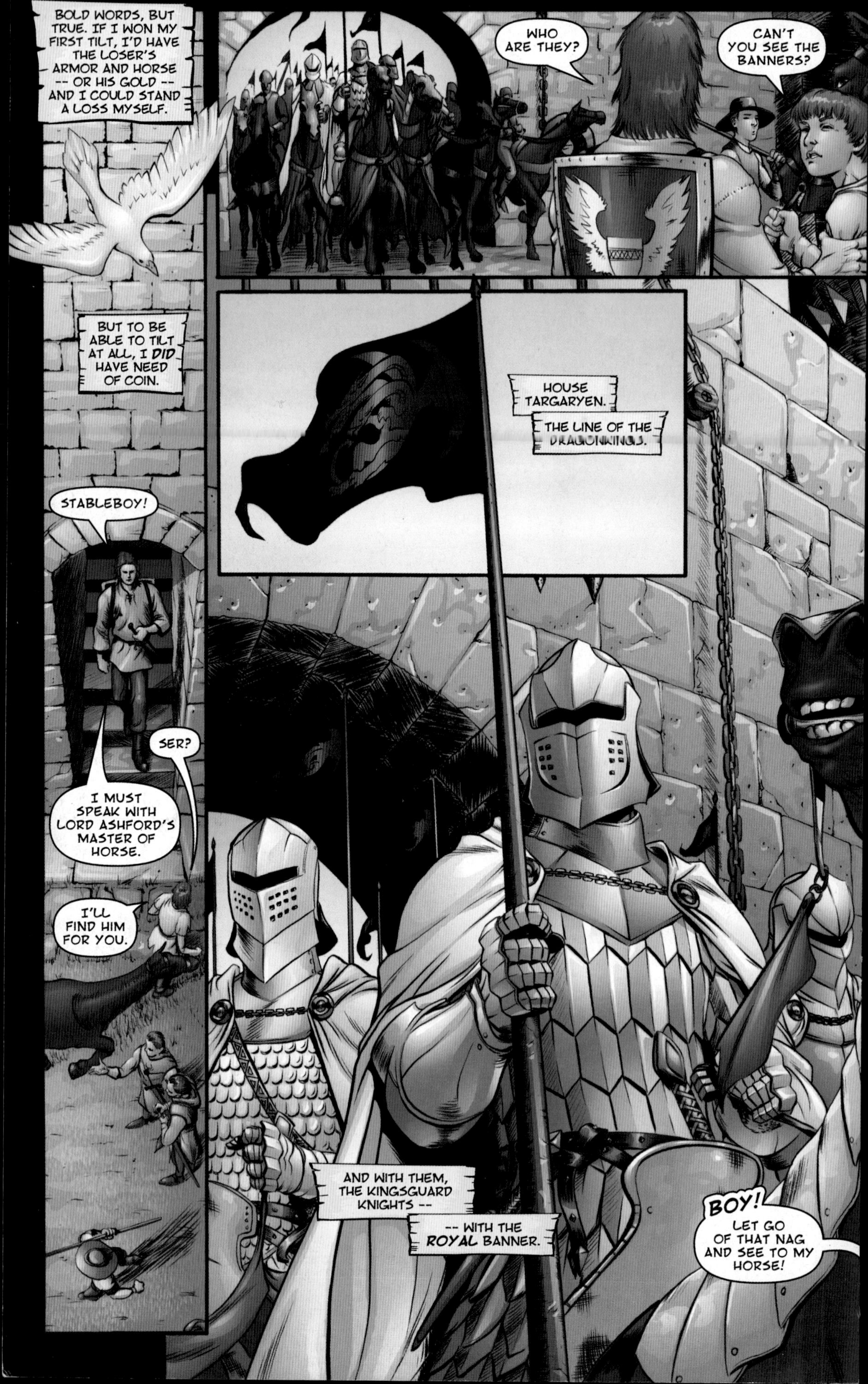

BOLD WORDS, BUT TRUE. IF I WON MY FIRST TILT, I'D HAVE THE LOSER'S ARMOR AND HORSE -- OR HIS GOLD -- AND I COULD STAND A LOSS MYSELF.
WHO ARE THEY?
CAN'T YOU SEE THE BANNERS?
BUT TO BE ABLE TO TILT AT ALL, I DID HAVE NEED OF COIN.
HOUSE TARGARYEN.
THE LINE OF THE DRAGONKINGS.
STABLEBOY!
SER?
I MUST SPEAK WITH LORD ASHFORD'S MASTER OF HORSE.
I'LL FIND HIM FOR YOU.
AND WITH THEM, THE KINGSGUARD KNIGHTS --
-- WITH THE ROYAL BANNER.
BOY! LET GO OF THAT NAG AND SEE TO MY HORSE!

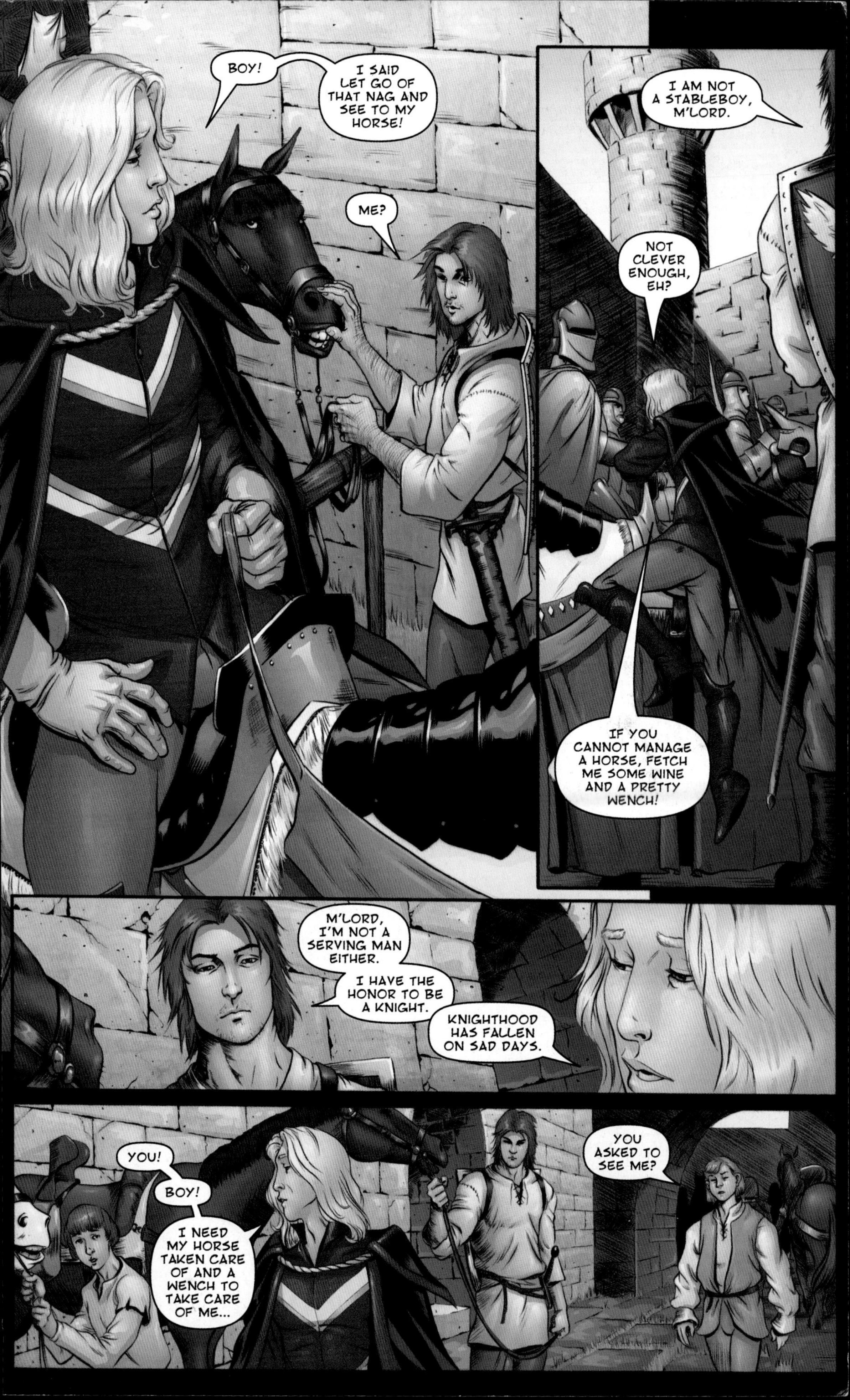
BOY!
I SAID LET GO OF THAT NAG AND SEE TO MY HORSE!
ME?
I AM NOT A STABLEBOY, M'LORD.
NOT CLEVER ENOUGH, EH?
IF YOU CANNOT MANAGE A HORSE, FETCH ME SOME WINE AND A PRETTY WENCH!
M'LORD, I'M NOT A SERVING MAN EITHER.
I HAVE THE HONOR TO BE A KNIGHT.
KNIGHTHOOD HAS FALLEN ON SAD DAYS.
YOU!
BOY!
I NEED MY HORSE TAKEN CARE OF AND A WENCH TO TAKE CARE OF ME...
YOU ASKED TO SEE ME?

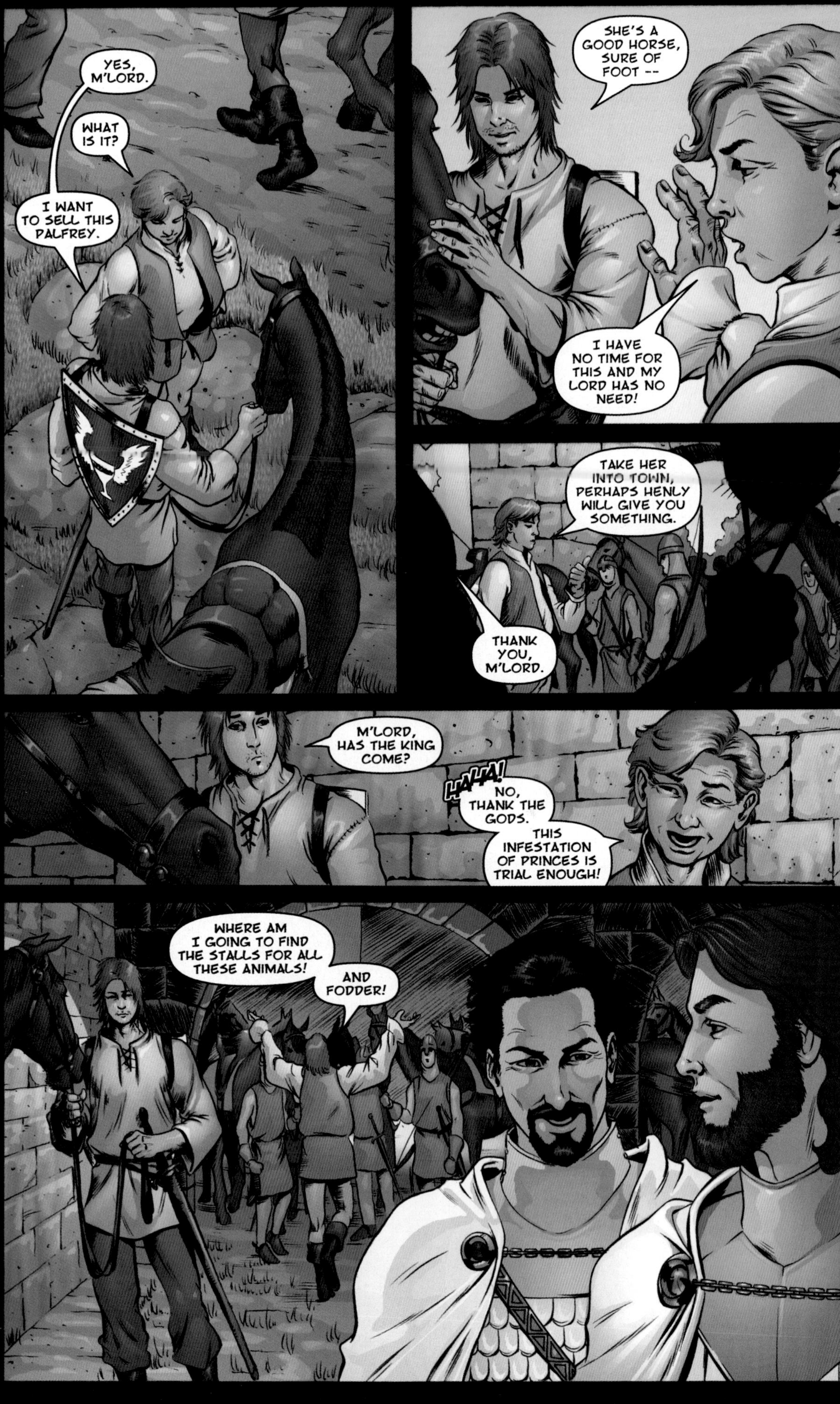
YES, M'LORD.
WHAT IS IT?
I WANT TO SELL THIS PALFREY.
SHE'S A GOOD HORSE, SURE OF FOOT --
I HAVE NO TIME FOR THIS AND MY LORD HAS NO NEED!
TAKE HER INTO TOWN, PERHAPS HENLY WILL GIVE YOU SOMETHING.
THANK YOU, M'LORD.
M'LORD, HAS THE KING COME?
HAHA!
NO, THANK THE GODS.
THIS INFESTATION OF PRINCES IS TRIAL ENOUGH!
WHERE AM I GOING TO FIND THE STALLS FOR ALL THESE ANIMALS!
AND FODDER!

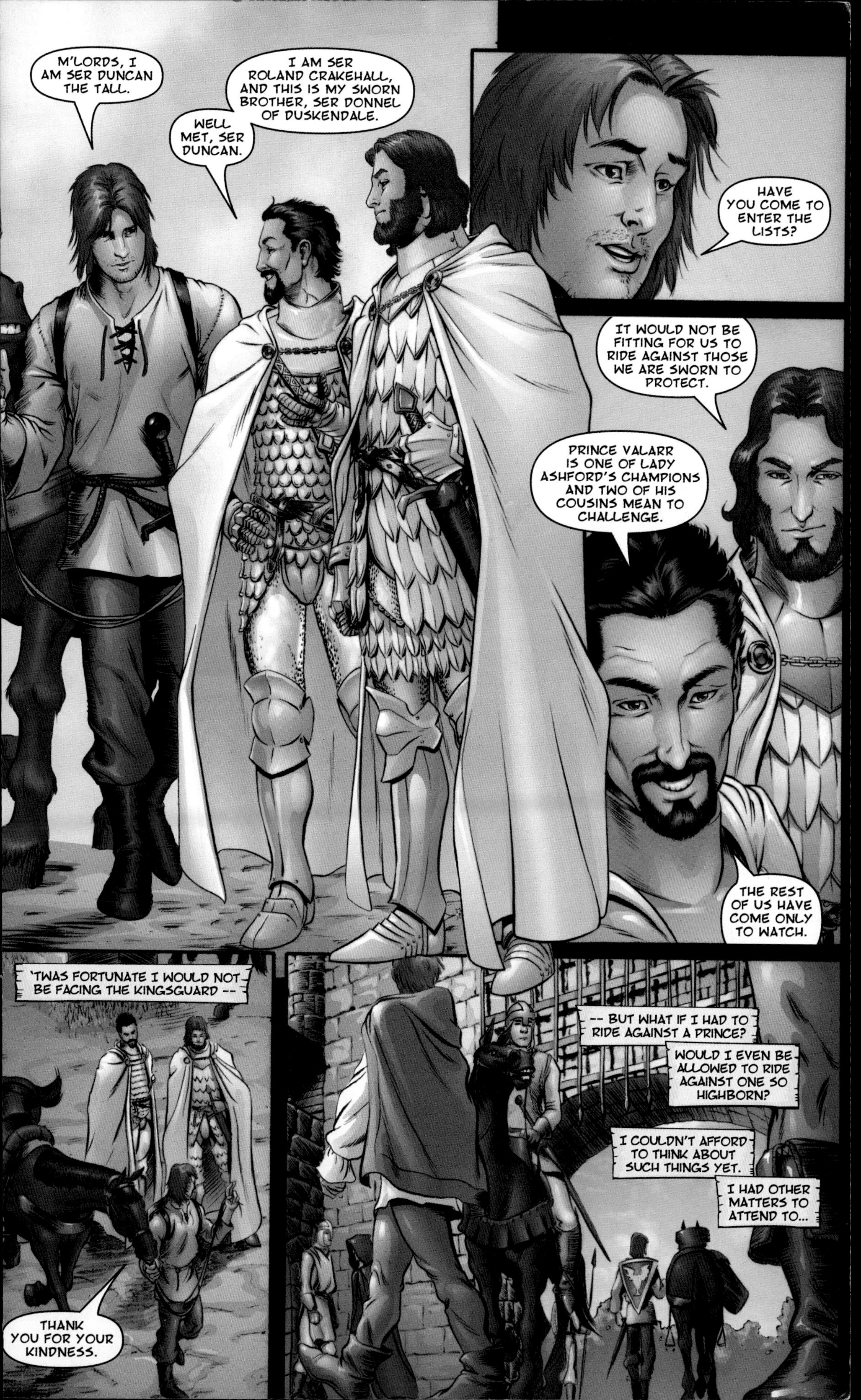
M'LORDS, I AM SER DUNCAN THE TALL.
I AM SER ROLAND CRAKEHALL, AND THIS IS MY SWORN BROTHER, SER DONNEL OF DUSKENDALE.
WELL MET, SER DUNCAN.
HAVE YOU COME TO ENTER THE LISTS?
IT WOULD NOT BE FITTING FOR US TO RIDE AGAINST THOSE WE ARE SWORN TO PROTECT.
PRINCE VALARR IS ONE OF LADY ASHFORD'S CHAMPIONS AND TWO OF HIS COUSINS MEAN TO CHALLENGE.
THE REST OF US HAVE COME ONLY TO WATCH.
'TWAS FORTUNATE I WOULD NOT BE FACING THE KINGSGUARD --
THANK YOU FOR YOUR KINDNESS.
-- BUT WHAT IF I HAD TO RIDE AGAINST A PRINCE?
WOULD I EVEN BE ALLOWED TO RIDE AGAINST ONE SO HIGHBORN?
I COULDN'T AFFORD TO THINK ABOUT SUCH THINGS YET.
I HAD OTHER MATTERS TO ATTEND TO...

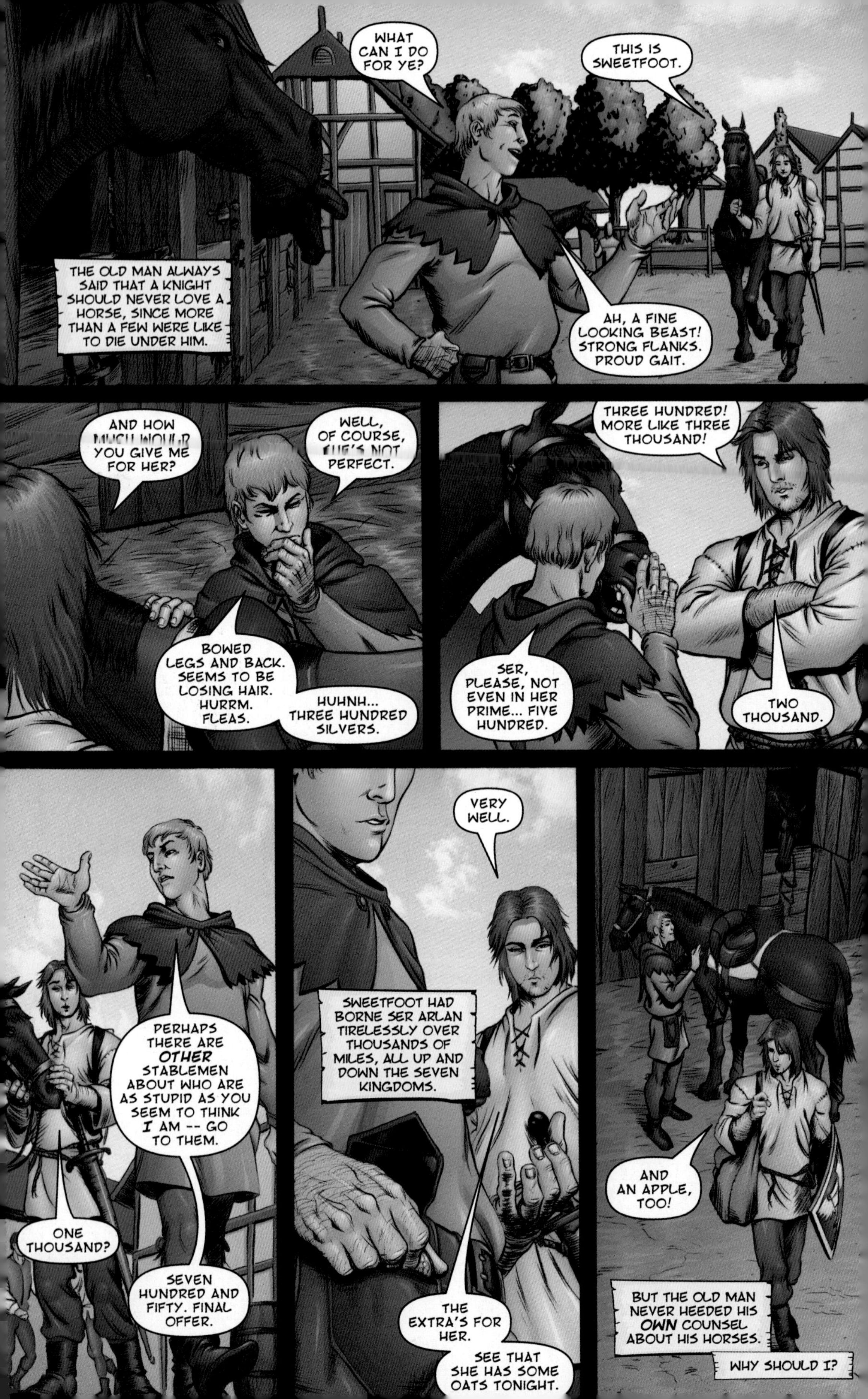
THE OLD MAN ALWAYS SAID THAT A KNIGHT SHOULD NEVER LOVE A HORSE, SINCE MORE THAN A FEW WERE LIKE TO DIE UNDER HIM.
WHAT CAN I DO FOR YE?
THIS IS SWEETFOOT.
AH, A FINE LOOKING BEAST! STRONG FLANKS. PROUD GAIT.
AND HOW MUCH WOULD YOU GIVE ME FOR HER?
WELL, OF COURSE, SHE'S NOT PERFECT.
BOWED LEGS AND BACK. SEEMS TO BE LOSING HAIR. HURRM. FLEAS.
HUHNH... THREE HUNDRED SILVERS.
THREE HUNDRED! MORE LIKE THREE THOUSAND!
SER, PLEASE, NOT EVEN IN HER PRIME... FIVE HUNDRED.
TWO THOUSAND.
PERHAPS THERE ARE *OTHER* STABLEMEN ABOUT WHO ARE AS STUPID AS YOU SEEM TO THINK *I* AM -- GO TO THEM.
ONE THOUSAND?
SEVEN HUNDRED AND FIFTY. FINAL OFFER.
VERY WELL.
SWEETFOOT HAD BORNE SER ARLAN TIRELESSLY OVER THOUSANDS OF MILES, ALL UP AND DOWN THE SEVEN KINGDOMS.
THE EXTRA'S FOR HER.
SEE THAT SHE HAS SOME OATS TONIGHT.
AND AN APPLE, TOO!
BUT THE OLD MAN NEVER HEEDED HIS *OWN* COUNSEL ABOUT HIS HORSES.
WHY SHOULD I?

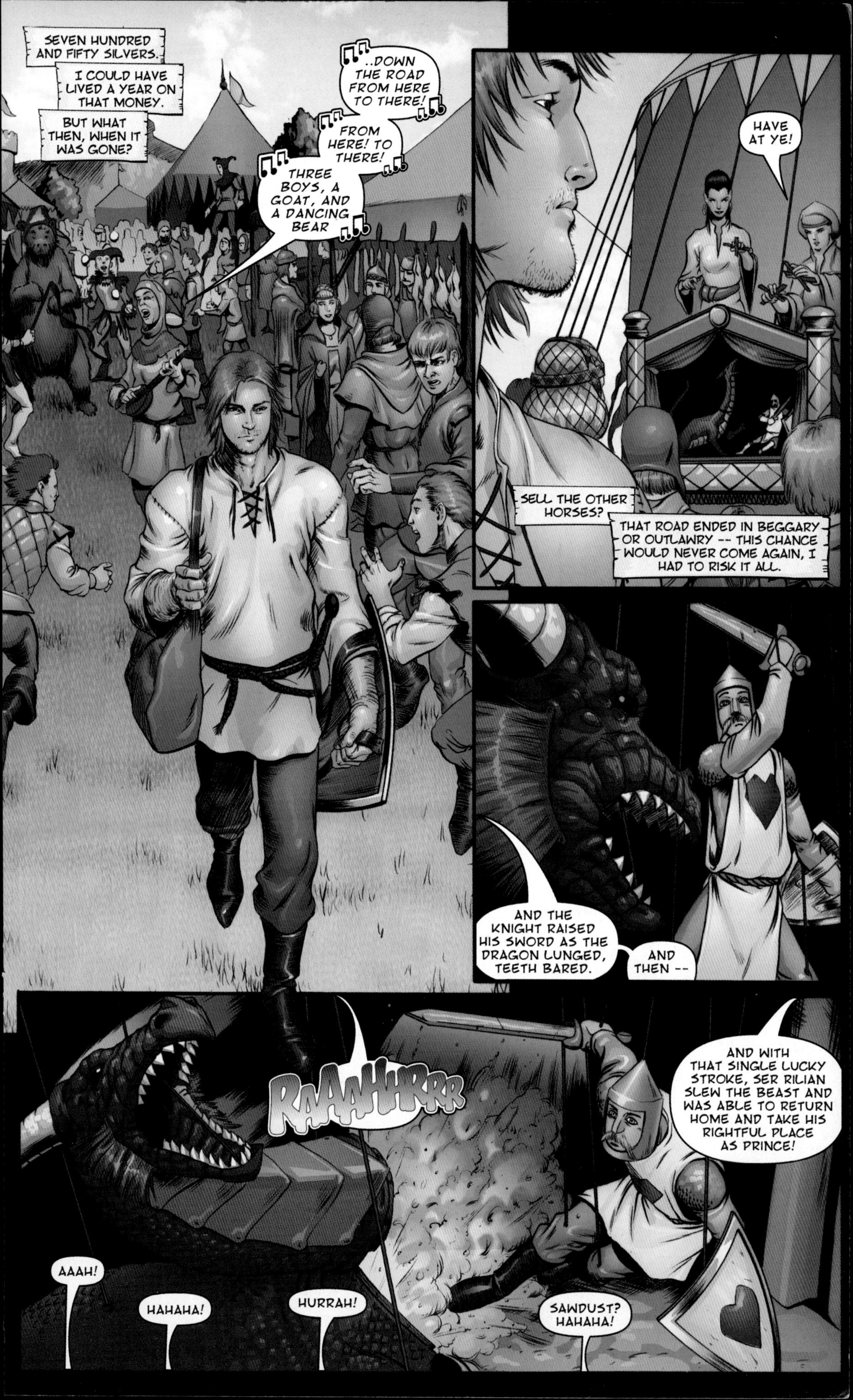
SEVEN HUNDRED AND FIFTY SILVERS.
I COULD HAVE LIVED A YEAR ON THAT MONEY.
BUT WHAT THEN, WHEN IT WAS GONE?
..DOWN THE ROAD FROM HERE TO THERE!
FROM HERE! TO THERE!
THREE BOYS, A GOAT, AND A DANCING BEAR
HAVE AT YE!
SELL THE OTHER HORSES?
THAT ROAD ENDED IN BEGGARY OR OUTLAWRY -- THIS CHANCE WOULD NEVER COME AGAIN, I HAD TO RISK IT ALL.
AND THE KNIGHT RAISED HIS SWORD AS THE DRAGON LUNGED, TEETH BARED.
AND THEN --
RAAAHHRRR
AND WITH THAT SINGLE LUCKY STROKE, SER RILIAN SLEW THE BEAST AND WAS ABLE TO RETURN HOME AND TAKE HIS RIGHTFUL PLACE AS PRINCE!
AAAH!
HAHAHA!
HURRAH!
SAWDUST? HAHAHA!

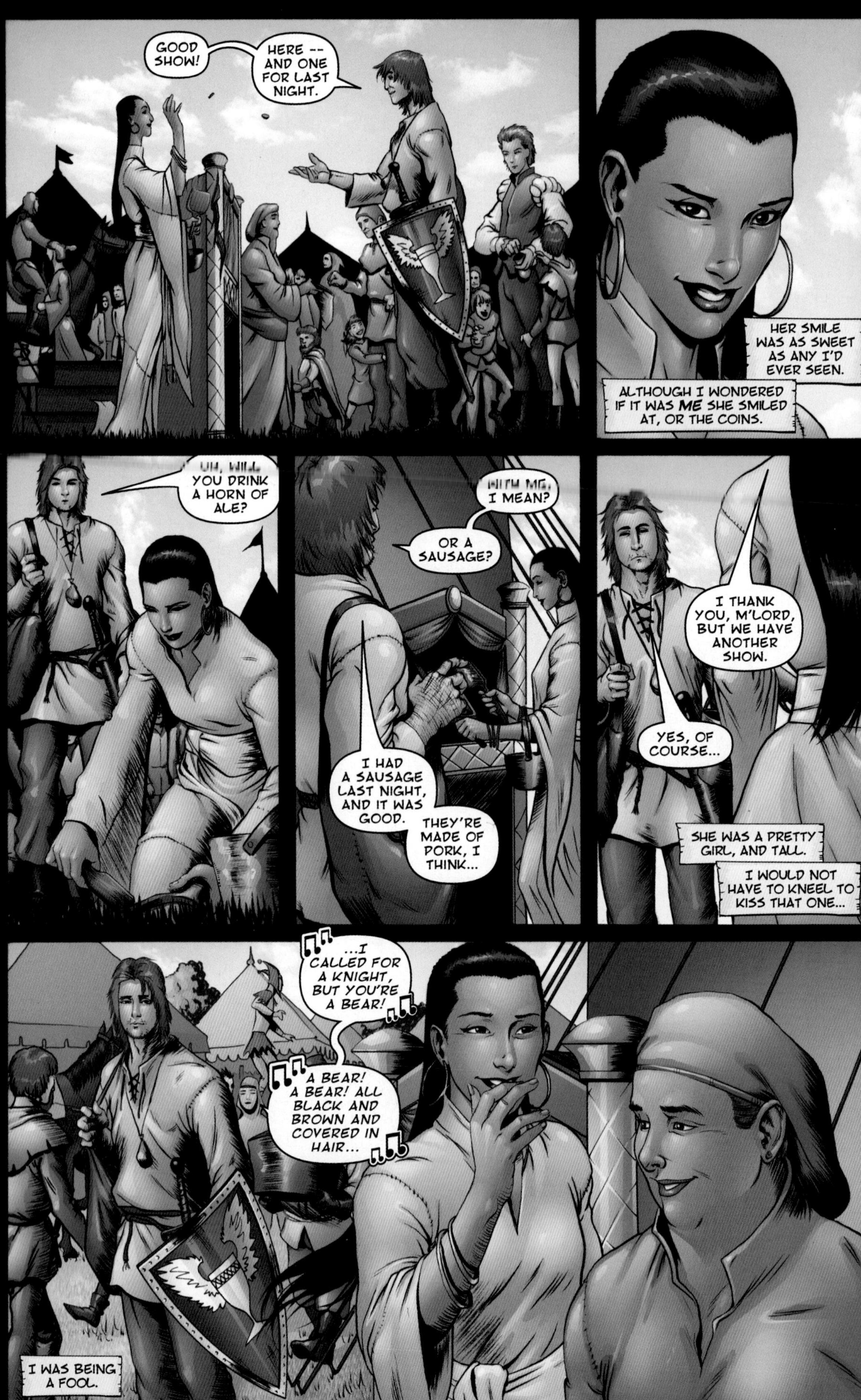
GOOD SHOW!
HERE -- AND ONE FOR LAST NIGHT.
HER SMILE WAS AS SWEET AS ANY I'D EVER SEEN.
ALTHOUGH I WONDERED IF IT WAS ME SHE SMILED AT, OR THE COINS.
YOU DRINK A HORN OF ALE?
I MEAN?
OR A SAUSAGE?
I HAD A SAUSAGE LAST NIGHT, AND IT WAS GOOD.
THEY'RE MADE OF PORK, I THINK...
I THANK YOU, M'LORD, BUT WE HAVE ANOTHER SHOW.
YES, OF COURSE...
SHE WAS A PRETTY GIRL, AND TALL.
I WOULD NOT HAVE TO KNEEL TO KISS THAT ONE...
...I CALLED FOR A KNIGHT, BUT YOU'RE A BEAR!
A BEAR! A BEAR! ALL BLACK AND BROWN AND COVERED IN HAIR...
I WAS BEING A FOOL.

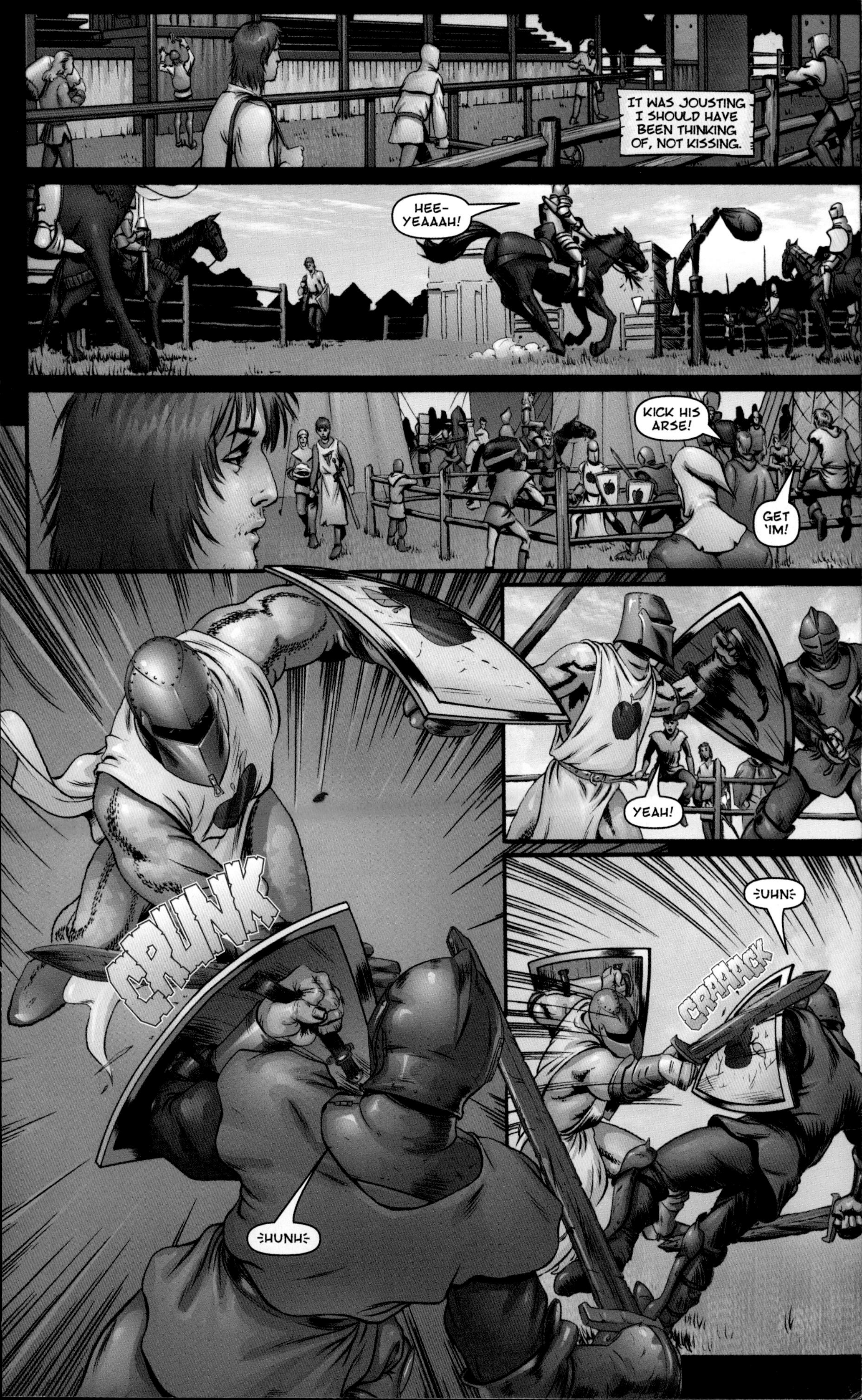
IT WAS JOUSTING I SHOULD HAVE BEEN THINKING OF, NOT KISSING.
HEE-YEAAAH!
KICK HIS ARSE!
GET 'IM!
YEAH!
CRUNK
HUNH
UHN
CRAAACK

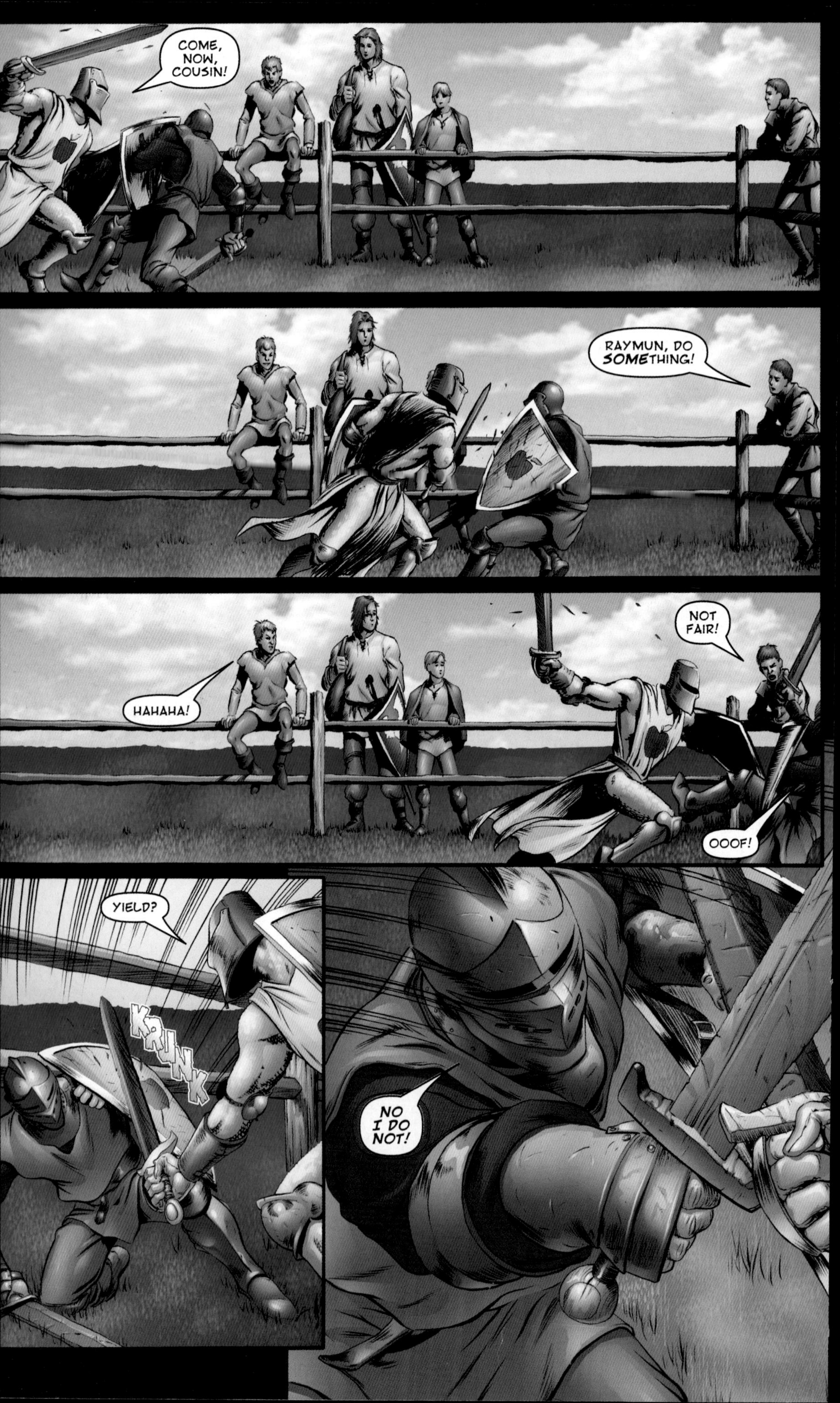
COME, NOW, COUSIN!
RAYMUN, DO SOMETHING!
HAHAHA!
NOT FAIR!
OOOF!
YIELD?
KRUNK
NO I DO NOT!

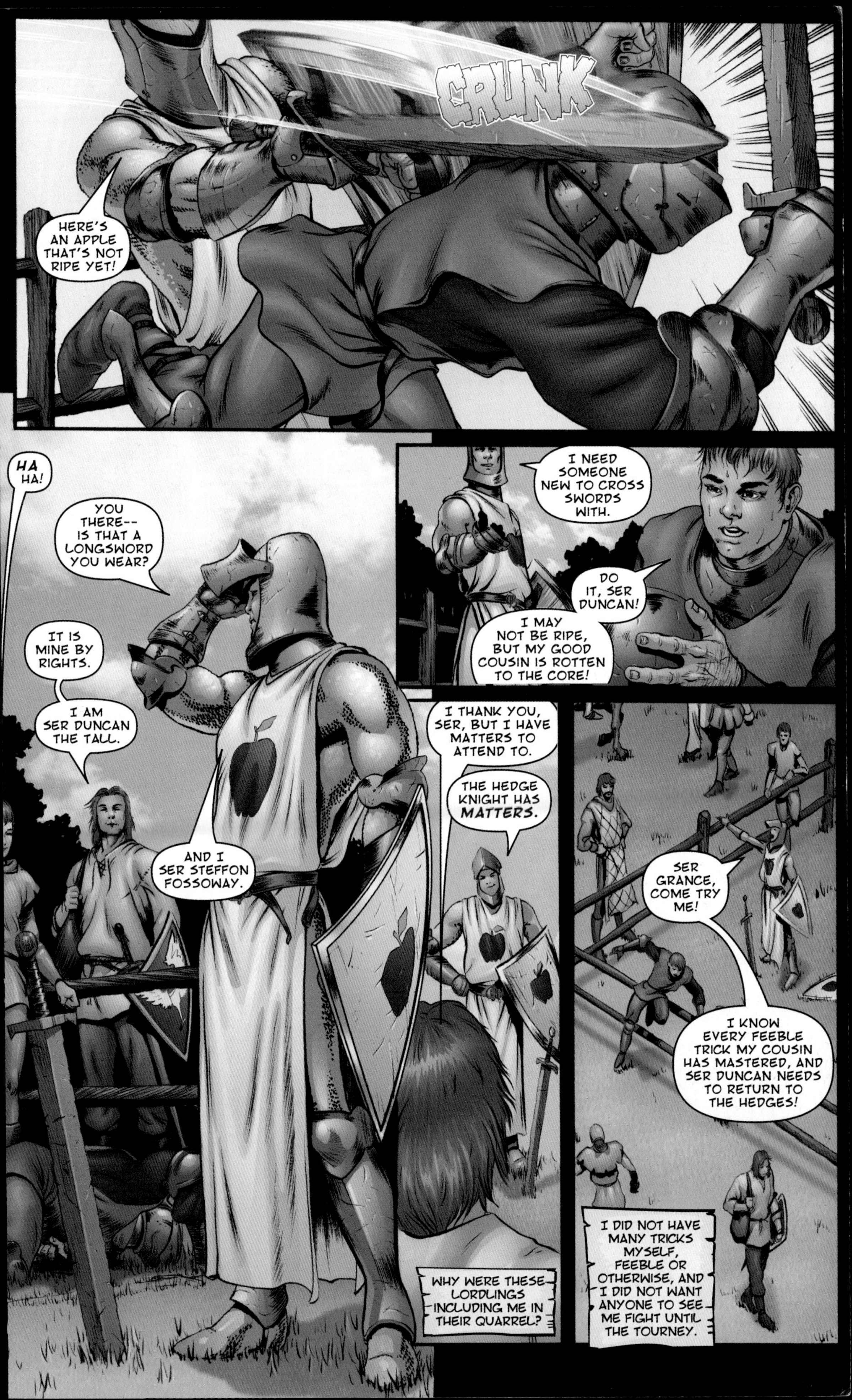
CRUNK
HERE'S AN APPLE THAT'S NOT RIPE YET!
HA HA!
YOU THERE-- IS THAT A LONGSWORD YOU WEAR?
IT IS MINE BY RIGHTS.
I AM SER DUNCAN THE TALL.
AND I SER STEFFON FOSSOWAY.
I NEED SOMEONE NEW TO CROSS SWORDS WITH.
DO IT, SER DUNCAN!
I MAY NOT BE RIPE, BUT MY GOOD COUSIN IS ROTTEN TO THE CORE!
I THANK YOU, SER, BUT I HAVE MATTERS TO ATTEND TO.
THE HEDGE KNIGHT HAS MATTERS.
WHY WERE THESE LORDLINGS INCLUDING ME IN THEIR QUARREL?
SER GRANCE, COME TRY ME!
I KNOW EVERY FEEBLE TRICK MY COUSIN HAS MASTERED, AND SER DUNCAN NEEDS TO RETURN TO THE HEDGES!
I DID NOT HAVE MANY TRICKS MYSELF, FEEBLE OR OTHERWISE, AND I DID NOT WANT ANYONE TO SEE ME FIGHT UNTIL THE TOURNEY.

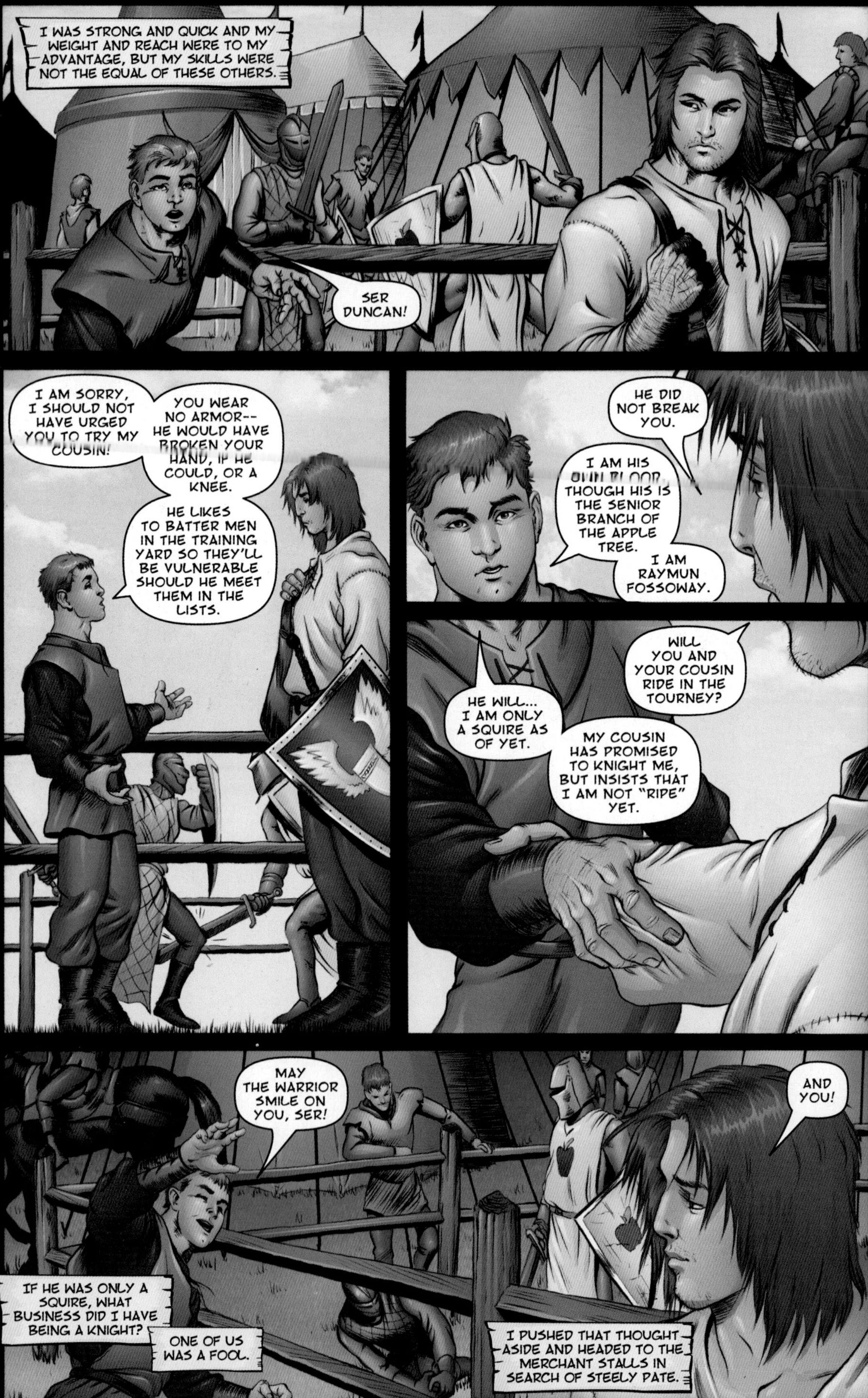

I WAS STRONG AND QUICK AND MY WEIGHT AND REACH WERE TO MY ADVANTAGE, BUT MY SKILLS WERE NOT THE EQUAL OF THESE OTHERS.
SER DUNCAN!
I AM SORRY, I SHOULD NOT HAVE URGED YOU TO TRY MY COUSIN!
YOU WEAR NO ARMOR-- HE WOULD HAVE BROKEN YOUR HAND, IF HE COULD, OR A KNEE.
HE LIKES TO BATTER MEN IN THE TRAINING YARD SO THEY'LL BE VULNERABLE SHOULD HE MEET THEM IN THE LISTS.
HE DID NOT BREAK YOU.
I AM HIS OWN BLOOD, THOUGH HIS IS THE SENIOR BRANCH OF THE APPLE TREE.
I AM RAYMUN FOSSOWAY.
WILL YOU AND YOUR COUSIN RIDE IN THE TOURNEY?
HE WILL... I AM ONLY A SQUIRE AS OF YET.
MY COUSIN HAS PROMISED TO KNIGHT ME, BUT INSISTS THAT I AM NOT "RIPE" YET.
MAY THE WARRIOR SMILE ON YOU, SER!
AND YOU!
IF HE WAS ONLY A SQUIRE, WHAT BUSINESS DID I HAVE BEING A KNIGHT?
ONE OF US WAS A FOOL.
I PUSHED THAT THOUGHT ASIDE AND HEADED TO THE MERCHANT STALLS IN SEARCH OF STEELY PATE.

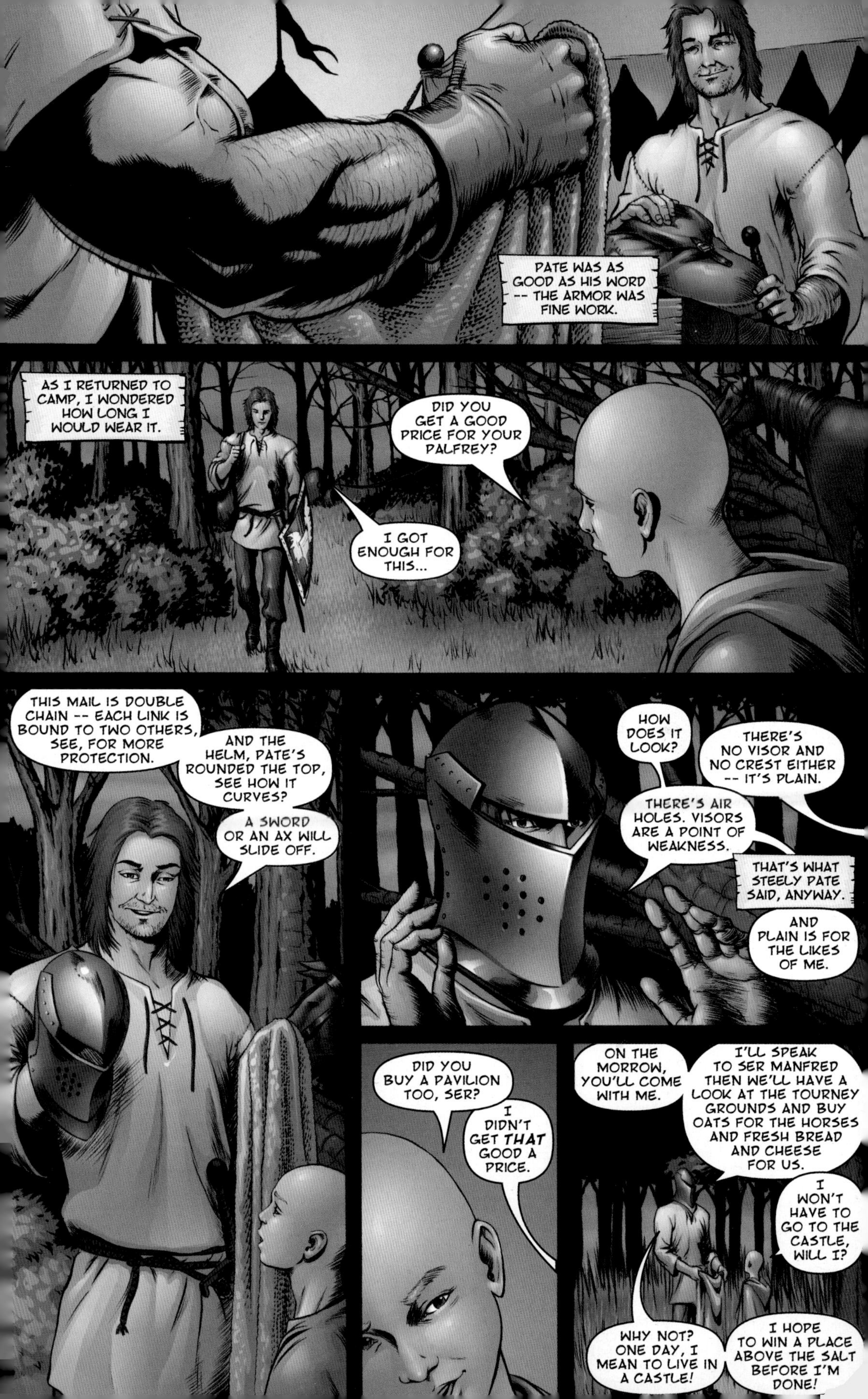
PATE WAS AS GOOD AS HIS WORD -- THE ARMOR WAS FINE WORK.
AS I RETURNED TO CAMP, I WONDERED HOW LONG I WOULD WEAR IT.
DID YOU GET A GOOD PRICE FOR YOUR PALFREY?
I GOT ENOUGH FOR THIS...
THIS MAIL IS DOUBLE CHAIN -- EACH LINK IS BOUND TO TWO OTHERS, SEE, FOR MORE PROTECTION.
AND THE HELM, PATE'S ROUNDED THE TOP, SEE HOW IT CURVES?
A SWORD OR AN AX WILL SLIDE OFF.
HOW DOES IT LOOK?
THERE'S NO VISOR AND NO CREST EITHER -- IT'S PLAIN.
THERE'S AIR HOLES. VISORS ARE A POINT OF WEAKNESS.
THAT'S WHAT STEELY PATE SAID, ANYWAY.
AND PLAIN IS FOR THE LIKES OF ME.
DID YOU BUY A PAVILION TOO, SER?
I DIDN'T GET *THAT* GOOD A PRICE.
ON THE MORROW, YOU'LL COME WITH ME.
I'LL SPEAK TO SER MANFRED THEN WE'LL HAVE A LOOK AT THE TOURNEY GROUNDS AND BUY OATS FOR THE HORSES AND FRESH BREAD AND CHEESE FOR US.
I WON'T HAVE TO GO TO THE CASTLE, WILL I?
WHY NOT? ONE DAY, I MEAN TO LIVE IN A CASTLE!
I HOPE TO WIN A PLACE ABOVE THE SALT BEFORE I'M DONE!

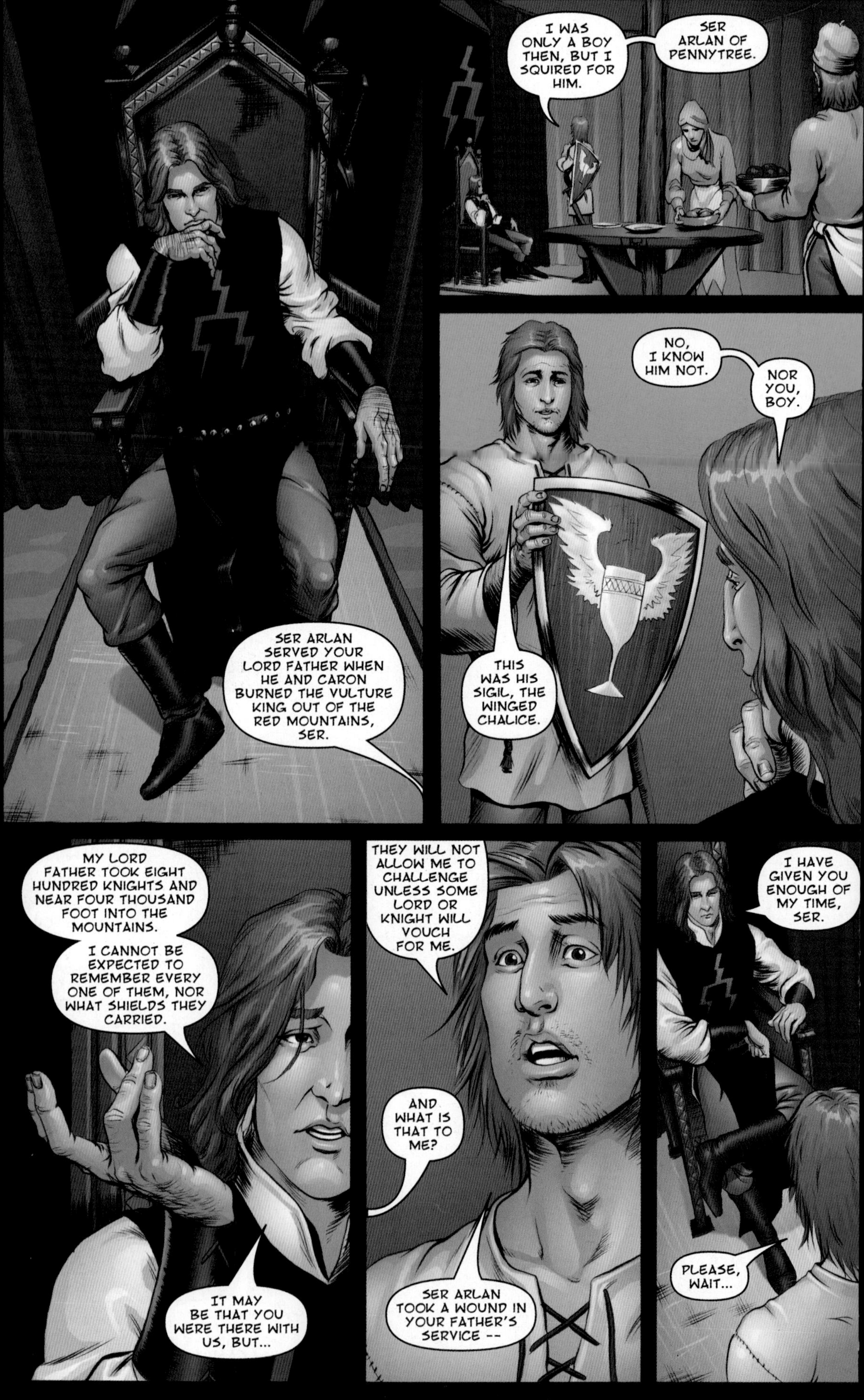
I WAS ONLY A BOY THEN, BUT I SQUIRED FOR HIM.
SER ARLAN OF PENNYTREE.
SER ARLAN SERVED YOUR LORD FATHER WHEN HE AND CARON BURNED THE VULTURE KING OUT OF THE RED MOUNTAINS, SER.
NO, I KNOW HIM NOT.
NOR YOU, BOY.
THIS WAS HIS SIGIL, THE WINGED CHALICE.
MY LORD FATHER TOOK EIGHT HUNDRED KNIGHTS AND NEAR FOUR THOUSAND FOOT INTO THE MOUNTAINS.
I CANNOT BE EXPECTED TO REMEMBER EVERY ONE OF THEM, NOR WHAT SHIELDS THEY CARRIED.
IT MAY BE THAT YOU WERE THERE WITH US, BUT...
THEY WILL NOT ALLOW ME TO CHALLENGE UNLESS SOME LORD OR KNIGHT WILL VOUCH FOR ME.
AND WHAT IS THAT TO ME?
SER ARLAN TOOK A WOUND IN YOUR FATHER'S SERVICE --
I HAVE GIVEN YOU ENOUGH OF MY TIME, SER.
PLEASE, WAIT...

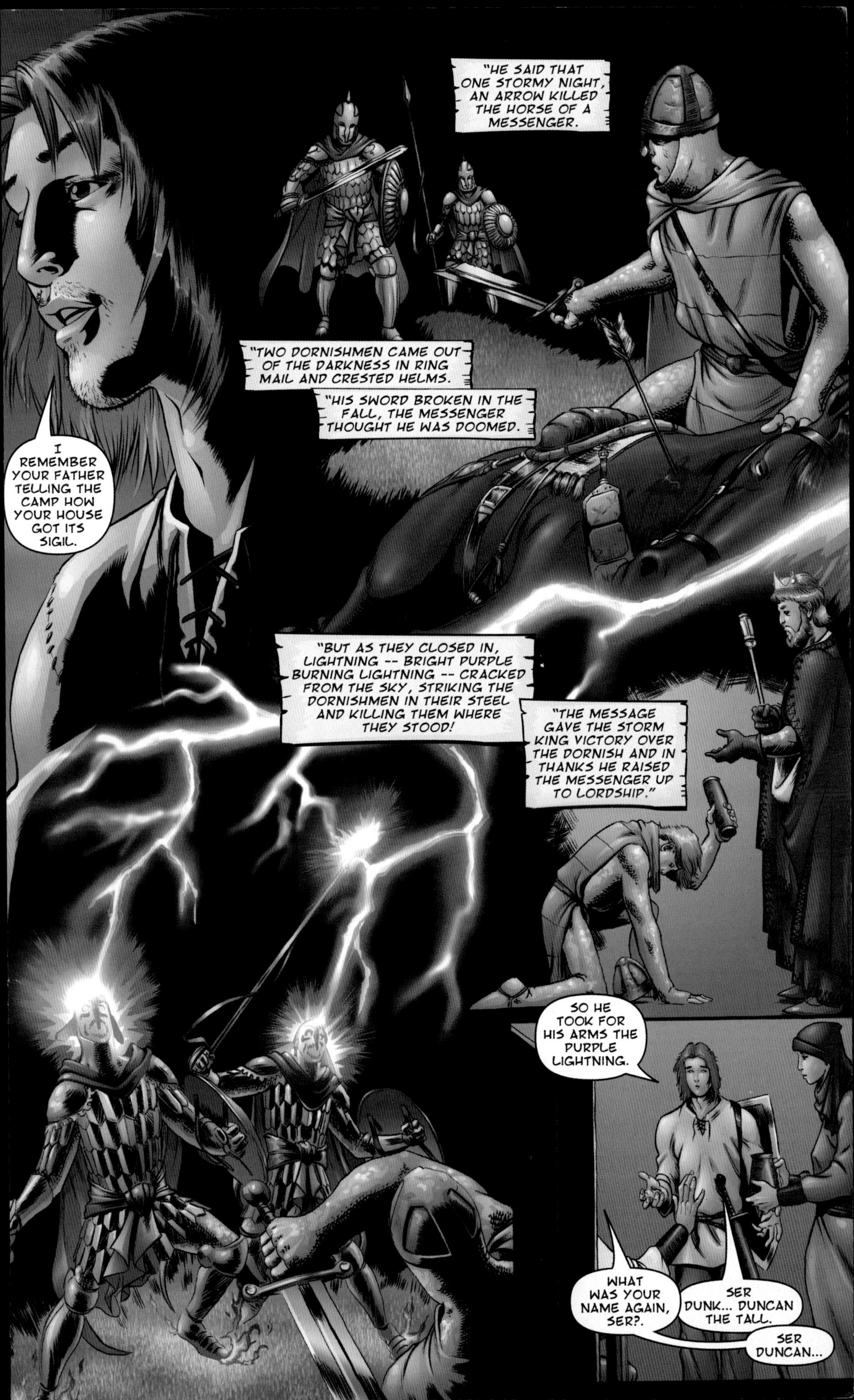
"HE SAID THAT ONE STORMY NIGHT, AN ARROW KILLED THE HORSE OF A MESSENGER.
I REMEMBER YOUR FATHER TELLING THE CAMP HOW YOUR HOUSE GOT ITS SIGIL.
"TWO DORNISHMEN CAME OUT OF THE DARKNESS IN RING MAIL AND CRESTED HELMS.
"HIS SWORD BROKEN IN THE FALL, THE MESSENGER THOUGHT HE WAS DOOMED.
"BUT AS THEY CLOSED IN, LIGHTNING -- BRIGHT PURPLE BURNING LIGHTNING -- CRACKED FROM THE SKY, STRIKING THE DORNISHMEN IN THEIR STEEL AND KILLING THEM WHERE THEY STOOD!
"THE MESSAGE GAVE THE STORM KING VICTORY OVER THE DORNISH AND IN THANKS HE RAISED THE MESSENGER UP TO LORDSHIP."
SO HE TOOK FOR HIS ARMS THE PURPLE LIGHTNING.
WHAT WAS YOUR NAME AGAIN, SER?.
SER DUNK... DUNCAN THE TALL.
SER DUNCAN...

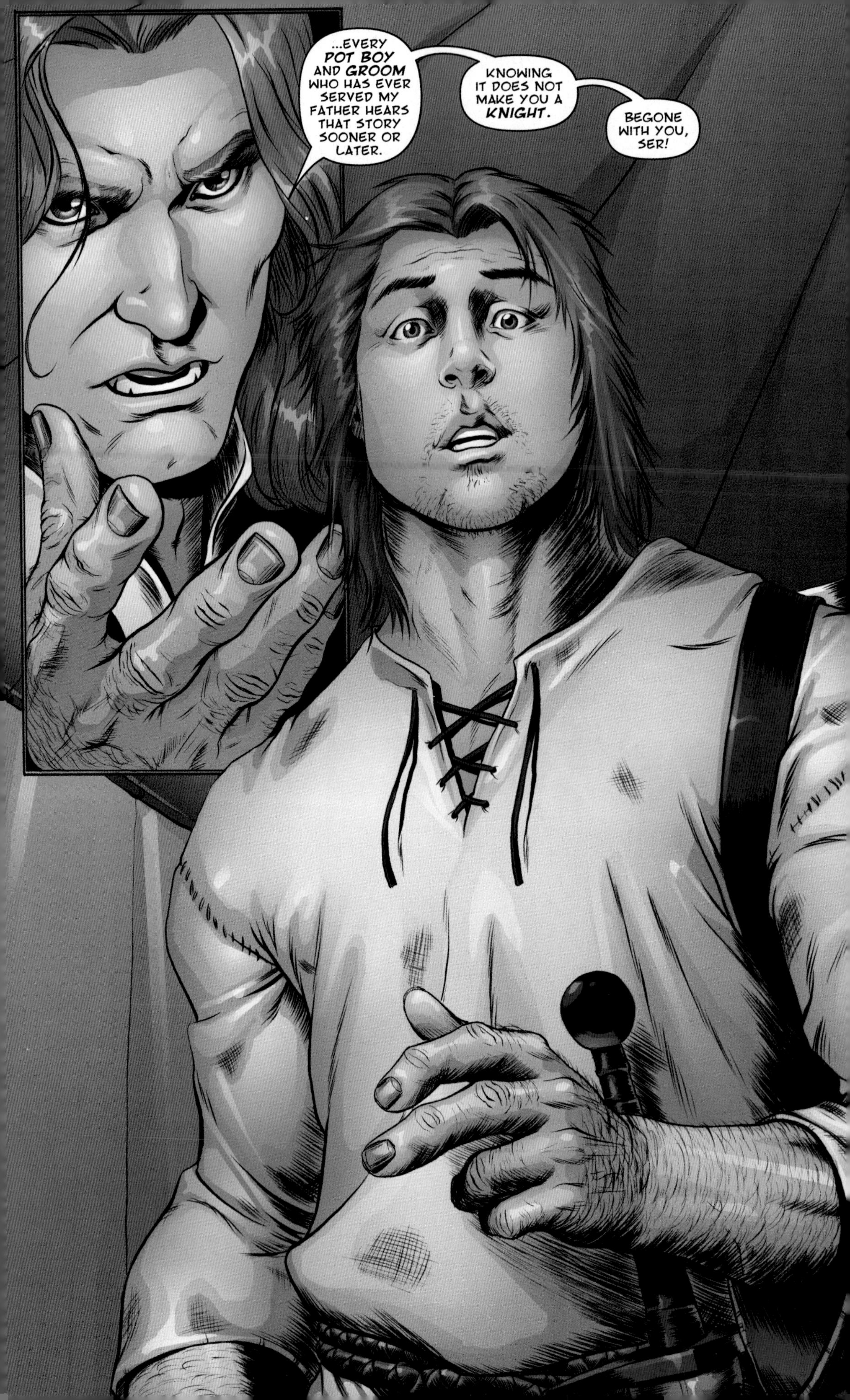
...EVERY POT BOY AND GROOM WHO HAS EVER SERVED MY FATHER HEARS THAT STORY SOONER OR LATER.
KNOWING IT DOES NOT MAKE YOU A KNIGHT.
BEGONE WITH YOU, SER!

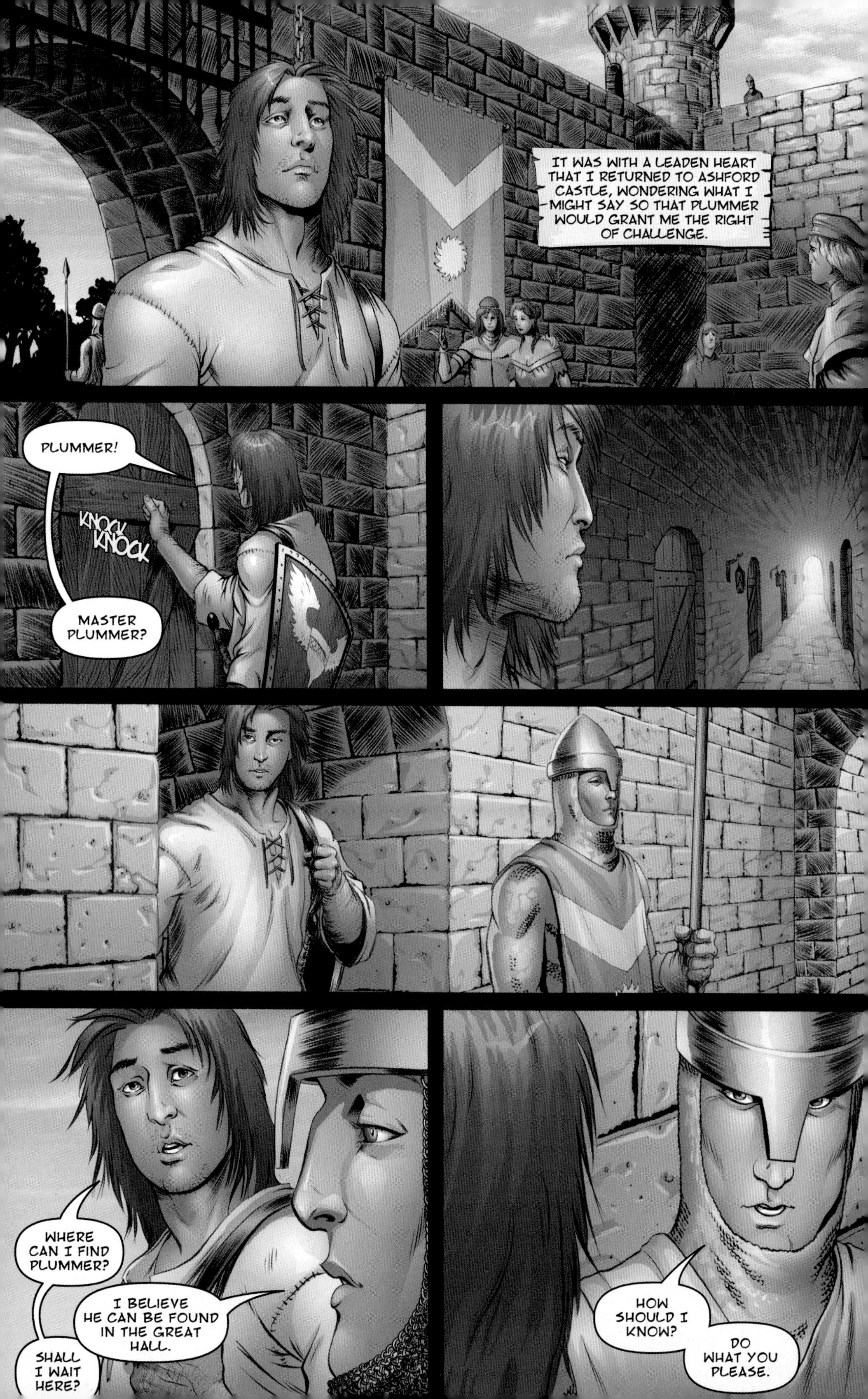
IT WAS WITH A LEADEN HEART THAT I RETURNED TO ASHFORD CASTLE, WONDERING WHAT I MIGHT SAY SO THAT PLUMMER WOULD GRANT ME THE RIGHT OF CHALLENGE.
PLUMMER!
KNOCK KNOCK
MASTER PLUMMER?
WHERE CAN I FIND PLUMMER?
I BELIEVE HE CAN BE FOUND IN THE GREAT HALL.
SHALL I WAIT HERE?
HOW SHOULD I KNOW?
DO WHAT YOU PLEASE.

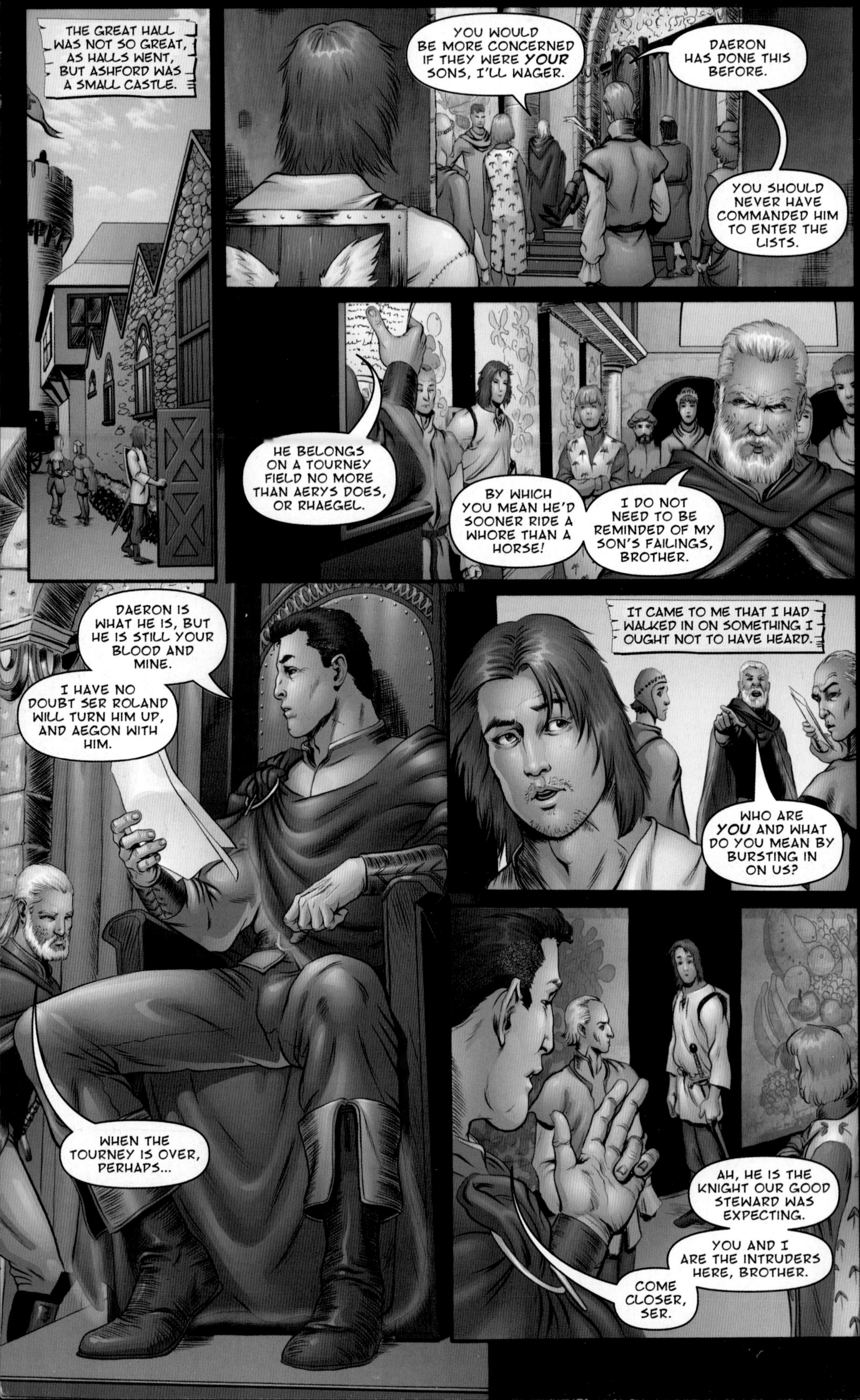

THE GREAT HALL WAS NOT SO GREAT, AS HALLS WENT, BUT ASHFORD WAS A SMALL CASTLE.
YOU WOULD BE MORE CONCERNED IF THEY WERE YOUR SONS, I'LL WAGER.
DAERON HAS DONE THIS BEFORE.
YOU SHOULD NEVER HAVE COMMANDED HIM TO ENTER THE LISTS.
HE BELONGS ON A TOURNEY FIELD NO MORE THAN AERYS DOES, OR RHAEGEL.
BY WHICH YOU MEAN HE'D SOONER RIDE A WHORE THAN A HORSE!
I DO NOT NEED TO BE REMINDED OF MY SON'S FAILINGS, BROTHER.
DAERON IS WHAT HE IS, BUT HE IS STILL YOUR BLOOD AND MINE.
I HAVE NO DOUBT SER ROLAND WILL TURN HIM UP, AND AEGON WITH HIM.
WHEN THE TOURNEY IS OVER, PERHAPS...
IT CAME TO ME THAT I HAD WALKED IN ON SOMETHING I OUGHT NOT TO HAVE HEARD.
WHO ARE YOU AND WHAT DO YOU MEAN BY BURSTING IN ON US?
AH, HE IS THE KNIGHT OUR GOOD STEWARD WAS EXPECTING.
YOU AND I ARE THE INTRUDERS HERE, BROTHER.
COME CLOSER, SER.

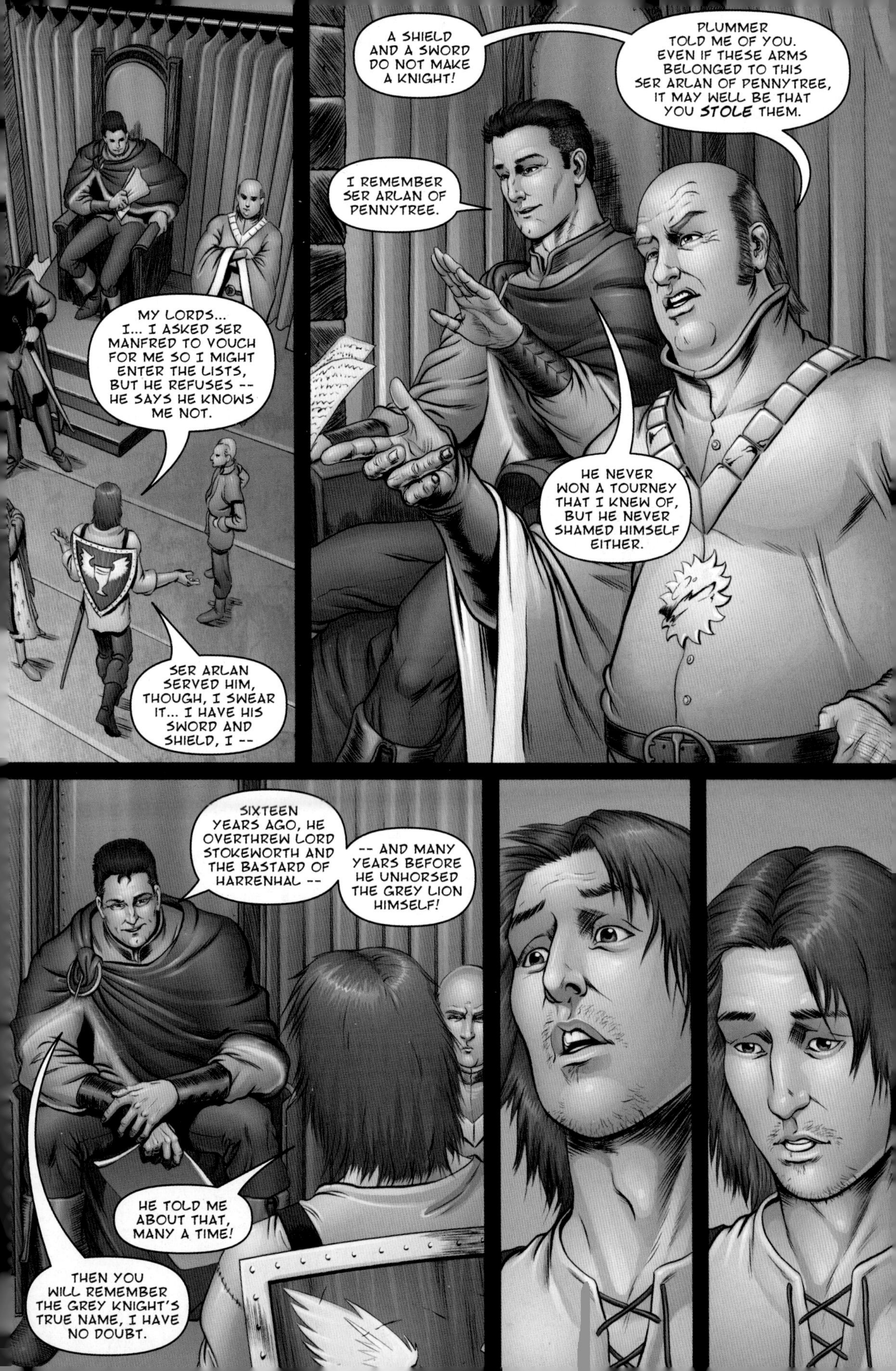
MY LORDS... I... I ASKED SER MANFRED TO VOUCH FOR ME SO I MIGHT ENTER THE LISTS, BUT HE REFUSES -- HE SAYS HE KNOWS ME NOT.
SER ARLAN SERVED HIM, THOUGH, I SWEAR IT... I HAVE HIS SWORD AND SHIELD, I --
A SHIELD AND A SWORD DO NOT MAKE A KNIGHT!
PLUMMER TOLD ME OF YOU. EVEN IF THESE ARMS BELONGED TO THIS SER ARLAN OF PENNYTREE, IT MAY WELL BE THAT YOU STOLE THEM.
I REMEMBER SER ARLAN OF PENNYTREE.
HE NEVER WON A TOURNEY THAT I KNEW OF, BUT HE NEVER SHAMED HIMSELF EITHER.
SIXTEEN YEARS AGO, HE OVERTHREW LORD STOKEWORTH AND THE BASTARD OF HARRENHAL --
-- AND MANY YEARS BEFORE HE UNHORSED THE GREY LION HIMSELF!
HE TOLD ME ABOUT THAT, MANY A TIME!
THEN YOU WILL REMEMBER THE GREY KNIGHT'S TRUE NAME, I HAVE NO DOUBT.

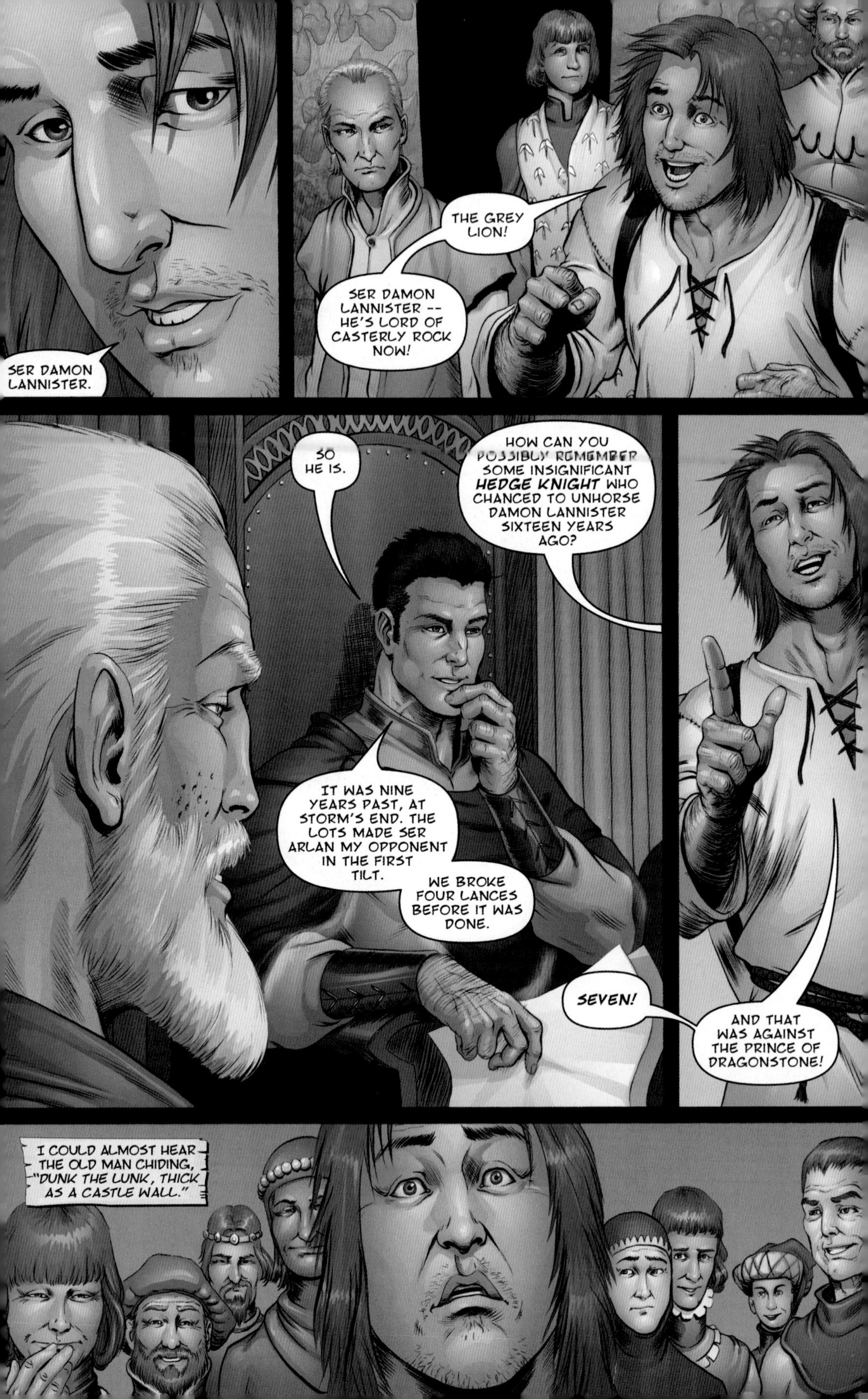
SER DAMON LANNISTER.
THE GREY LION!
SER DAMON LANNISTER -- HE'S LORD OF CASTERLY ROCK NOW!
SO HE IS.
HOW CAN YOU POSSIBLY REMEMBER SOME INSIGNIFICANT **HEDGE KNIGHT** WHO CHANCED TO UNHORSE DAMON LANNISTER SIXTEEN YEARS AGO?
IT WAS NINE YEARS PAST, AT STORM'S END. THE LOTS MADE SER ARLAN MY OPPONENT IN THE FIRST TILT.
WE BROKE FOUR LANCES BEFORE IT WAS DONE.
*SEVEN!*
AND THAT WAS AGAINST THE PRINCE OF DRAGONSTONE!
I COULD ALMOST HEAR THE OLD MAN CHIDING, "DUNK THE LUNK, THICK AS A CASTLE WALL."

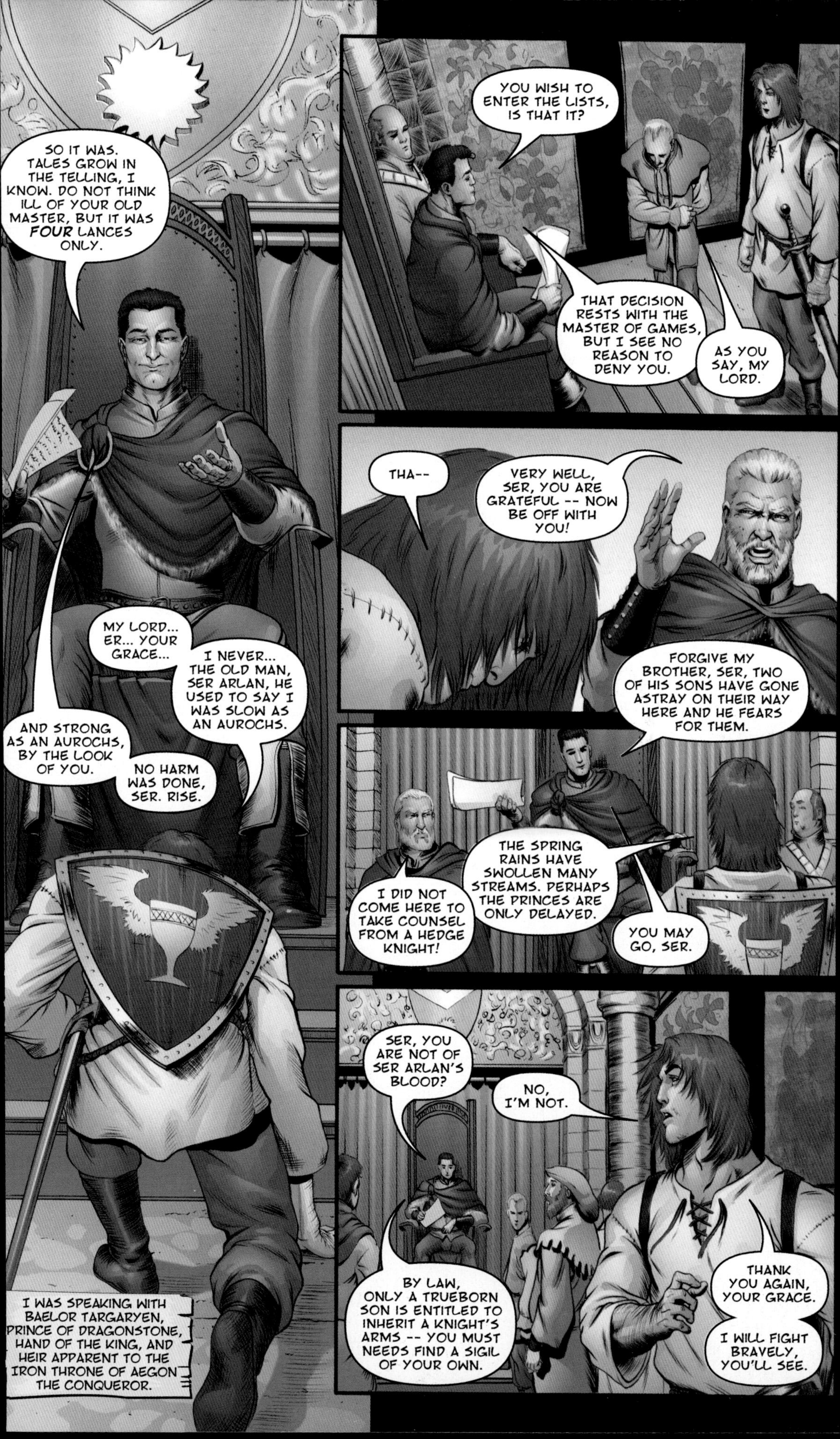
SO IT WAS. TALES GROW IN THE TELLING, I KNOW. DO NOT THINK ILL OF YOUR OLD MASTER, BUT IT WAS FOUR LANCES ONLY.
MY LORD... ER... YOUR GRACE...
I NEVER... THE OLD MAN, SER ARLAN, HE USED TO SAY I WAS SLOW AS AN AUROCHS.
AND STRONG AS AN AUROCHS, BY THE LOOK OF YOU.
NO HARM WAS DONE, SER. RISE.
I WAS SPEAKING WITH BAELOR TARGARYEN, PRINCE OF DRAGONSTONE, HAND OF THE KING, AND HEIR APPARENT TO THE IRON THRONE OF AEGON THE CONQUEROR.
YOU WISH TO ENTER THE LISTS, IS THAT IT?
THAT DECISION RESTS WITH THE MASTER OF GAMES, BUT I SEE NO REASON TO DENY YOU.
AS YOU SAY, MY LORD.
THA--
VERY WELL, SER, YOU ARE GRATEFUL -- NOW BE OFF WITH YOU!
FORGIVE MY BROTHER, SER, TWO OF HIS SONS HAVE GONE ASTRAY ON THEIR WAY HERE AND HE FEARS FOR THEM.
THE SPRING RAINS HAVE SWOLLEN MANY STREAMS. PERHAPS THE PRINCES ARE ONLY DELAYED.
I DID NOT COME HERE TO TAKE COUNSEL FROM A HEDGE KNIGHT!
YOU MAY GO, SER.
SER, YOU ARE NOT OF SER ARLAN'S BLOOD?
NO, I'M NOT.
BY LAW, ONLY A TRUEBORN SON IS ENTITLED TO INHERIT A KNIGHT'S ARMS -- YOU MUST NEEDS FIND A SIGIL OF YOUR OWN.
THANK YOU AGAIN, YOUR GRACE.
I WILL FIGHT BRAVELY, YOU'LL SEE.

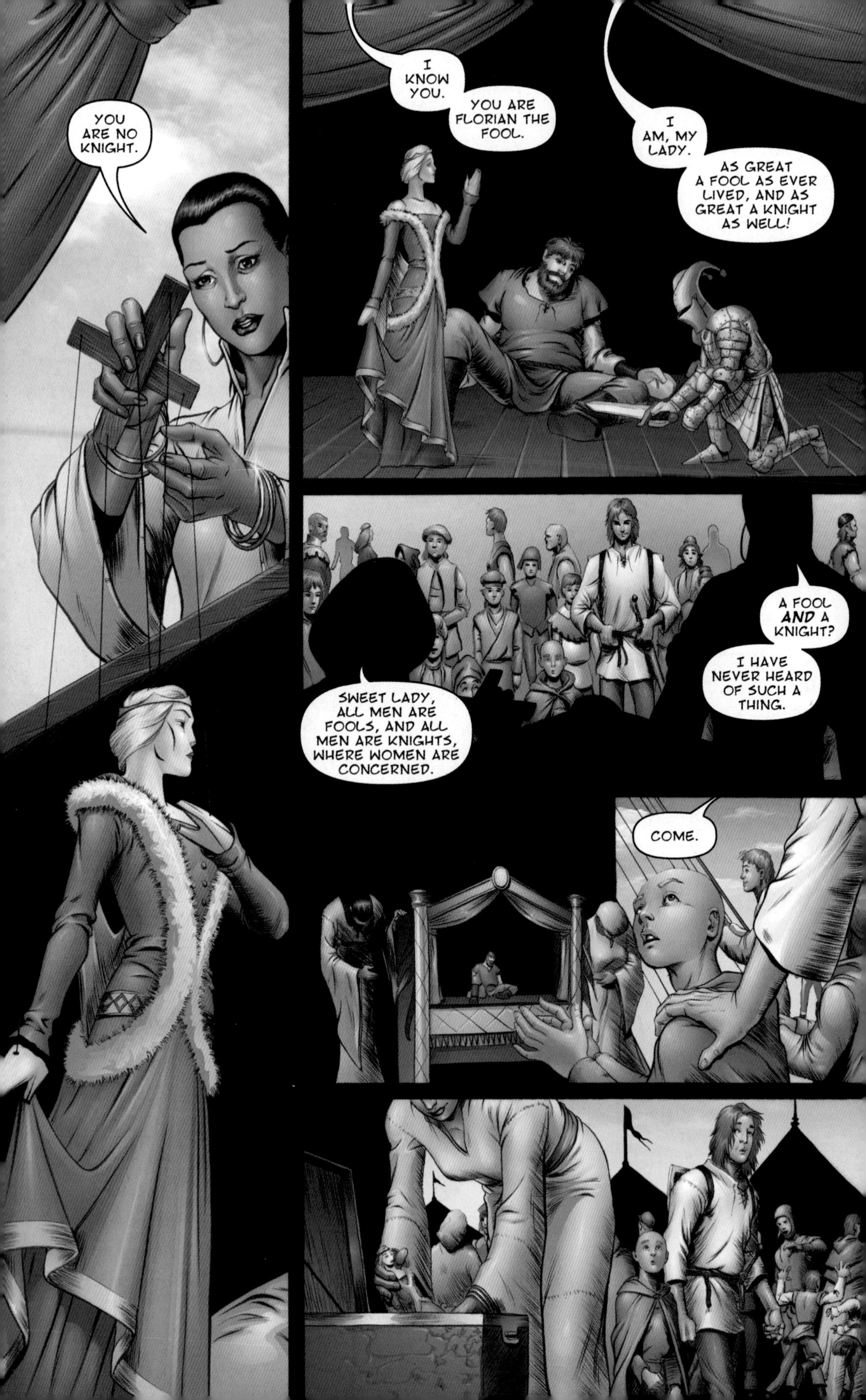
YOU ARE NO KNIGHT.
I KNOW YOU.
YOU ARE FLORIAN THE FOOL.
I AM, MY LADY.
AS GREAT A FOOL AS EVER LIVED, AND AS GREAT A KNIGHT AS WELL!
A FOOL **AND** A KNIGHT?
I HAVE NEVER HEARD OF SUCH A THING.
SWEET LADY, ALL MEN ARE FOOLS, AND ALL MEN ARE KNIGHTS, WHERE WOMEN ARE CONCERNED.
COME.

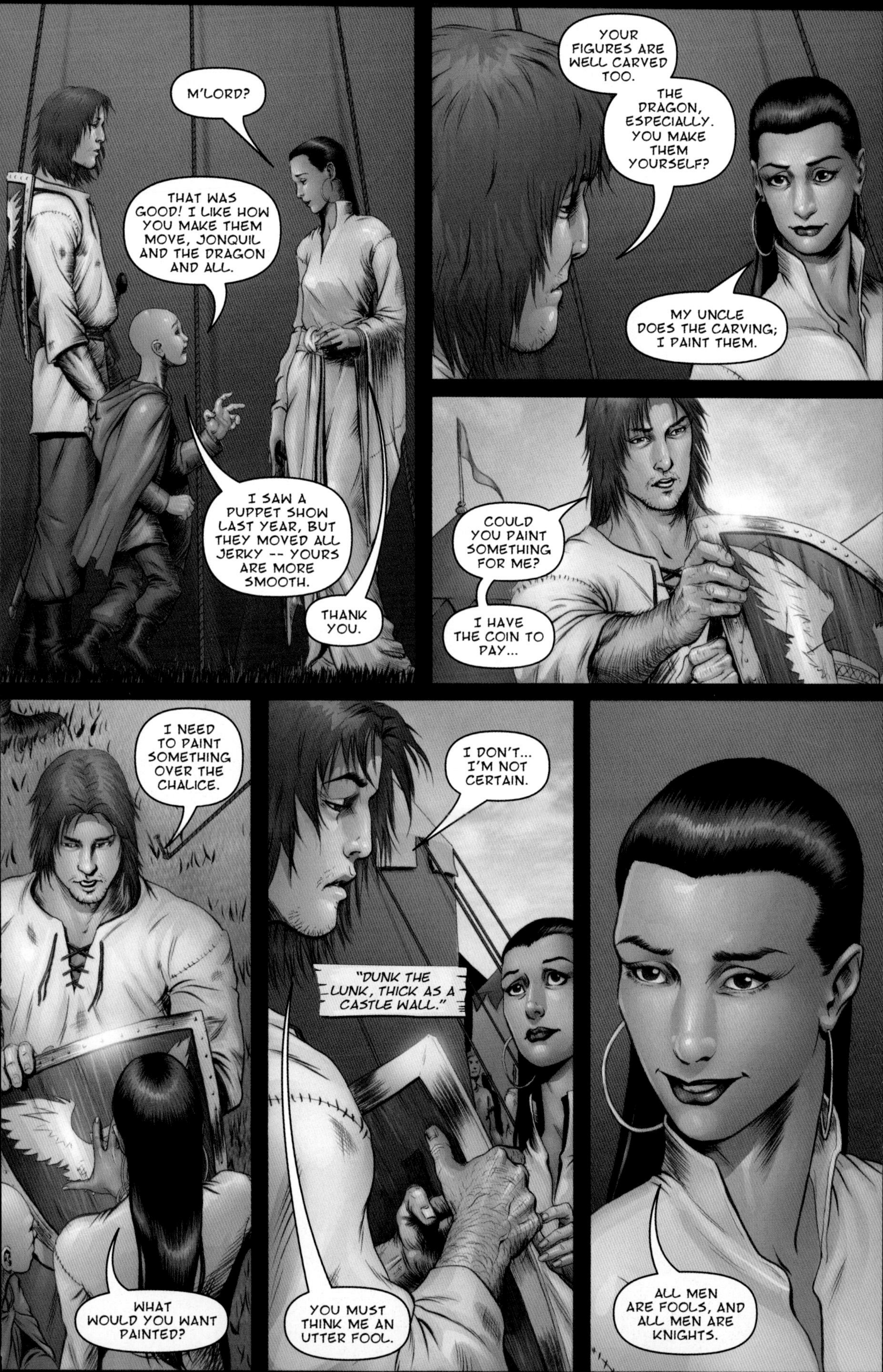
M'LORD?
THAT WAS GOOD! I LIKE HOW YOU MAKE THEM MOVE, JONQUIL AND THE DRAGON AND ALL.
I SAW A PUPPET SHOW LAST YEAR, BUT THEY MOVED ALL JERKY -- YOURS ARE MORE SMOOTH.
THANK YOU.
YOUR FIGURES ARE WELL CARVED TOO.
THE DRAGON, ESPECIALLY. YOU MAKE THEM YOURSELF?
MY UNCLE DOES THE CARVING; I PAINT THEM.
COULD YOU PAINT SOMETHING FOR ME?
I HAVE THE COIN TO PAY...
I NEED TO PAINT SOMETHING OVER THE CHALICE.
WHAT WOULD YOU WANT PAINTED?
I DON'T... I'M NOT CERTAIN.
"DUNK THE LUNK, THICK AS A CASTLE WALL."
YOU MUST THINK ME AN UTTER FOOL.
ALL MEN ARE FOOLS, AND ALL MEN ARE KNIGHTS.

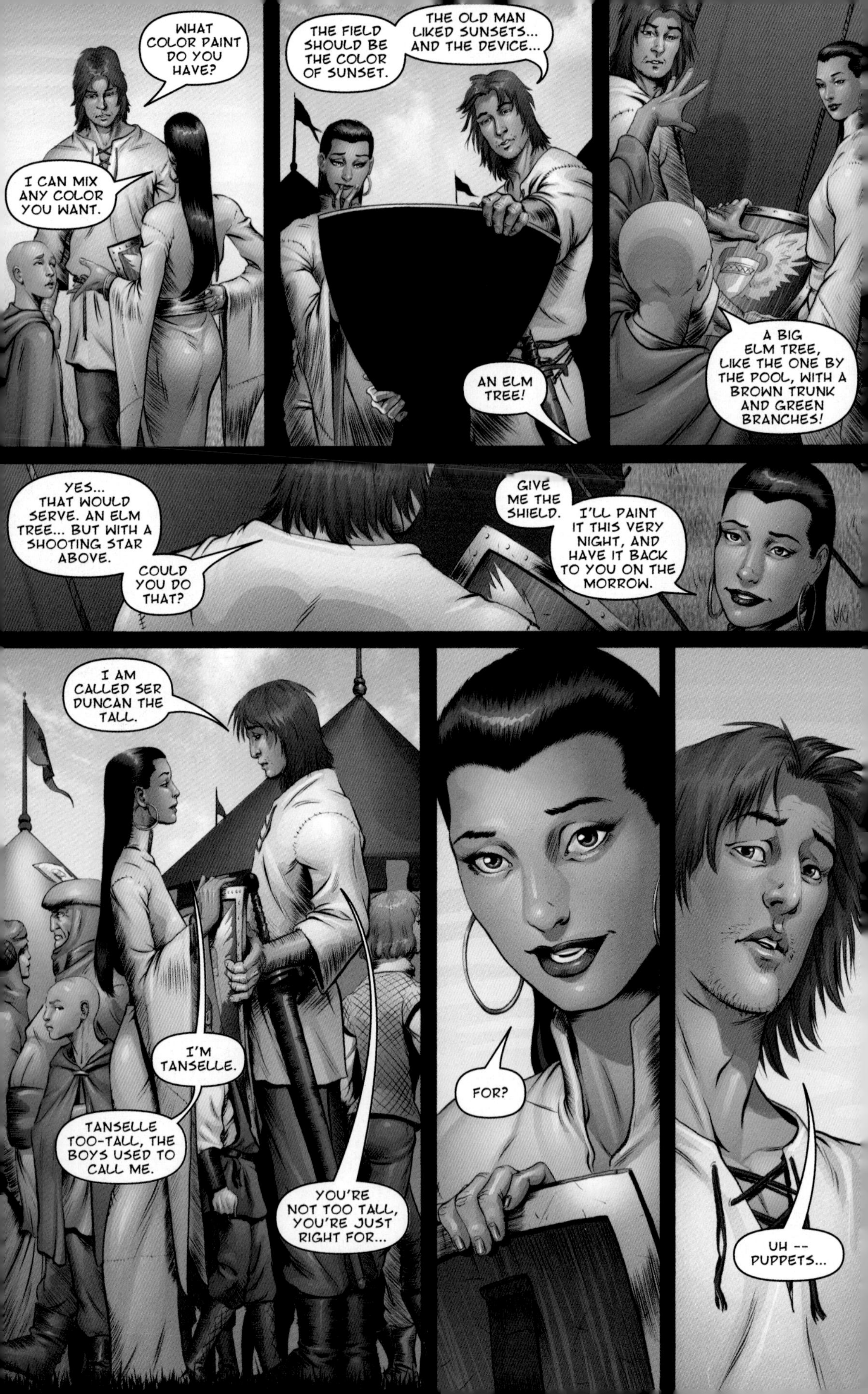
WHAT COLOR PAINT DO YOU HAVE?
I CAN MIX ANY COLOR YOU WANT.
THE FIELD SHOULD BE THE COLOR OF SUNSET.
THE OLD MAN LIKED SUNSETS... AND THE DEVICE...
AN ELM TREE!
A BIG ELM TREE, LIKE THE ONE BY THE POOL, WITH A BROWN TRUNK AND GREEN BRANCHES!
YES... THAT WOULD SERVE. AN ELM TREE... BUT WITH A SHOOTING STAR ABOVE.
COULD YOU DO THAT?
GIVE ME THE SHIELD.
I'LL PAINT IT THIS VERY NIGHT, AND HAVE IT BACK TO YOU ON THE MORROW.
I AM CALLED SER DUNCAN THE TALL.
I'M TANSELLE.
TANSELLE TOO-TALL, THE BOYS USED TO CALL ME.
YOU'RE NOT TOO TALL, YOU'RE JUST RIGHT FOR...
FOR?
UH -- PUPPETS...

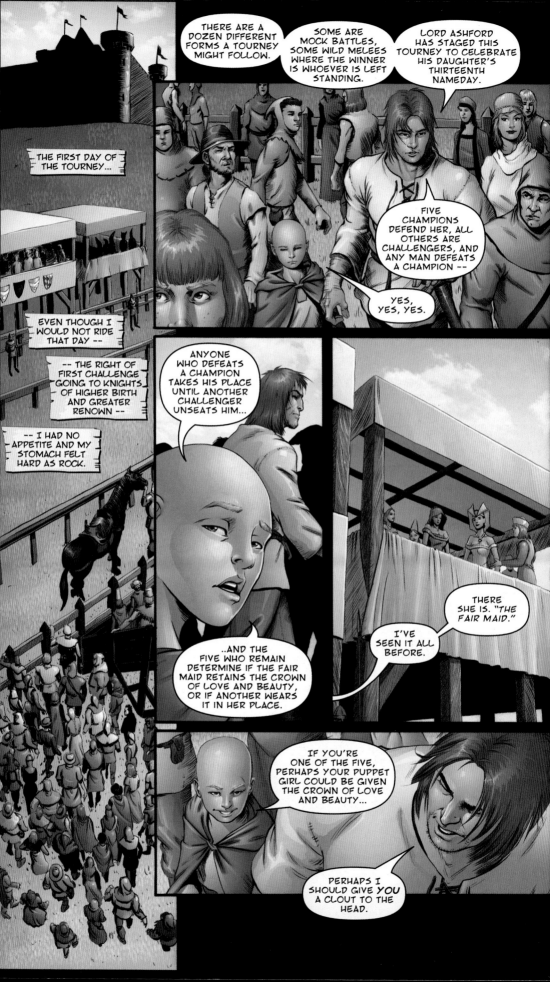

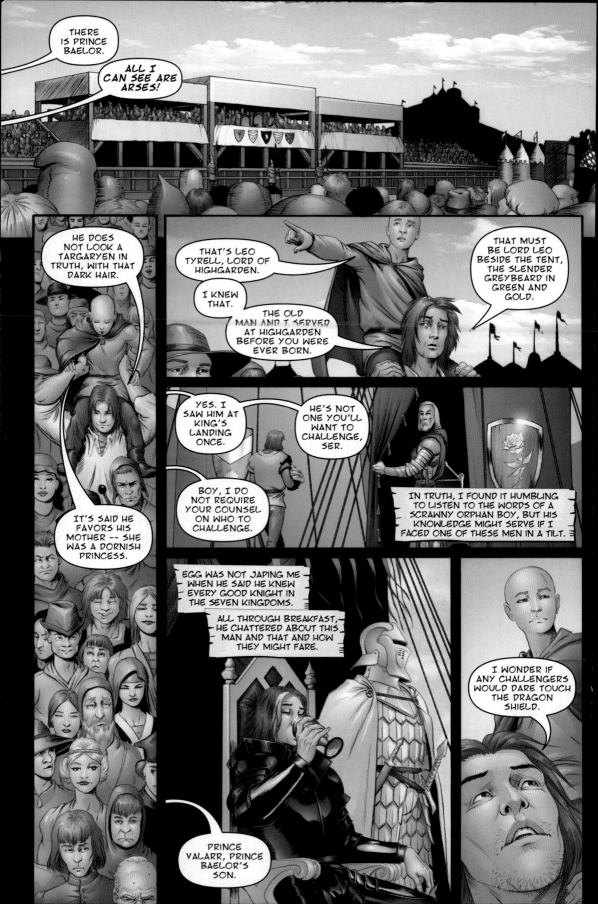

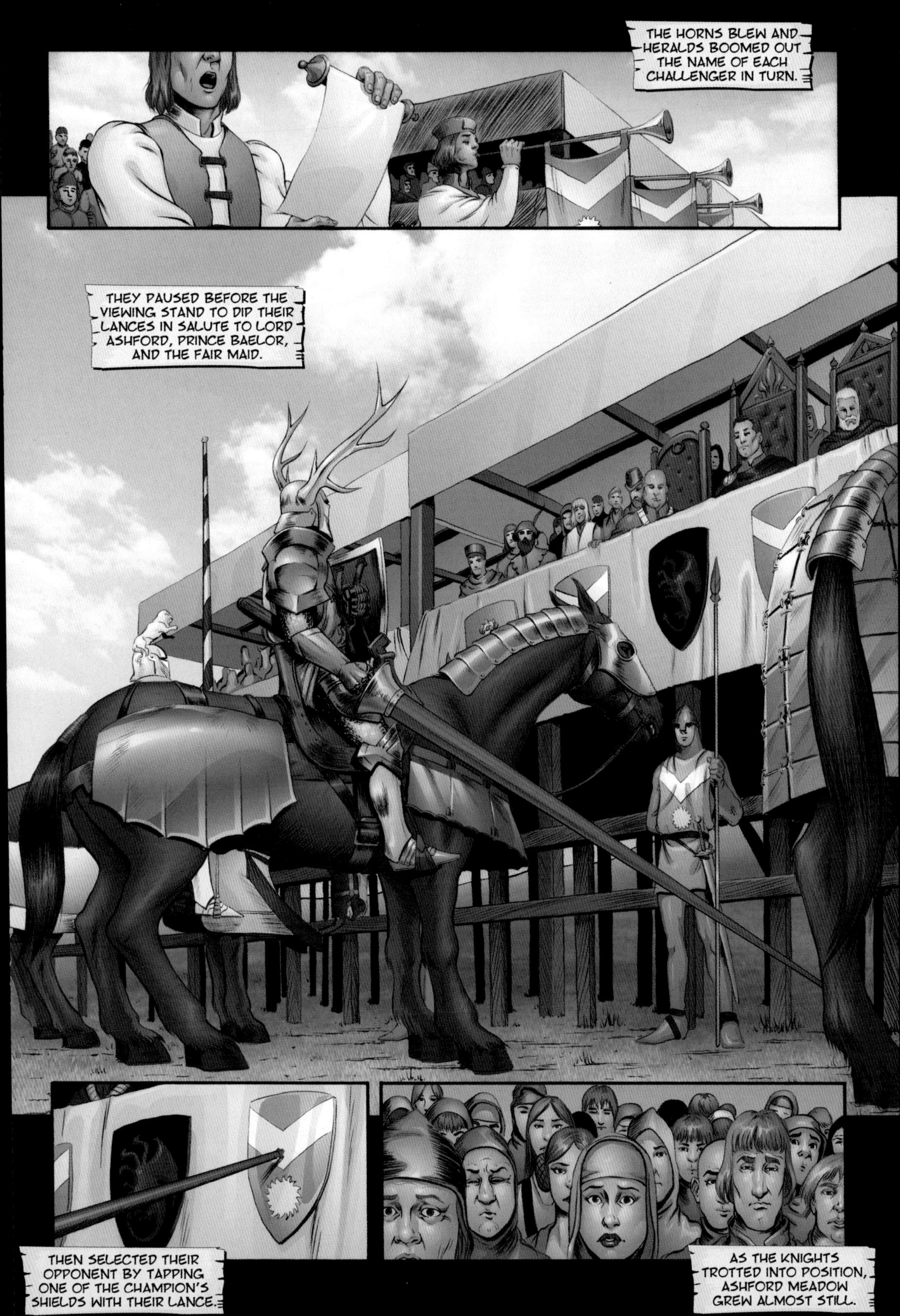
THE HORNS BLEW AND HERALDS BOOMED OUT THE NAME OF EACH CHALLENGER IN TURN.
THEY PAUSED BEFORE THE VIEWING STAND TO DIP THEIR LANCES IN SALUTE TO LORD ASHFORD, PRINCE BAELOR, AND THE FAIR MAID.
THEN SELECTED THEIR OPPONENT BY TAPPING ONE OF THE CHAMPION'S SHIELDS WITH THEIR LANCE.
AS THE KNIGHTS TROTTED INTO POSITION, ASHFORD MEADOW GREW ALMOST STILL.

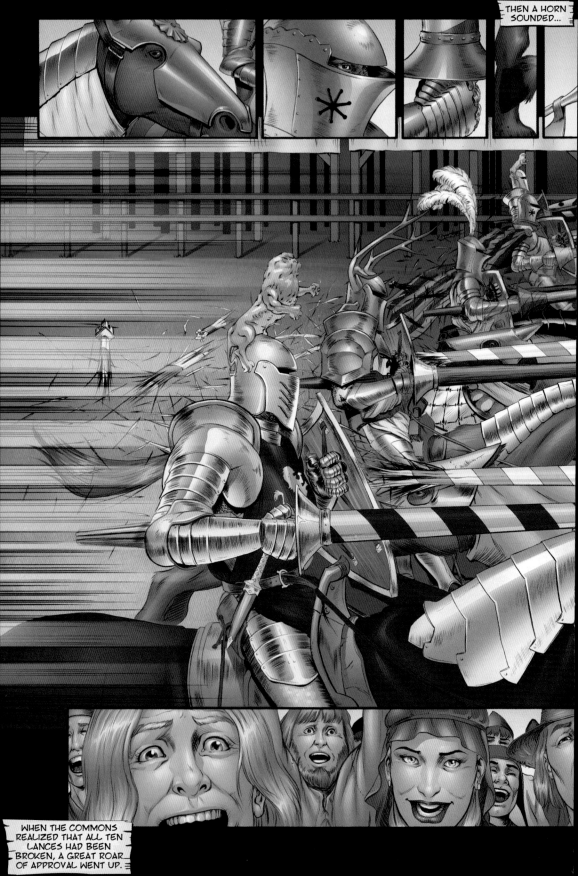

THEN A HORN SOUNDED...

WHEN THE COMMONS REALIZED THAT ALL TEN LANCES HAD BEEN BROKEN, A GREAT ROAR OF APPROVAL WENT UP.

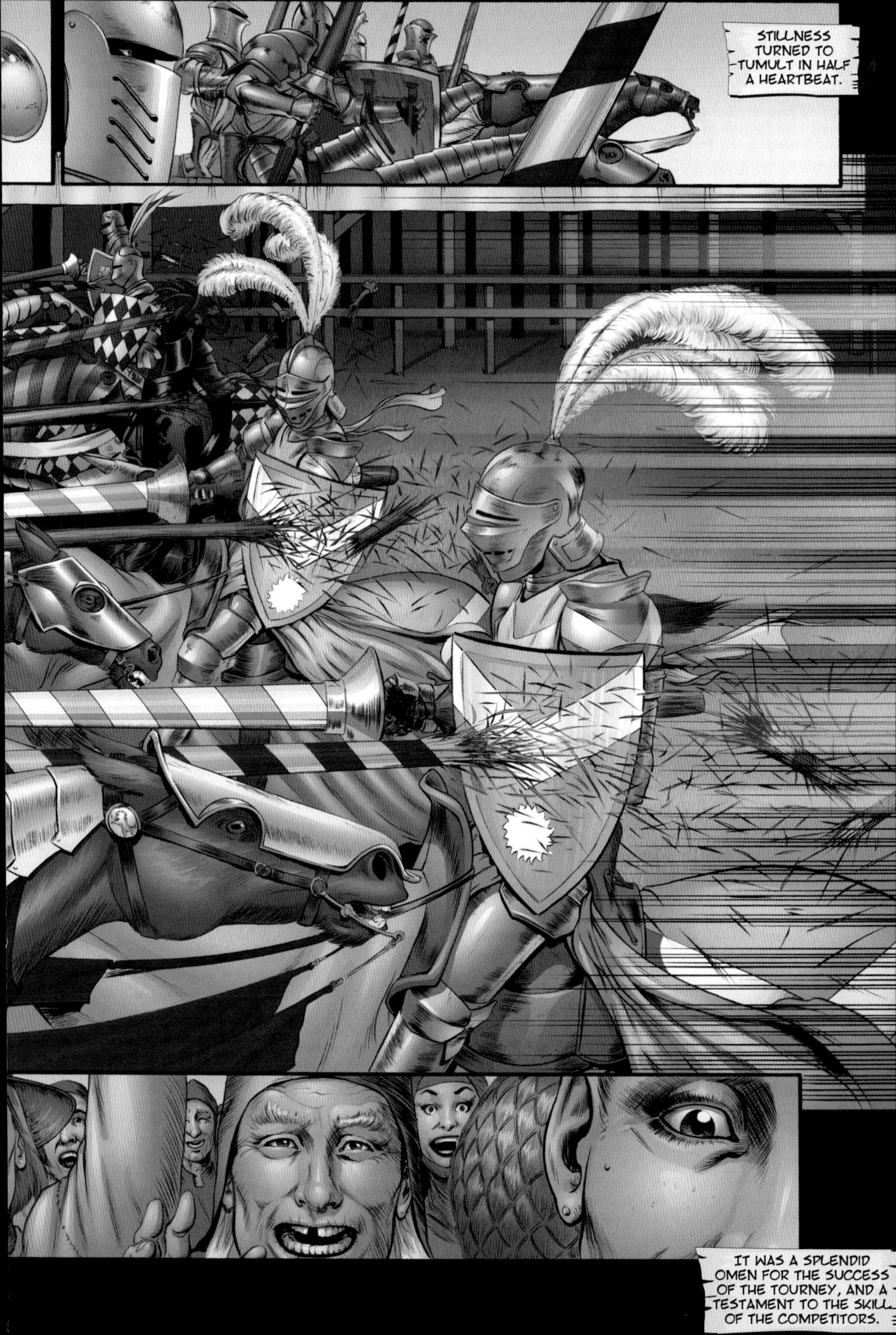
STILLNESS TURNED TO TUMULT IN HALF A HEARTBEAT.
IT WAS A SPLENDID OMEN FOR THE SUCCESS OF THE TOURNEY, AND A TESTAMENT TO THE SKILL OF THE COMPETITORS.

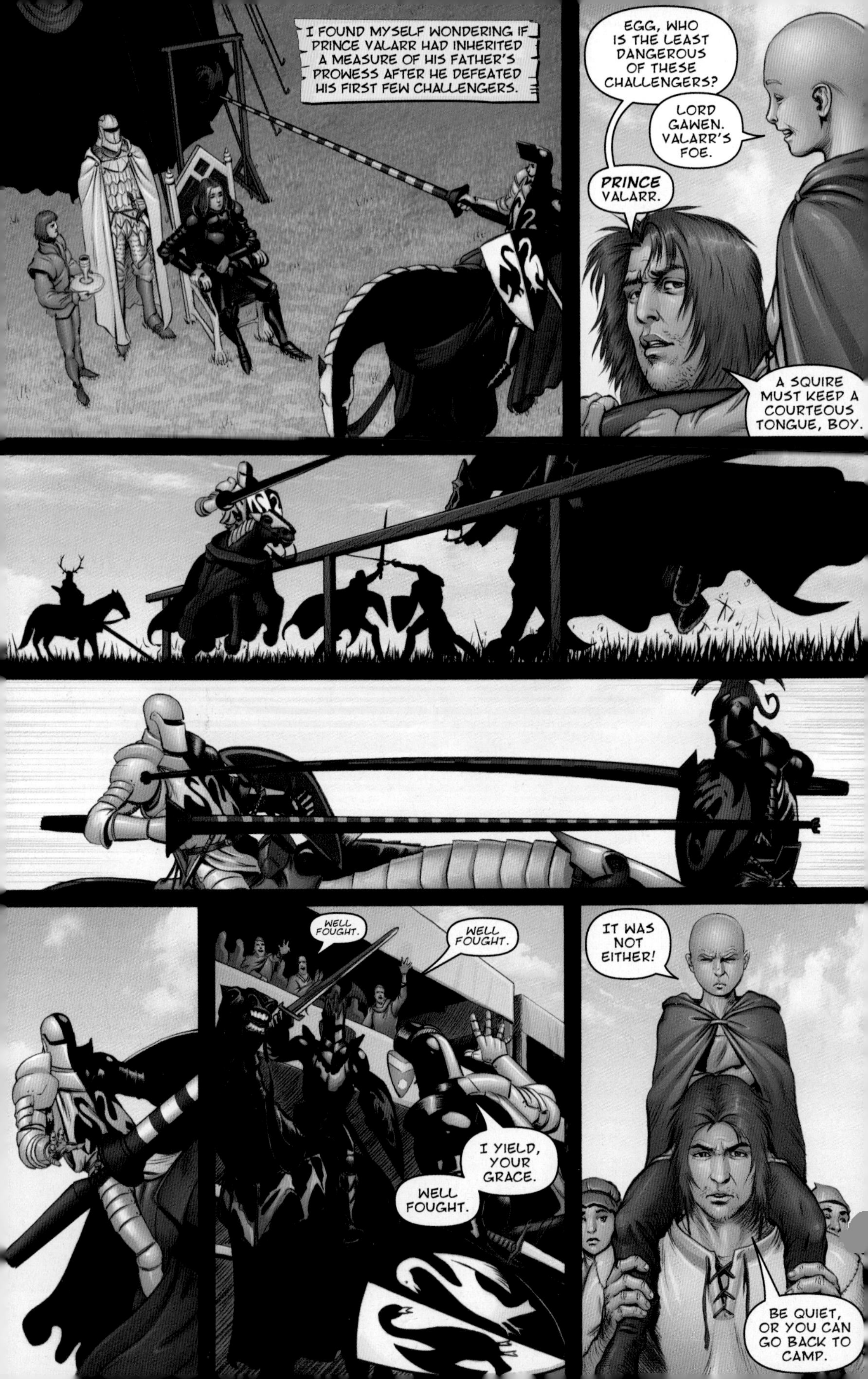
I FOUND MYSELF WONDERING IF PRINCE VALARR HAD INHERITED A MEASURE OF HIS FATHER'S PROWESS AFTER HE DEFEATED HIS FIRST FEW CHALLENGERS.
EGG, WHO IS THE LEAST DANGEROUS OF THESE CHALLENGERS?
LORD GAWEN. VALARR'S FOE.
PRINCE VALARR.
A SQUIRE MUST KEEP A COURTEOUS TONGUE, BOY.
WELL FOUGHT.
WELL FOUGHT.
I YIELD, YOUR GRACE.
WELL FOUGHT.
IT WAS NOT EITHER!
BE QUIET, OR YOU CAN GO BACK TO CAMP.

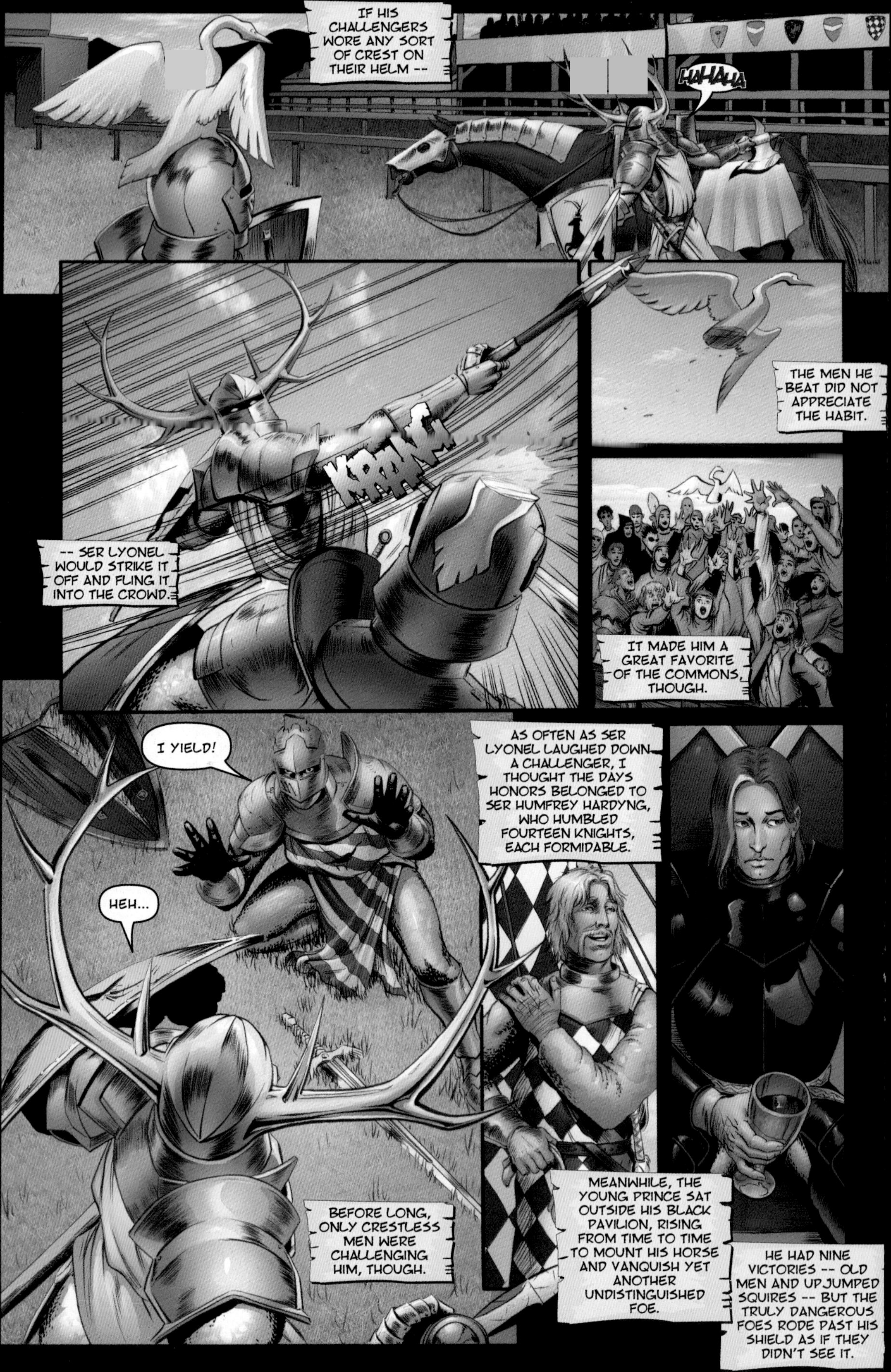
IF HIS CHALLENGERS WORE ANY SORT OF CREST ON THEIR HELM --
HAHAHA
-- SER LYONEL WOULD STRIKE IT OFF AND FLING IT INTO THE CROWD.
KRANG
THE MEN HE BEAT DID NOT APPRECIATE THE HABIT.
IT MADE HIM A GREAT FAVORITE OF THE COMMONS, THOUGH.
I YIELD!
HEH...
BEFORE LONG, ONLY CRESTLESS MEN WERE CHALLENGING HIM, THOUGH.
AS OFTEN AS SER LYONEL LAUGHED DOWN A CHALLENGER, I THOUGHT THE DAYS HONORS BELONGED TO SER HUMFREY HARDYNG, WHO HUMBLED FOURTEEN KNIGHTS, EACH FORMIDABLE.
MEANWHILE, THE YOUNG PRINCE SAT OUTSIDE HIS BLACK PAVILION, RISING FROM TIME TO TIME TO MOUNT HIS HORSE AND VANQUISH YET ANOTHER UNDISTINGUISHED FOE.
HE HAD NINE VICTORIES -- OLD MEN AND UPJUMPED SQUIRES -- BUT THE TRULY DANGEROUS FOES RODE PAST HIS SHIELD AS IF THEY DIDN'T SEE IT.

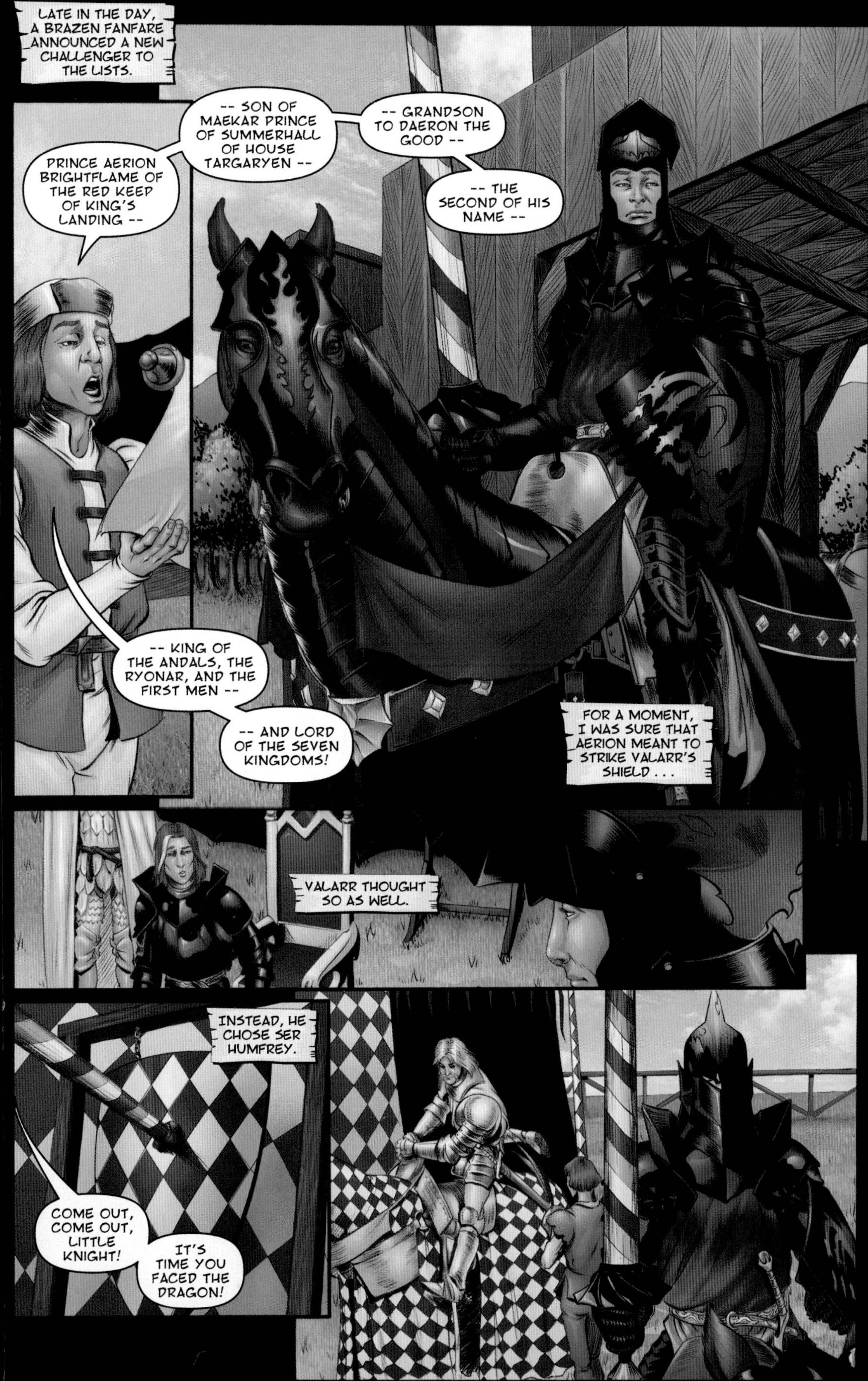
LATE IN THE DAY, A BRAZEN FANFARE ANNOUNCED A NEW CHALLENGER TO THE LISTS.
PRINCE AERION BRIGHTFLAME OF THE RED KEEP OF KING'S LANDING --
-- SON OF MAEKAR PRINCE OF SUMMERHALL OF HOUSE TARGARYEN --
-- GRANDSON TO DAERON THE GOOD --
-- THE SECOND OF HIS NAME --
-- KING OF THE ANDALS, THE RYONAR, AND THE FIRST MEN --
-- AND LORD OF THE SEVEN KINGDOMS!
FOR A MOMENT, I WAS SURE THAT AERION MEANT TO STRIKE VALARR'S SHIELD . . .
VALARR THOUGHT SO AS WELL.
INSTEAD, HE CHOSE SER HUMFREY.
COME OUT, COME OUT, LITTLE KNIGHT!
IT'S TIME YOU FACED THE DRAGON!

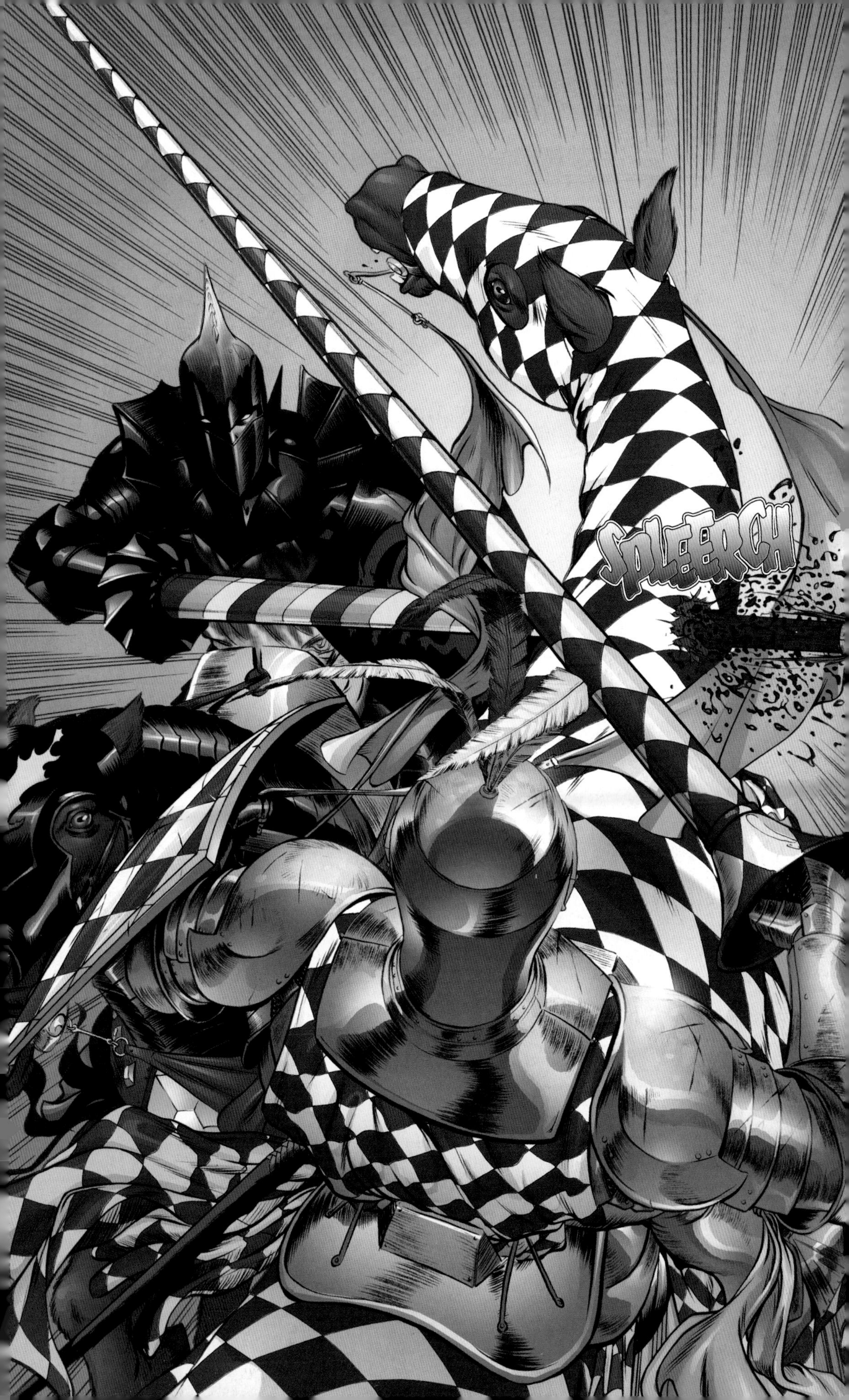
SPLEERCH

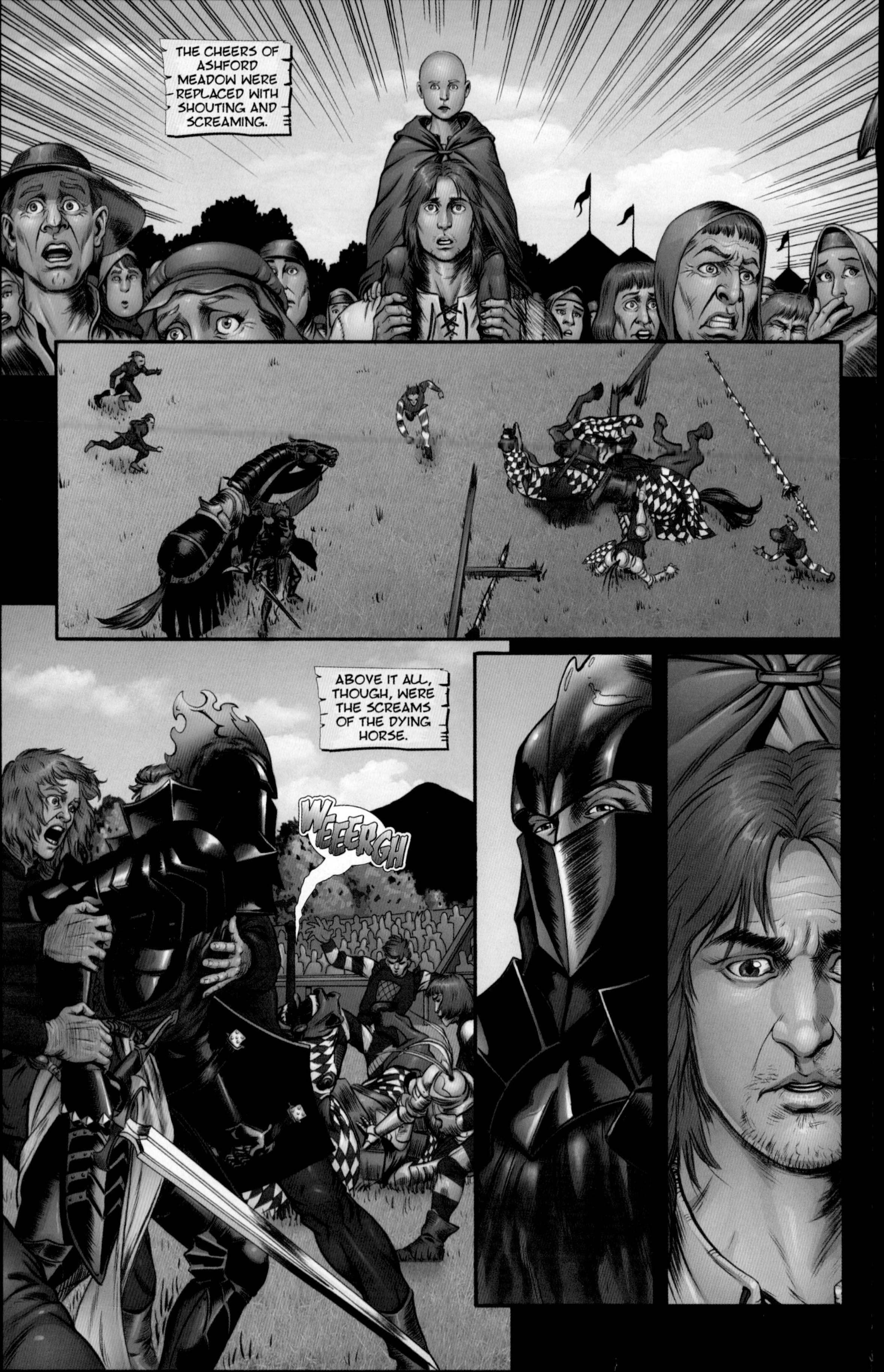
THE CHEERS OF ASHFORD MEADOW WERE REPLACED WITH SHOUTING AND SCREAMING.
ABOVE IT ALL, THOUGH, WERE THE SCREAMS OF THE DYING HORSE.
WEEERGH

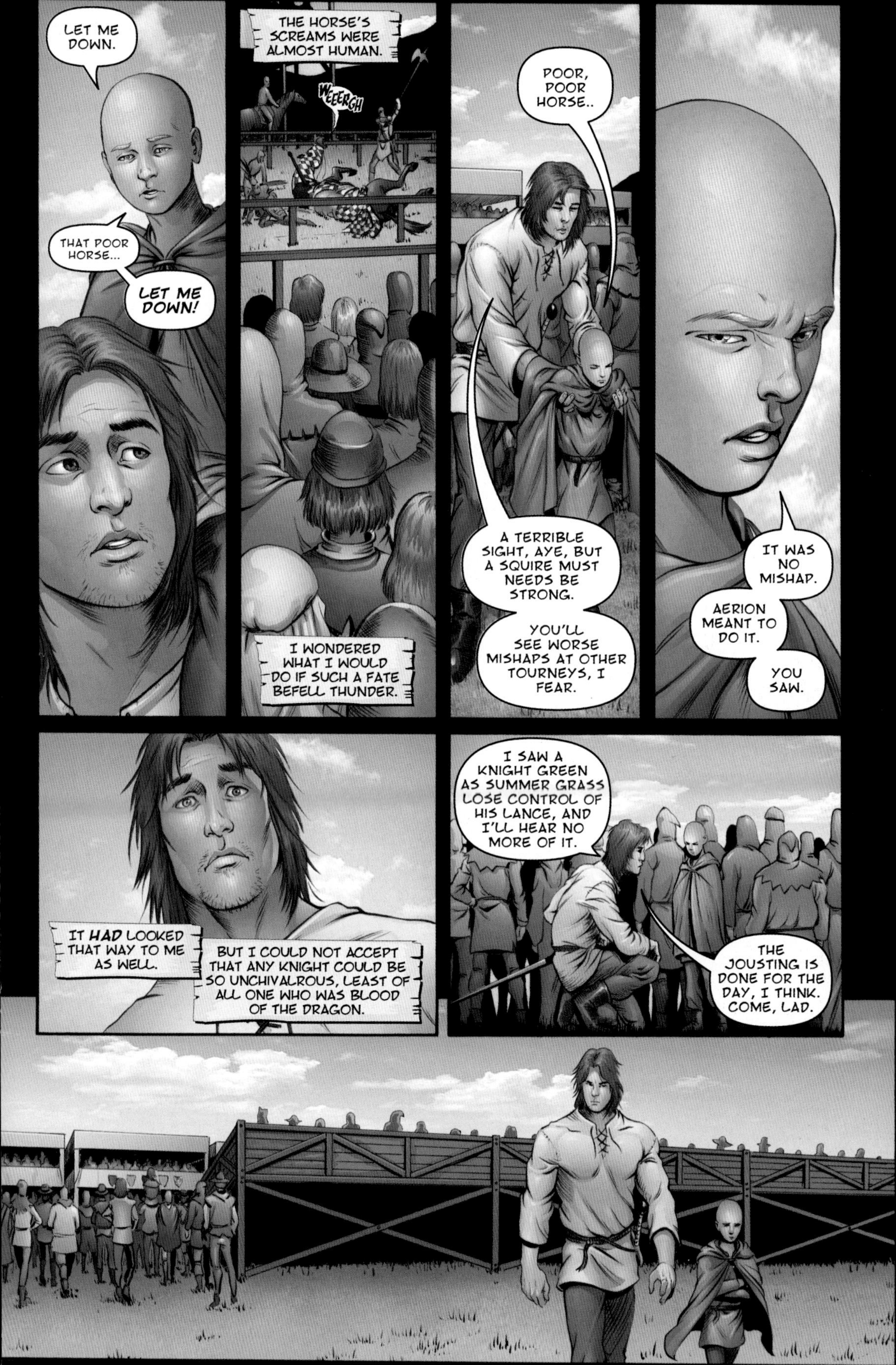
LET ME DOWN.
THAT POOR HORSE...
LET ME DOWN!
THE HORSE'S SCREAMS WERE ALMOST HUMAN.
WEEERGH
I WONDERED WHAT I WOULD DO IF SUCH A FATE BEFELL THUNDER.
POOR, POOR HORSE..
A TERRIBLE SIGHT, AYE, BUT A SQUIRE MUST NEEDS BE STRONG.
YOU'LL SEE WORSE MISHAPS AT OTHER TOURNEYS, I FEAR.
IT WAS NO MISHAP.
AERION MEANT TO DO IT.
YOU SAW.
IT HAD LOOKED THAT WAY TO ME AS WELL.
BUT I COULD NOT ACCEPT THAT ANY KNIGHT COULD BE SO UNCHIVALROUS, LEAST OF ALL ONE WHO WAS BLOOD OF THE DRAGON.
I SAW A KNIGHT GREEN AS SUMMER GRASS LOSE CONTROL OF HIS LANCE, AND I'LL HEAR NO MORE OF IT.
THE JOUSTING IS DONE FOR THE DAY, I THINK. COME, LAD.

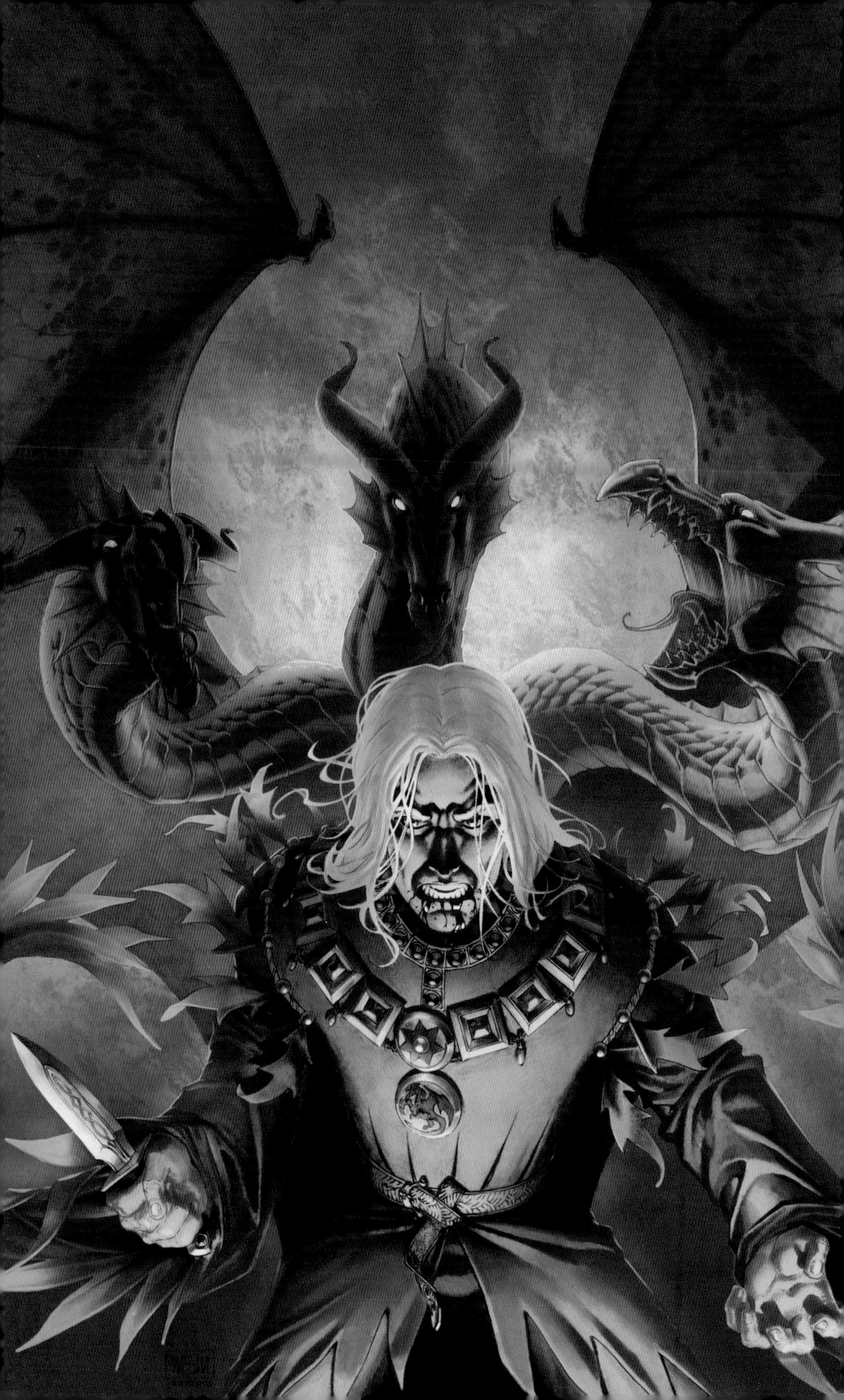

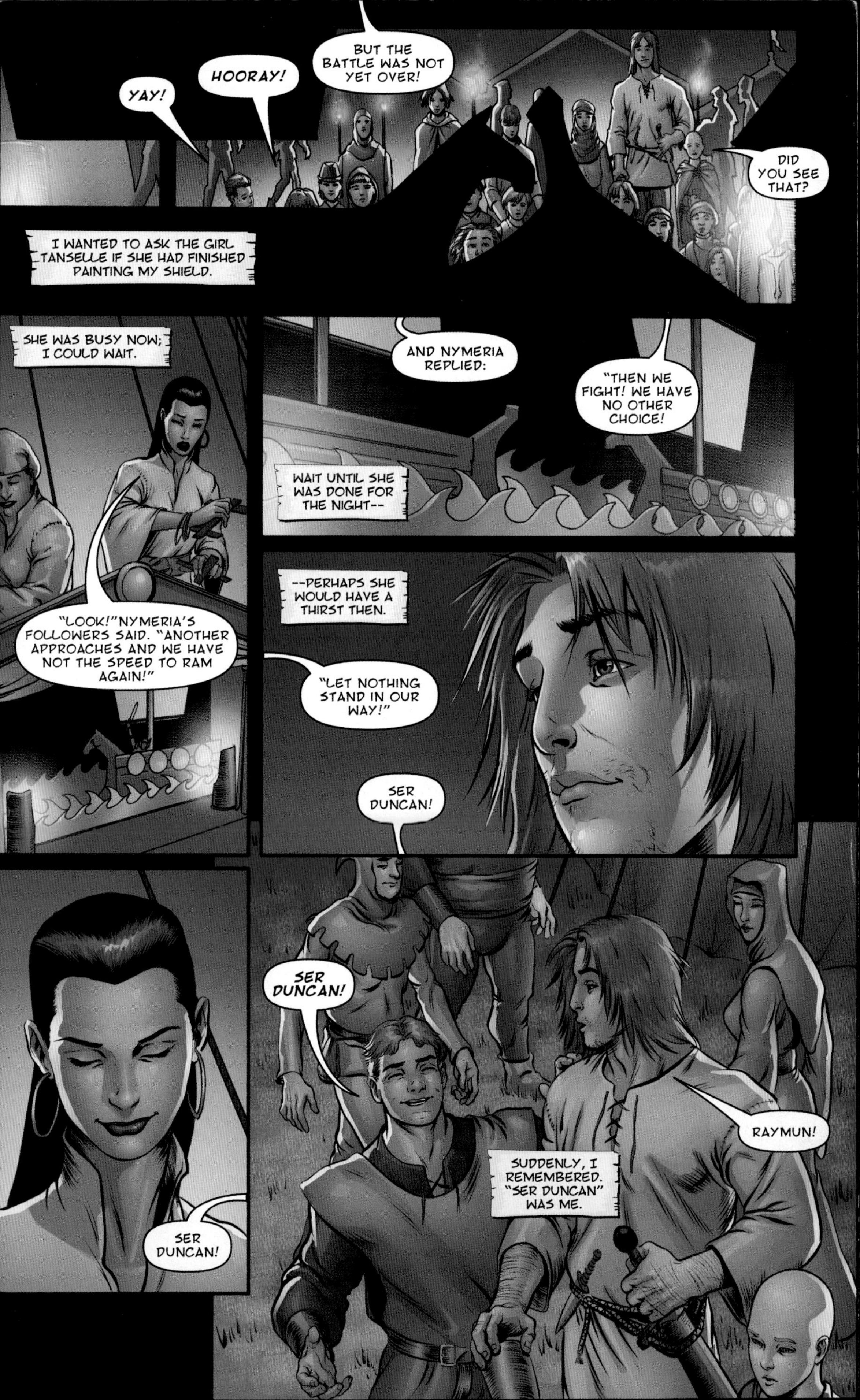
YAY!
HOORAY!
BUT THE BATTLE WAS NOT YET OVER!
DID YOU SEE THAT?
I WANTED TO ASK THE GIRL TANSELLE IF SHE HAD FINISHED PAINTING MY SHIELD.
SHE WAS BUSY NOW; I COULD WAIT.
AND NYMERIA REPLIED:
"THEN WE FIGHT! WE HAVE NO OTHER CHOICE!
WAIT UNTIL SHE WAS DONE FOR THE NIGHT--
"LOOK!" NYMERIA'S FOLLOWERS SAID. "ANOTHER APPROACHES AND WE HAVE NOT THE SPEED TO RAM AGAIN!"
--PERHAPS SHE WOULD HAVE A THIRST THEN.
"LET NOTHING STAND IN OUR WAY!"
SER DUNCAN!
SER DUNCAN!
RAYMUN!
SUDDENLY, I REMEMBERED. "SER DUNCAN" WAS ME.
SER DUNCAN!

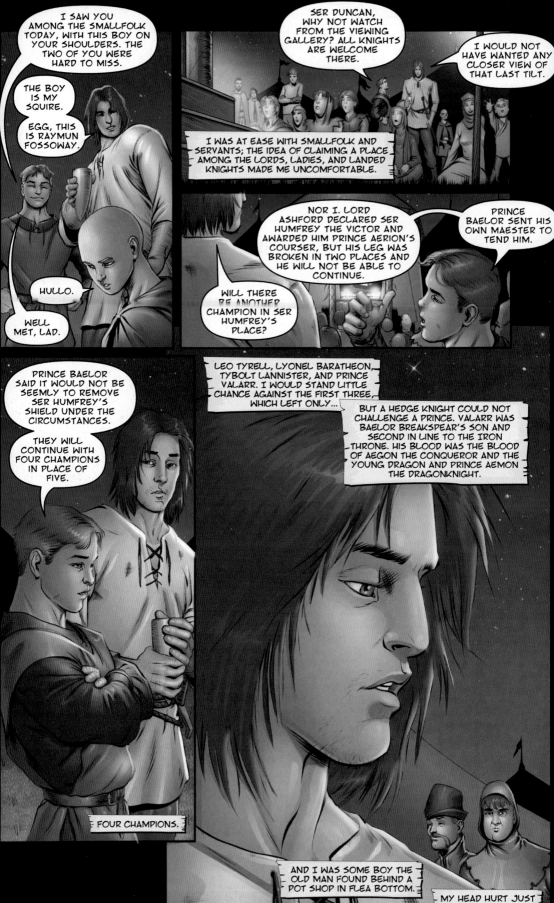

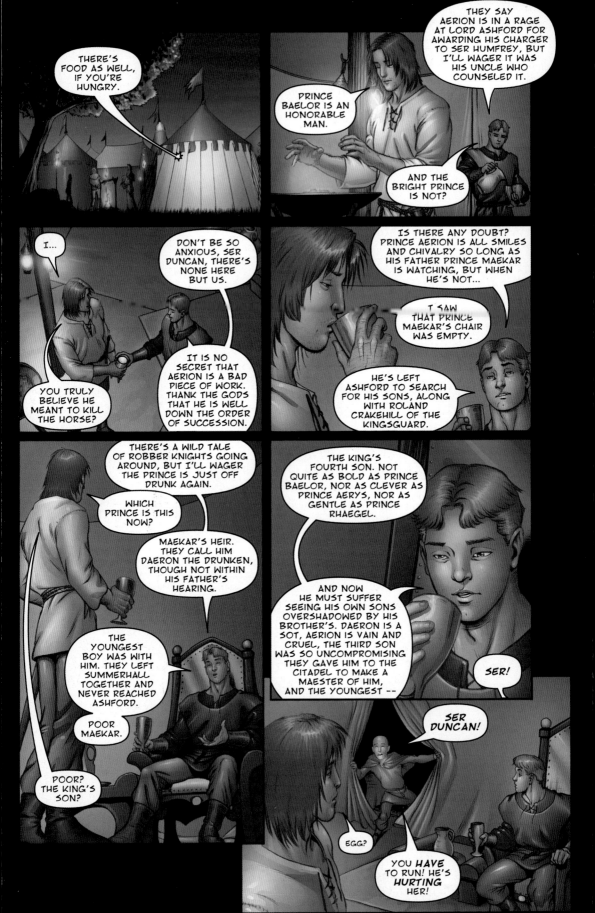

THERE'S FOOD AS WELL, IF YOU'RE HUNGRY.

THEY SAY AERION IS IN A RAGE AT LORD ASHFORD FOR AWARDING HIS CHARGER TO SER HUMFREY, BUT I'LL WAGER IT WAS HIS UNCLE WHO COUNSELED IT.

PRINCE BAELOR IS AN HONORABLE MAN.

AND THE BRIGHT PRINCE IS NOT?

I...

DON'T BE SO ANXIOUS, SER DUNCAN, THERE'S NONE HERE BUT US.

IT IS NO SECRET THAT AERION IS A BAD PIECE OF WORK. THANK THE GODS THAT HE IS WELL DOWN THE ORDER OF SUCCESSION.

YOU TRULY BELIEVE HE MEANT TO KILL THE HORSE?

IS THERE ANY DOUBT? PRINCE AERION IS ALL SMILES AND CHIVALRY SO LONG AS HIS FATHER PRINCE MAEKAR IS WATCHING, BUT WHEN HE'S NOT...

I SAW THAT PRINCE MAEKAR'S CHAIR WAS EMPTY.

HE'S LEFT ASHFORD TO SEARCH FOR HIS SONS, ALONG WITH ROLAND CRAKEHILL OF THE KINGSGUARD.

THERE'S A WILD TALE OF ROBBER KNIGHTS GOING AROUND, BUT I'LL WAGER THE PRINCE IS JUST OFF DRUNK AGAIN.

WHICH PRINCE IS THIS NOW?

MAEKAR'S HEIR. THEY CALL HIM DAERON THE DRUNKEN, THOUGH NOT WITHIN HIS FATHER'S HEARING.

THE YOUNGEST BOY WAS WITH HIM. THEY LEFT SUMMERHALL TOGETHER AND NEVER REACHED ASHFORD.

POOR MAEKAR.

POOR? THE KING'S SON?

THE KING'S FOURTH SON. NOT QUITE AS BOLD AS PRINCE BAELOR, NOR AS CLEVER AS PRINCE AERYS, NOR AS GENTLE AS PRINCE RHAEGEL.

AND NOW HE MUST SUFFER SEEING HIS OWN SONS OVERSHADOWED BY HIS BROTHER'S. DAERON IS A SOT, AERION IS VAIN AND CRUEL, THE THIRD SON WAS SO UNCOMPROMISING THEY GAVE HIM TO THE CITADEL TO MAKE A MAESTER OF HIM, AND THE YOUNGEST --

SER!

SER DUNCAN!

EGG?

YOU *HAVE* TO RUN! HE'S *HURTING* HER!

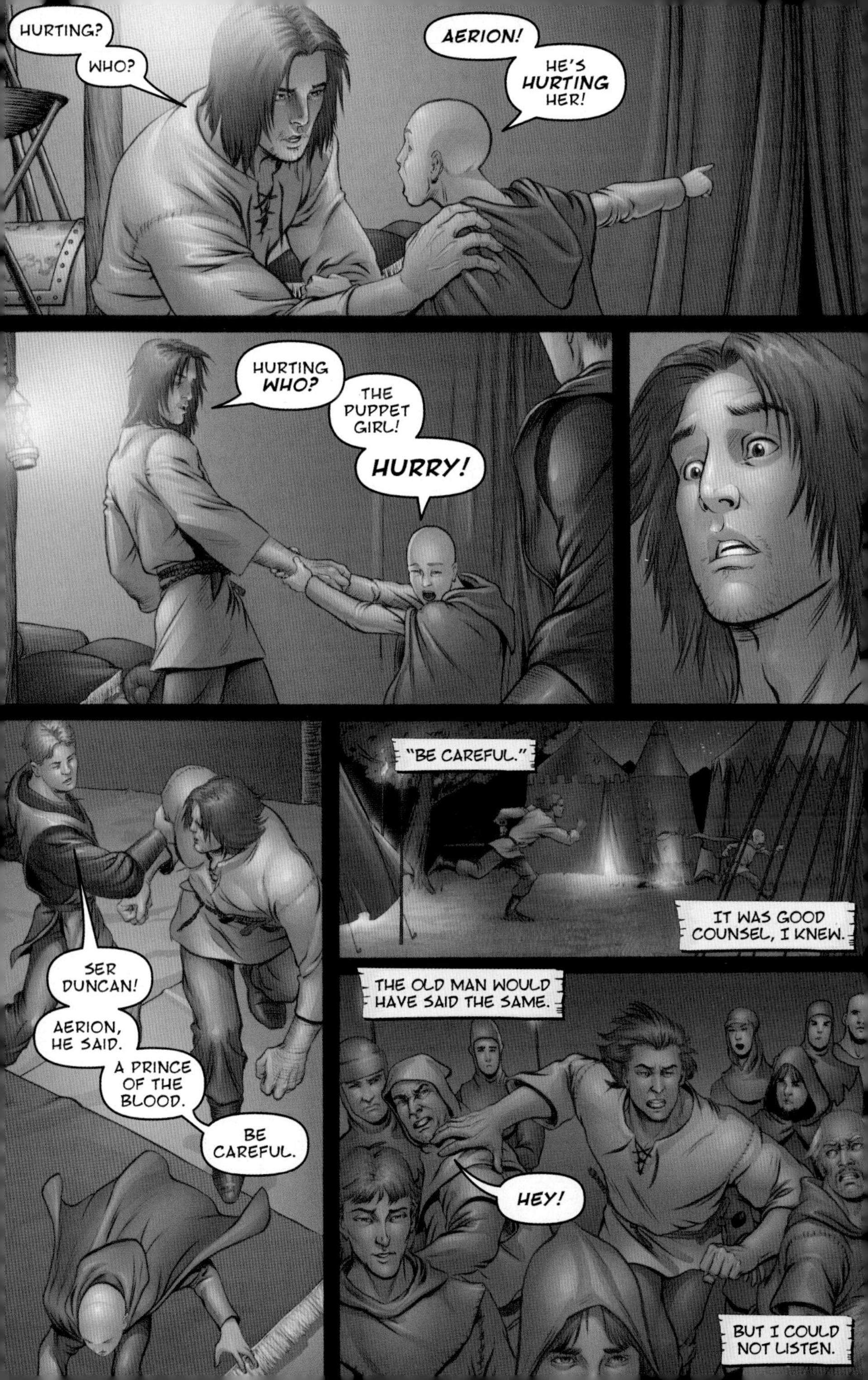
HURTING?
WHO?
AERION!
HE'S HURTING HER!
HURTING WHO?
THE PUPPET GIRL!
HURRY!
SER DUNCAN!
AERION, HE SAID.
A PRINCE OF THE BLOOD.
BE CAREFUL.
"BE CAREFUL."
IT WAS GOOD COUNSEL, I KNEW.
THE OLD MAN WOULD HAVE SAID THE SAME.
HEY!
BUT I COULD NOT LISTEN.

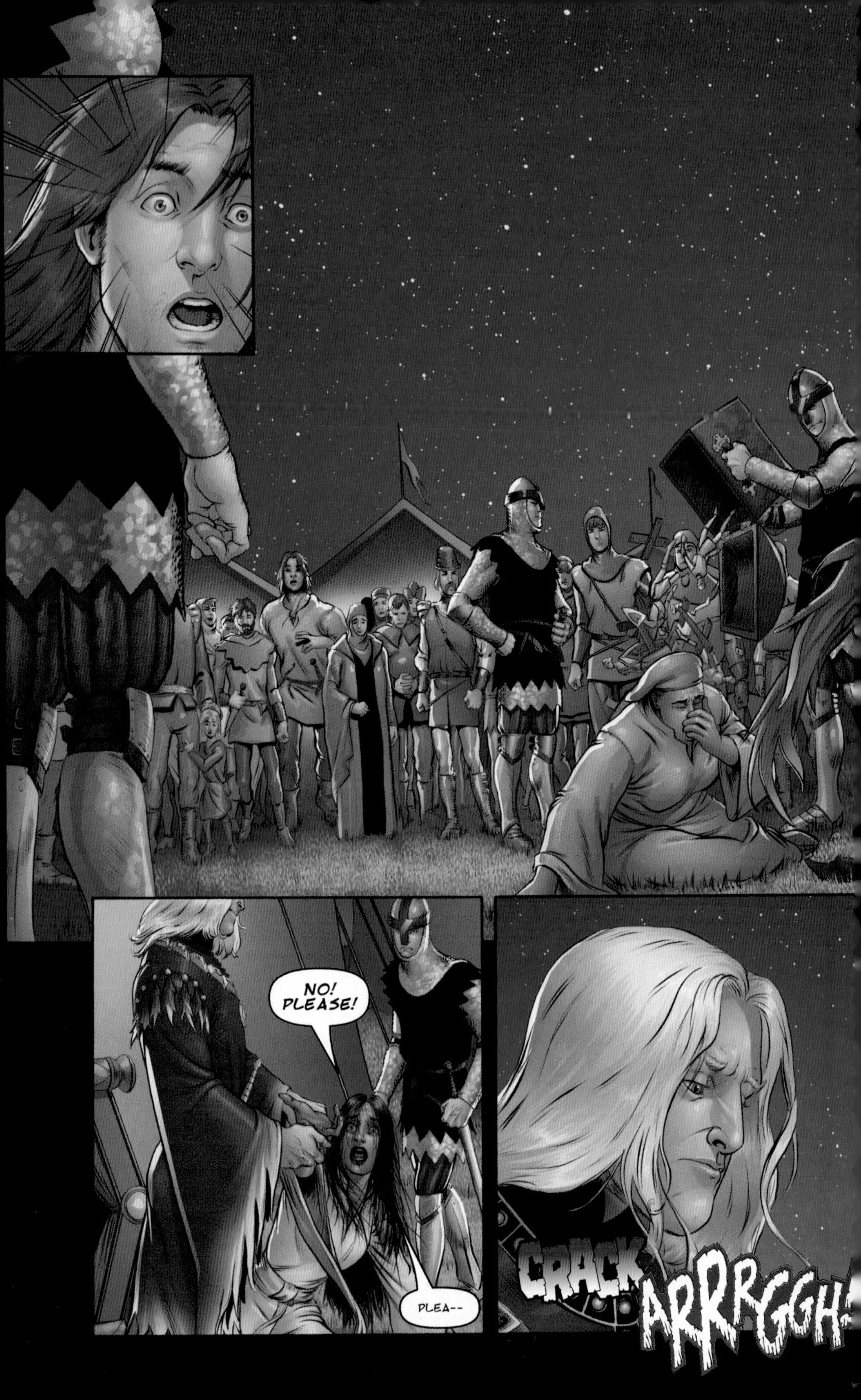
NO! PLEASE!
PLEA--
CRACK
ARRRGGH!

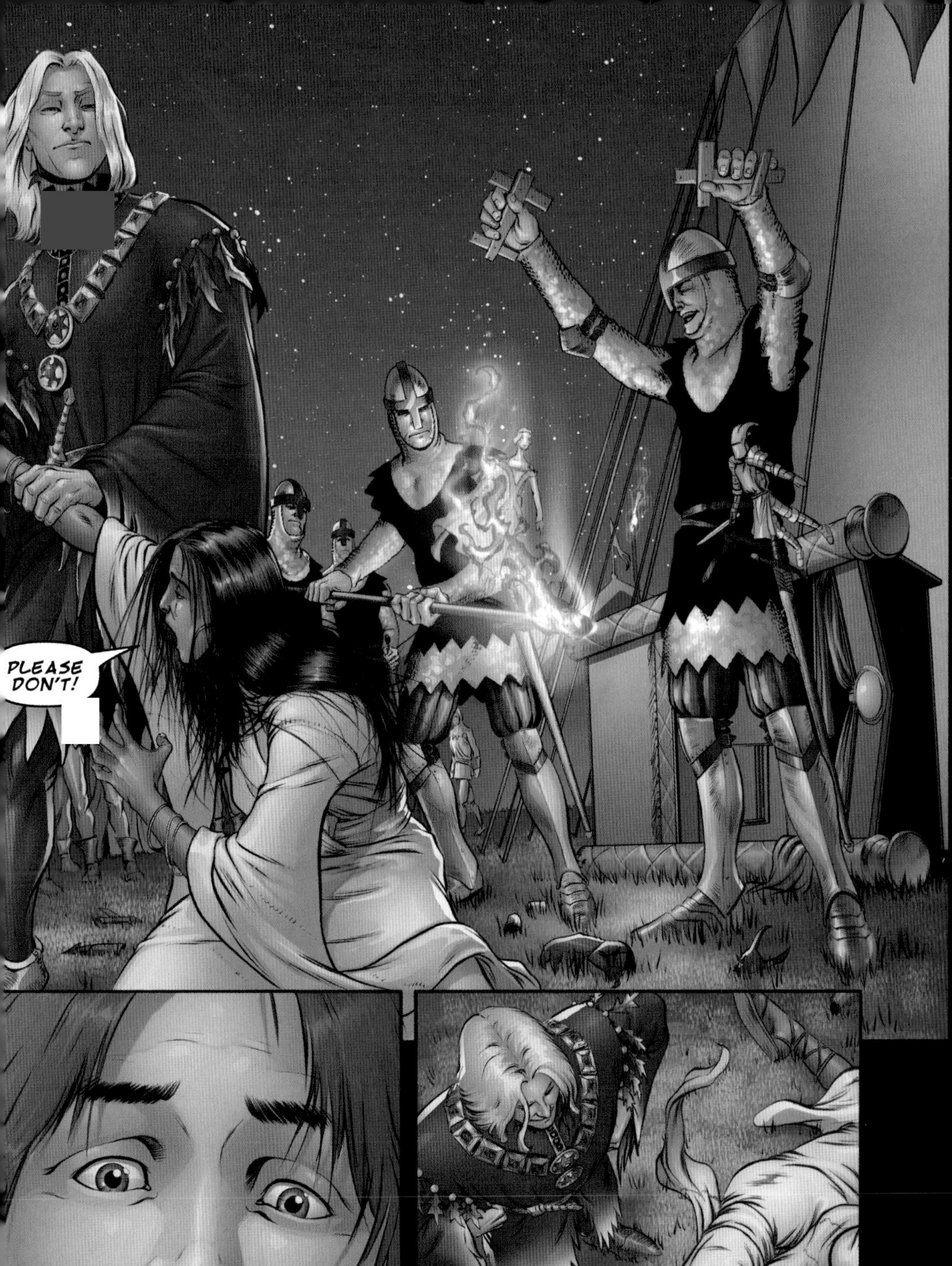
PLEASE DON'T!

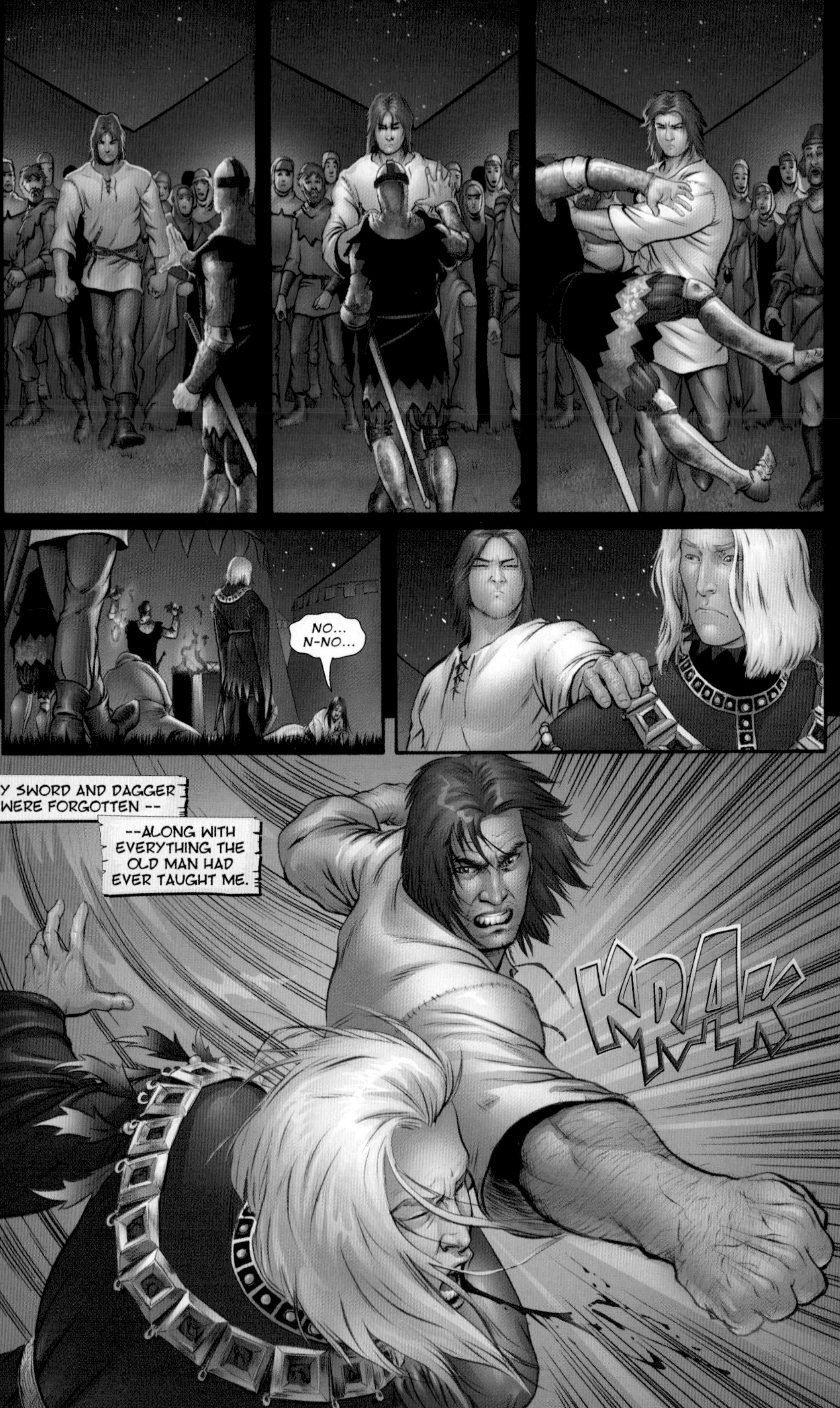
NO... N-NO...
MY SWORD AND DAGGER WERE FORGOTTEN --
--ALONG WITH EVERYTHING THE OLD MAN HAD EVER TAUGHT ME.
KRAK

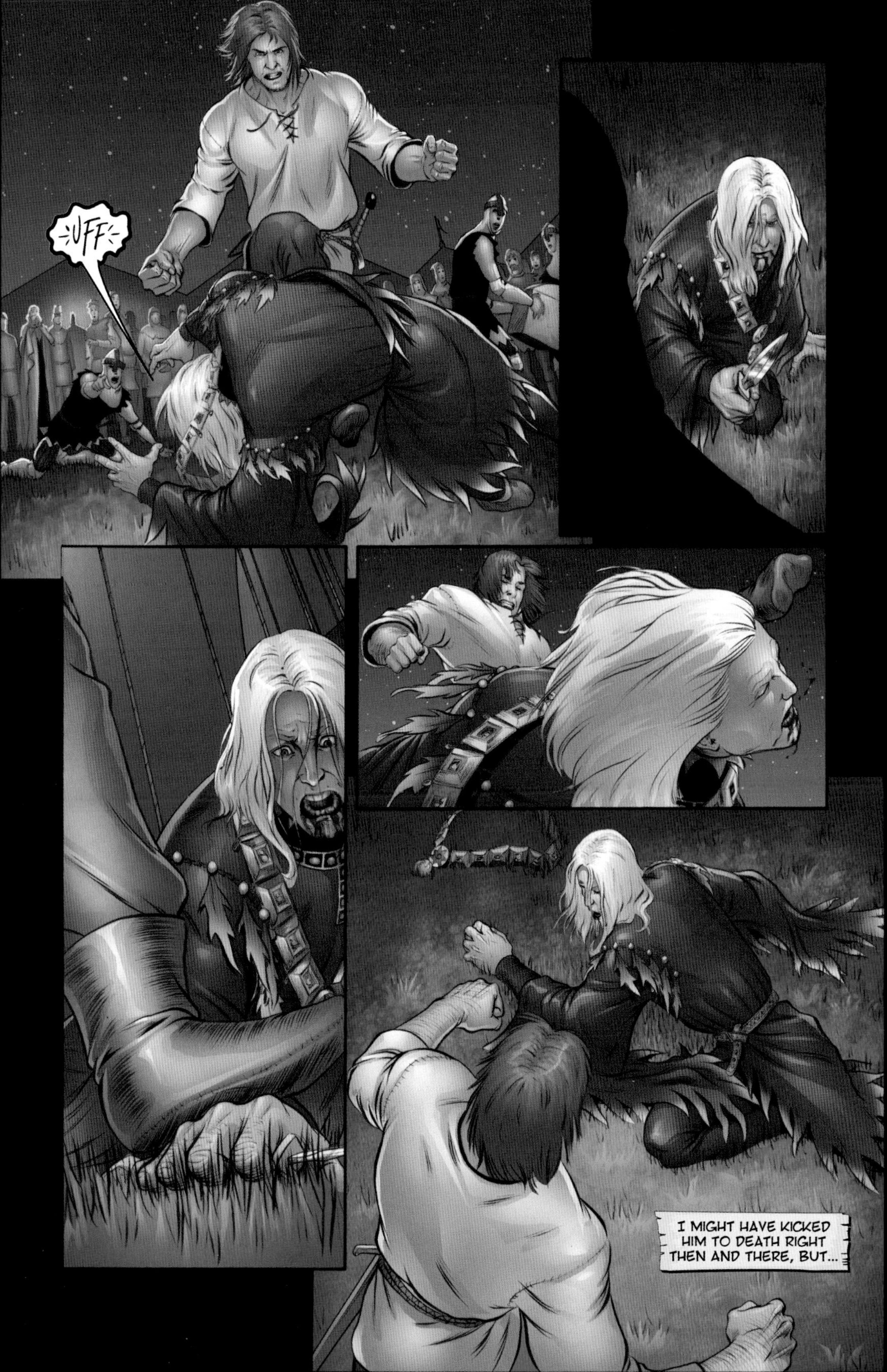
UFF
I MIGHT HAVE KICKED HIM TO DEATH RIGHT THEN AND THERE, BUT...

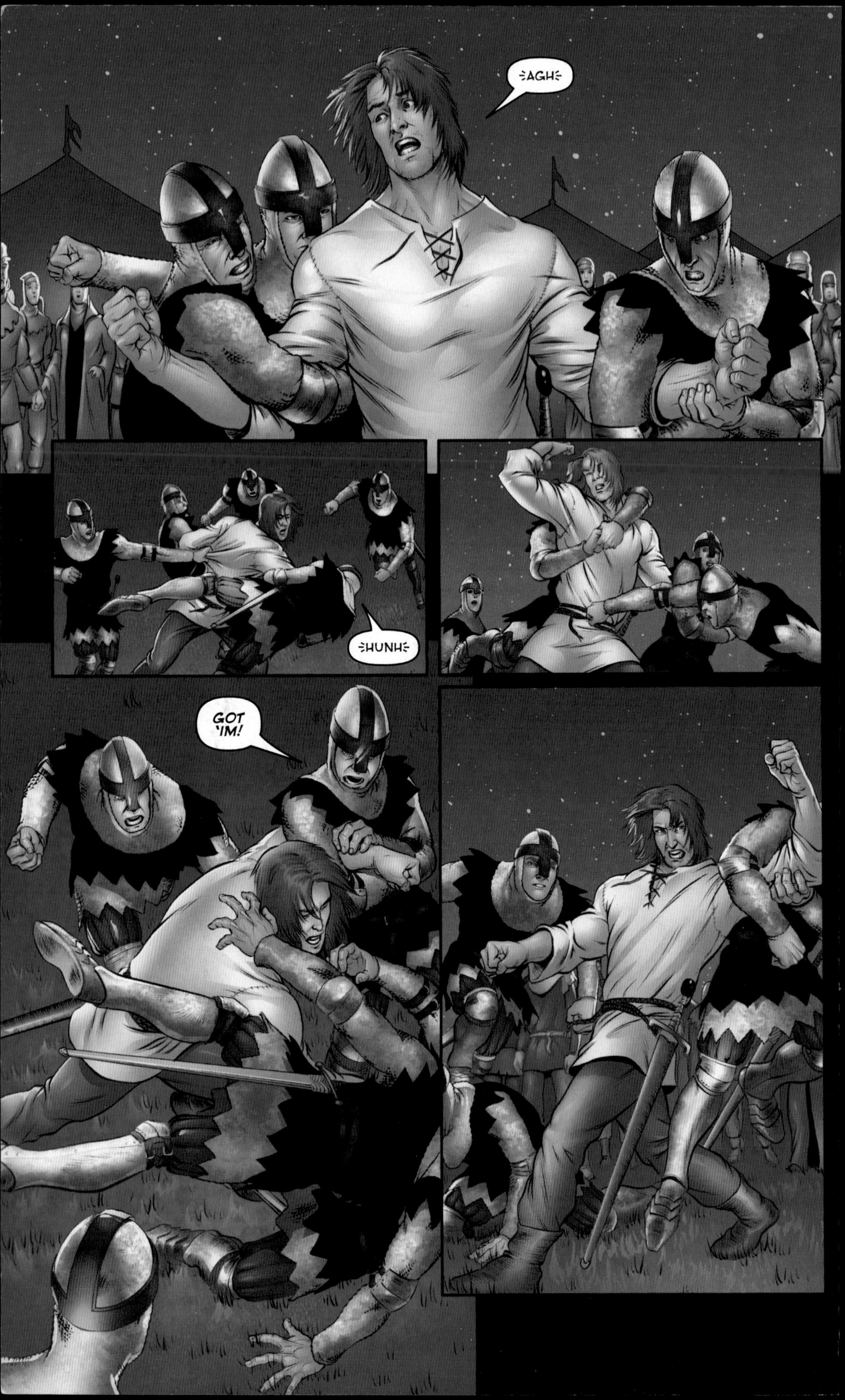

AGH
HUNH
GOT 'IM!

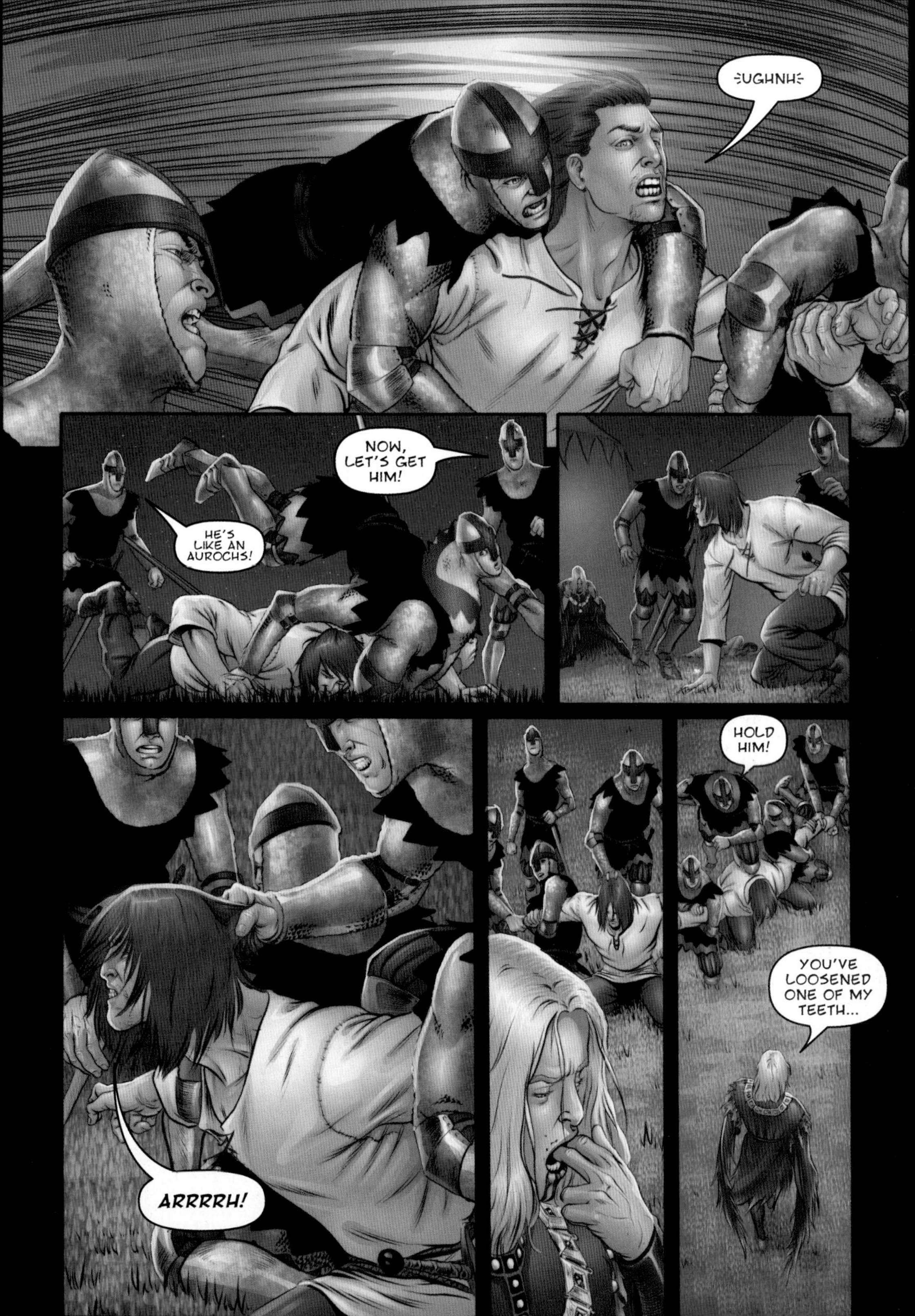

UGHNH
NOW, LET'S GET HIM!
HE'S LIKE AN AUROCHS!
ARRRRH!
HOLD HIM!
YOU'VE LOOSENED ONE OF MY TEETH...

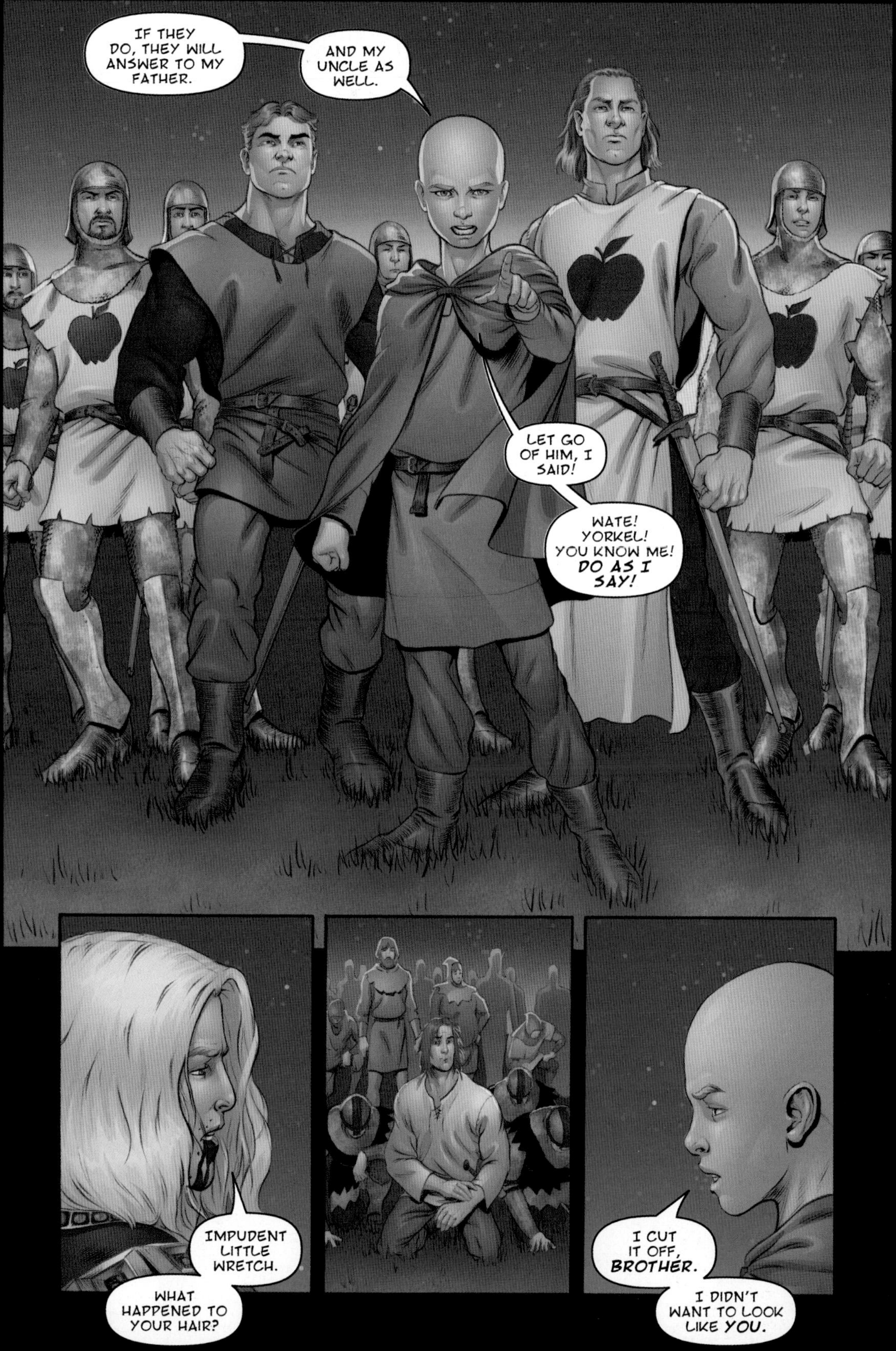

IF THEY DO, THEY WILL ANSWER TO MY FATHER.
AND MY UNCLE AS WELL.
LET GO OF HIM, I SAID!
WATE! YORKEL! YOU KNOW ME! **DO AS I SAY!**
IMPUDENT LITTLE WRETCH.
WHAT HAPPENED TO YOUR HAIR?
I CUT IT OFF, **BROTHER**.
I DIDN'T WANT TO LOOK LIKE **YOU**.

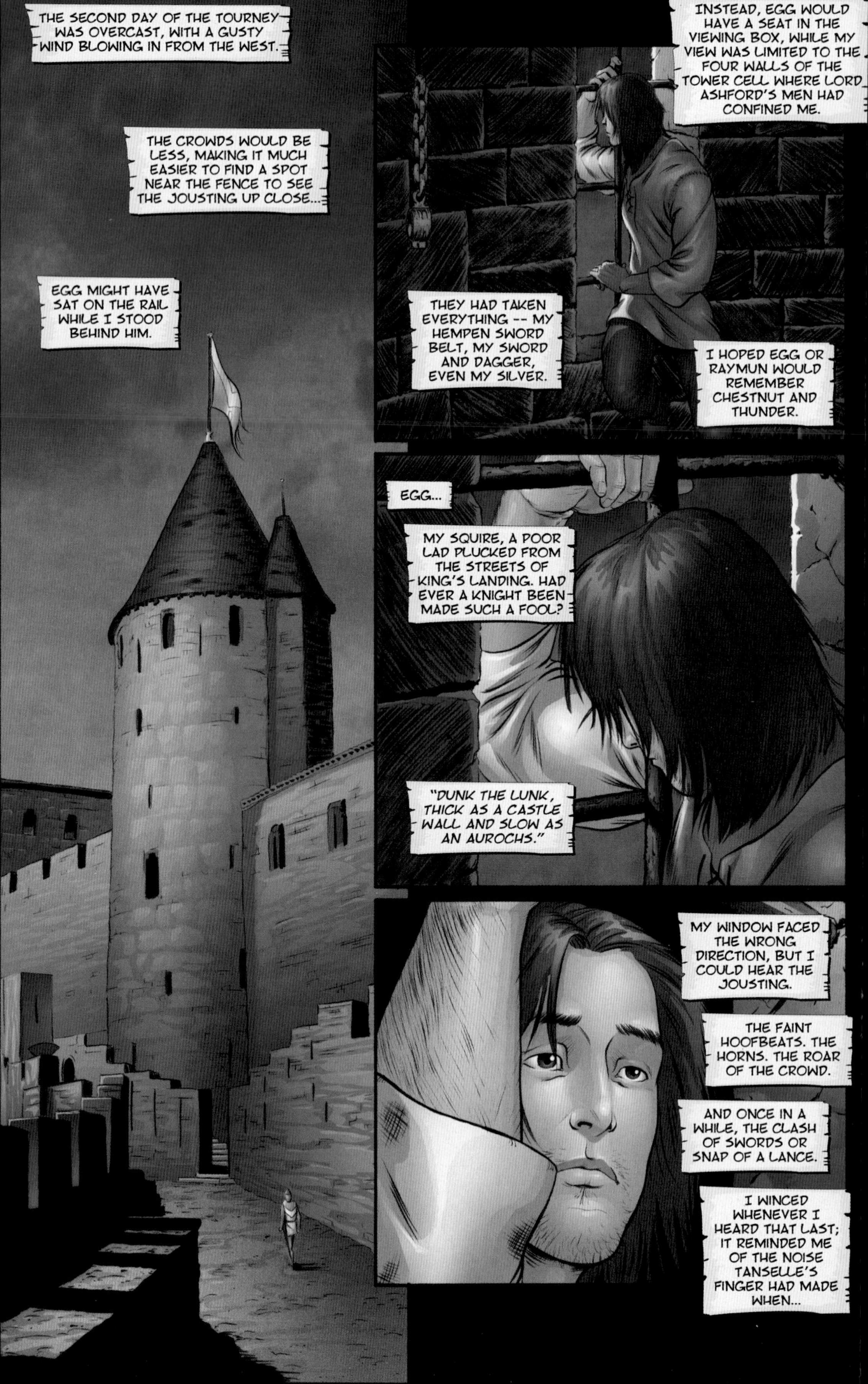
THE SECOND DAY OF THE TOURNEY WAS OVERCAST, WITH A GUSTY WIND BLOWING IN FROM THE WEST.
THE CROWDS WOULD BE LESS, MAKING IT MUCH EASIER TO FIND A SPOT NEAR THE FENCE TO SEE THE JOUSTING UP CLOSE...
EGG MIGHT HAVE SAT ON THE RAIL WHILE I STOOD BEHIND HIM.
INSTEAD, EGG WOULD HAVE A SEAT IN THE VIEWING BOX, WHILE MY VIEW WAS LIMITED TO THE FOUR WALLS OF THE TOWER CELL WHERE LORD ASHFORD'S MEN HAD CONFINED ME.
THEY HAD TAKEN EVERYTHING -- MY HEMPEN SWORD BELT, MY SWORD AND DAGGER, EVEN MY SILVER.
I HOPED EGG OR RAYMUN WOULD REMEMBER CHESTNUT AND THUNDER.
EGG...
MY SQUIRE, A POOR LAD PLUCKED FROM THE STREETS OF KING'S LANDING. HAD EVER A KNIGHT BEEN MADE SUCH A FOOL?
"DUNK THE LUNK, THICK AS A CASTLE WALL AND SLOW AS AN AUROCHS."
MY WINDOW FACED THE WRONG DIRECTION, BUT I COULD HEAR THE JOUSTING.
THE FAINT HOOFBEATS. THE HORNS. THE ROAR OF THE CROWD.
AND ONCE IN A WHILE, THE CLASH OF SWORDS OR SNAP OF A LANCE.
I WINCED WHENEVER I HEARD THAT LAST; IT REMINDED ME OF THE NOISE TANSELLE'S FINGER HAD MADE WHEN...

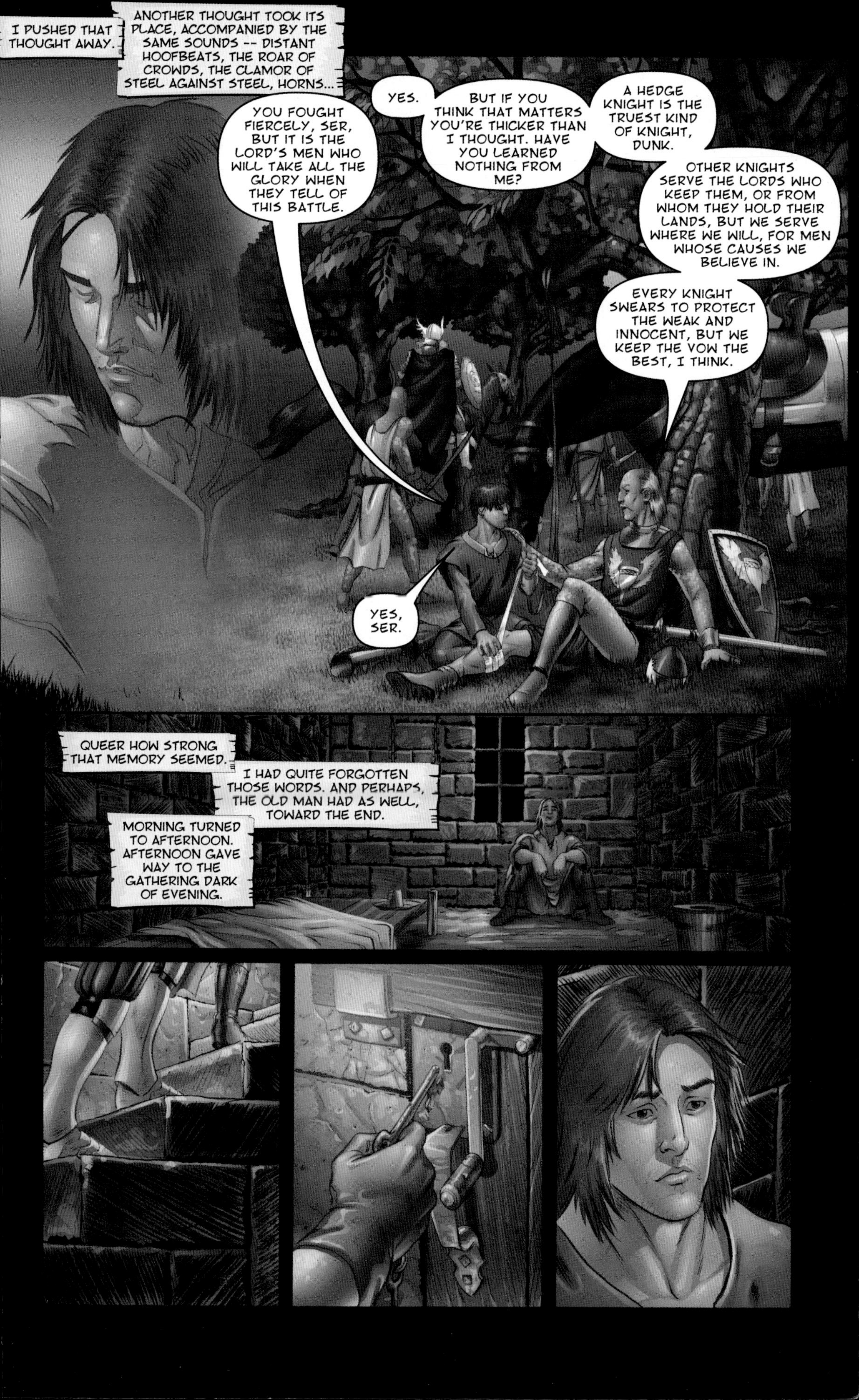
I PUSHED THAT THOUGHT AWAY.
ANOTHER THOUGHT TOOK ITS PLACE, ACCOMPANIED BY THE SAME SOUNDS -- DISTANT HOOFBEATS, THE ROAR OF CROWDS, THE CLAMOR OF STEEL AGAINST STEEL, HORNS...
YOU FOUGHT FIERCELY, SER, BUT IT IS THE LORD'S MEN WHO WILL TAKE ALL THE GLORY WHEN THEY TELL OF THIS BATTLE.
YES.
BUT IF YOU THINK THAT MATTERS YOU'RE THICKER THAN I THOUGHT. HAVE YOU LEARNED NOTHING FROM ME?
YES, SER.
A HEDGE KNIGHT IS THE TRUEST KIND OF KNIGHT, DUNK.
OTHER KNIGHTS SERVE THE LORDS WHO KEEP THEM, OR FROM WHOM THEY HOLD THEIR LANDS, BUT WE SERVE WHERE WE WILL, FOR MEN WHOSE CAUSES WE BELIEVE IN.
EVERY KNIGHT SWEARS TO PROTECT THE WEAK AND INNOCENT, BUT WE KEEP THE VOW THE BEST, I THINK.
QUEER HOW STRONG THAT MEMORY SEEMED.
I HAD QUITE FORGOTTEN THOSE WORDS. AND PERHAPS THE OLD MAN HAD AS WELL, TOWARD THE END.
MORNING TURNED TO AFTERNOON. AFTERNOON GAVE WAY TO THE GATHERING DARK OF EVENING.

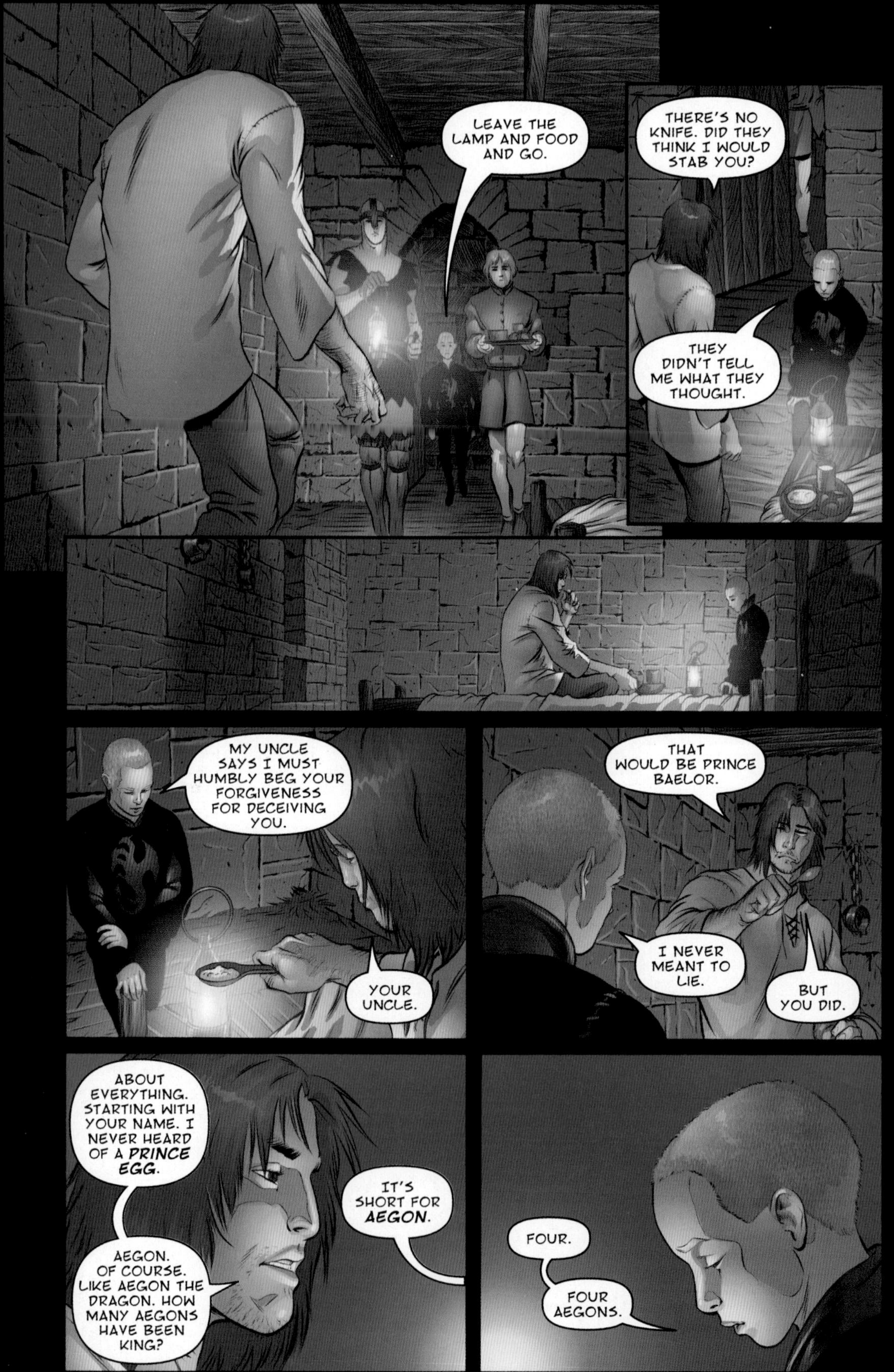
LEAVE THE LAMP AND FOOD AND GO.
THERE'S NO KNIFE. DID THEY THINK I WOULD STAB YOU?
THEY DIDN'T TELL ME WHAT THEY THOUGHT.
MY UNCLE SAYS I MUST HUMBLY BEG YOUR FORGIVENESS FOR DECEIVING YOU.
YOUR UNCLE.
THAT WOULD BE PRINCE BAELOR.
I NEVER MEANT TO LIE.
BUT YOU DID.
ABOUT EVERYTHING. STARTING WITH YOUR NAME. I NEVER HEARD OF A ***PRINCE EGG***.
IT'S SHORT FOR ***AEGON***.
AEGON. OF COURSE. LIKE AEGON THE DRAGON. HOW MANY AEGONS HAVE BEEN KING?
FOUR.
FOUR AEGONS.

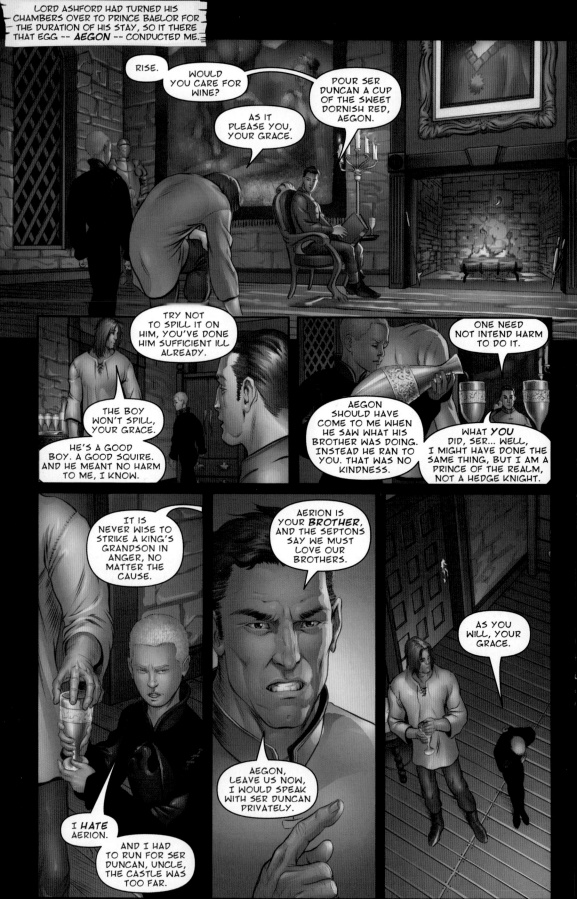

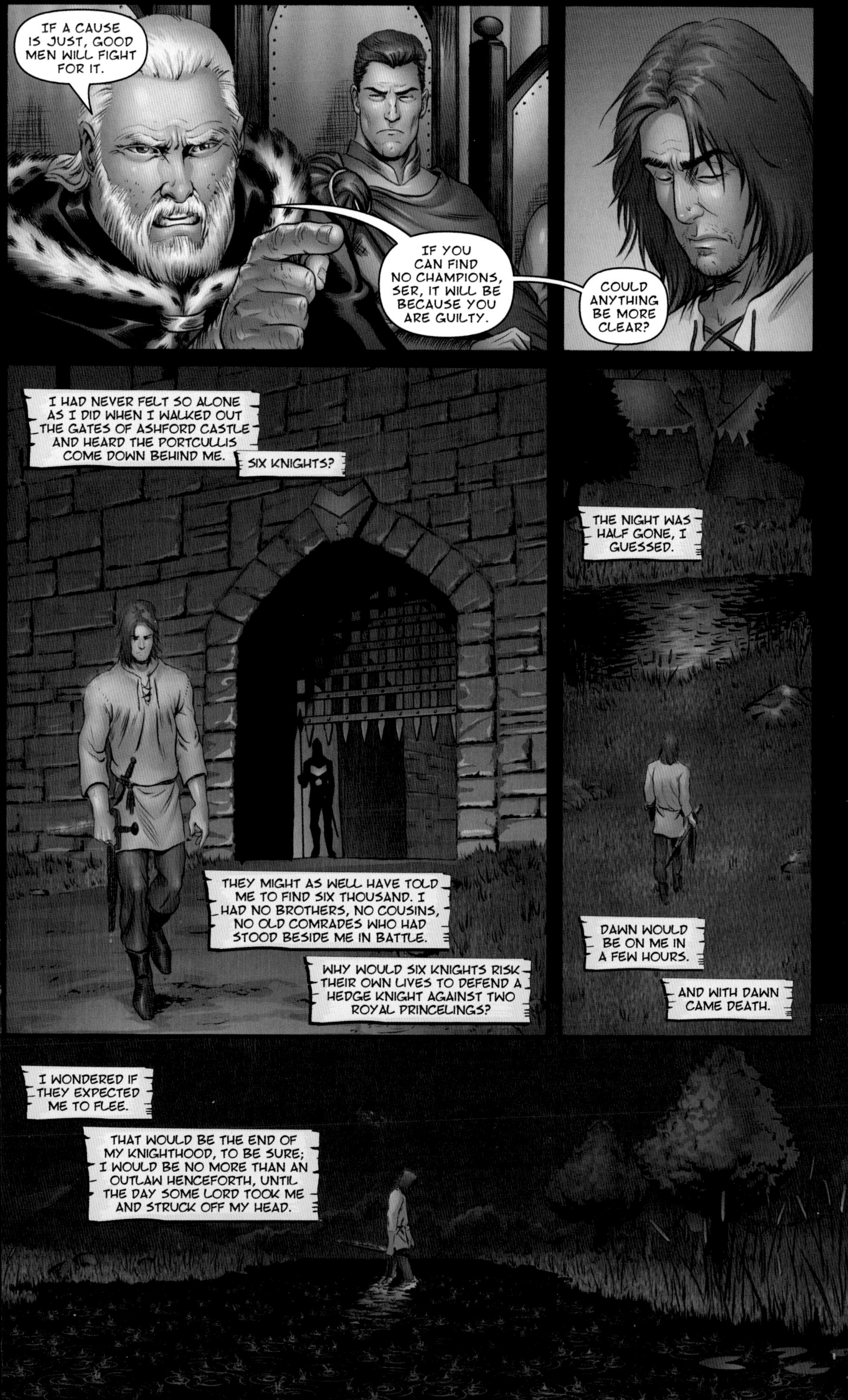
IF A CAUSE IS JUST, GOOD MEN WILL FIGHT FOR IT.
IF YOU CAN FIND NO CHAMPIONS, SER, IT WILL BE BECAUSE YOU ARE GUILTY.
COULD ANYTHING BE MORE CLEAR?
I HAD NEVER FELT SO ALONE AS I DID WHEN I WALKED OUT THE GATES OF ASHFORD CASTLE AND HEARD THE PORTCULLIS COME DOWN BEHIND ME.
SIX KNIGHTS?
THEY MIGHT AS WELL HAVE TOLD ME TO FIND SIX THOUSAND. I HAD NO BROTHERS, NO COUSINS, NO OLD COMRADES WHO HAD STOOD BESIDE ME IN BATTLE.
WHY WOULD SIX KNIGHTS RISK THEIR OWN LIVES TO DEFEND A HEDGE KNIGHT AGAINST TWO ROYAL PRINCELINGS?
THE NIGHT WAS HALF GONE, I GUESSED.
DAWN WOULD BE ON ME IN A FEW HOURS.
AND WITH DAWN CAME DEATH.
I WONDERED IF THEY EXPECTED ME TO FLEE.
THAT WOULD BE THE END OF MY KNIGHTHOOD, TO BE SURE; I WOULD BE NO MORE THAN AN OUTLAW HENCEFORTH, UNTIL THE DAY SOME LORD TOOK ME AND STRUCK OFF MY HEAD.

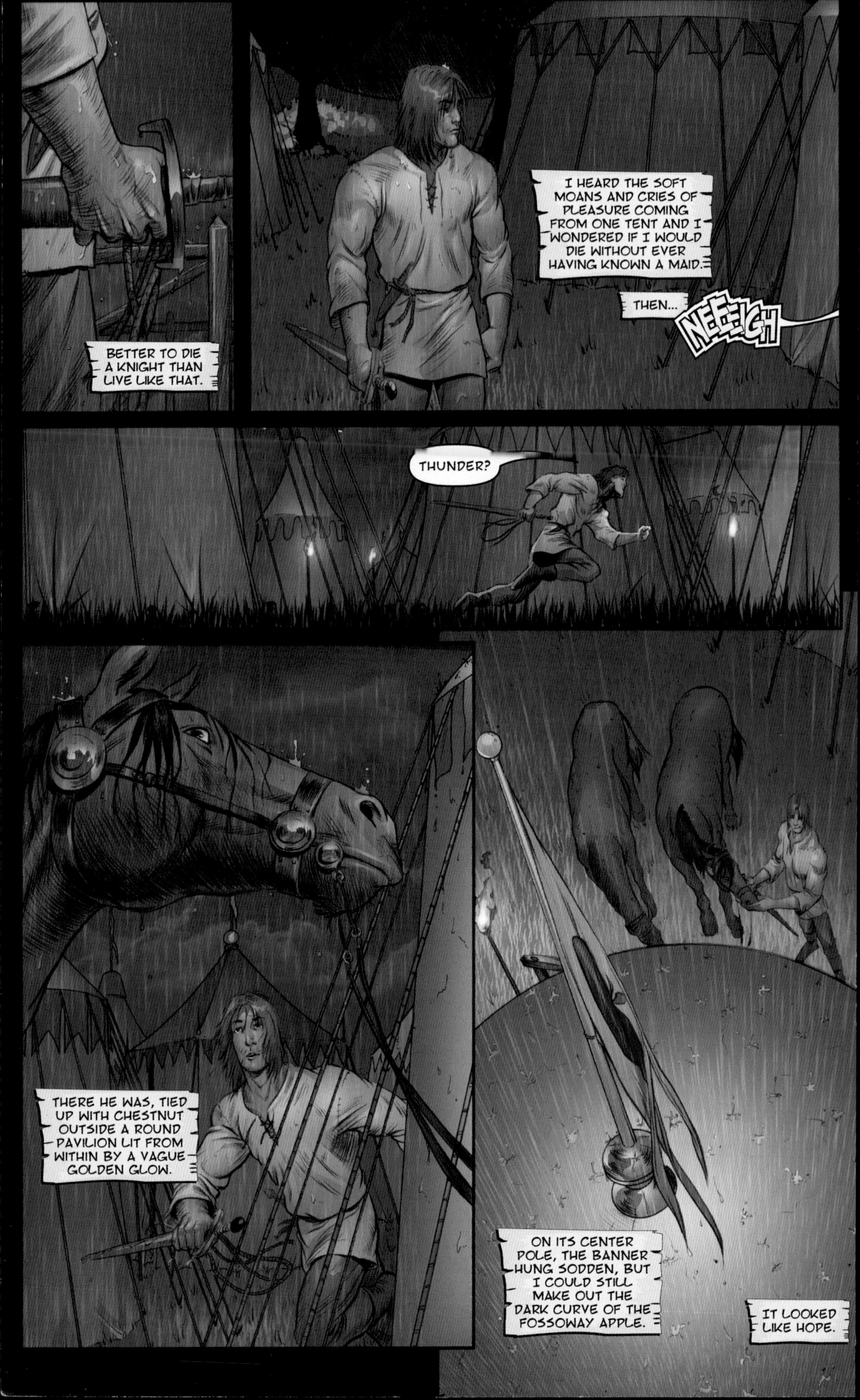
BETTER TO DIE A KNIGHT THAN LIVE LIKE THAT.
I HEARD THE SOFT MOANS AND CRIES OF PLEASURE COMING FROM ONE TENT AND I WONDERED IF I WOULD DIE WITHOUT EVER HAVING KNOWN A MAID.
THEN...
NEEEIGH
THUNDER?
THERE HE WAS, TIED UP WITH CHESTNUT OUTSIDE A ROUND PAVILION LIT FROM WITHIN BY A VAGUE GOLDEN GLOW.
ON ITS CENTER POLE, THE BANNER HUNG SODDEN, BUT I COULD STILL MAKE OUT THE DARK CURVE OF THE FOSSOWAY APPLE.
IT LOOKED LIKE HOPE.

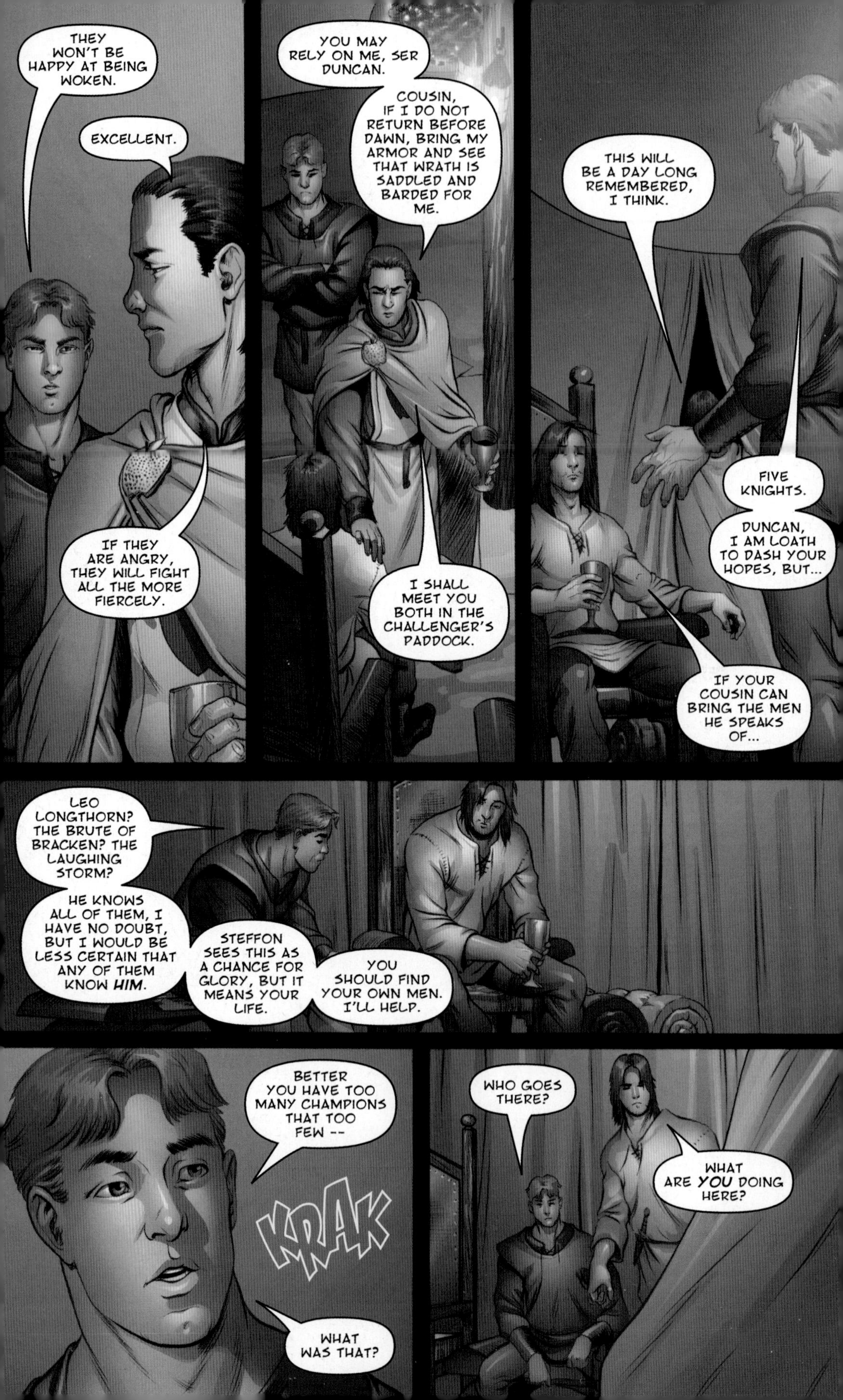

THEY WON'T BE HAPPY AT BEING WOKEN.
EXCELLENT.
IF THEY ARE ANGRY, THEY WILL FIGHT ALL THE MORE FIERCELY.
YOU MAY RELY ON ME, SER DUNCAN.
COUSIN, IF I DO NOT RETURN BEFORE DAWN, BRING MY ARMOR AND SEE THAT WRATH IS SADDLED AND BARDED FOR ME.
I SHALL MEET YOU BOTH IN THE CHALLENGER'S PADDOCK.
THIS WILL BE A DAY LONG REMEMBERED, I THINK.
FIVE KNIGHTS.
DUNCAN, I AM LOATH TO DASH YOUR HOPES, BUT...
IF YOUR COUSIN CAN BRING THE MEN HE SPEAKS OF...
LEO LONGTHORN? THE BRUTE OF BRACKEN? THE LAUGHING STORM?
HE KNOWS ALL OF THEM, I HAVE NO DOUBT, BUT I WOULD BE LESS CERTAIN THAT ANY OF THEM KNOW ***HIM***.
STEFFON SEES THIS AS A CHANCE FOR GLORY, BUT IT MEANS YOUR LIFE.
YOU SHOULD FIND YOUR OWN MEN. I'LL HELP.
BETTER YOU HAVE TOO MANY CHAMPIONS THAT TOO FEW --
KRAK
WHAT WAS THAT?
WHO GOES THERE?
WHAT ARE ***YOU*** DOING HERE?

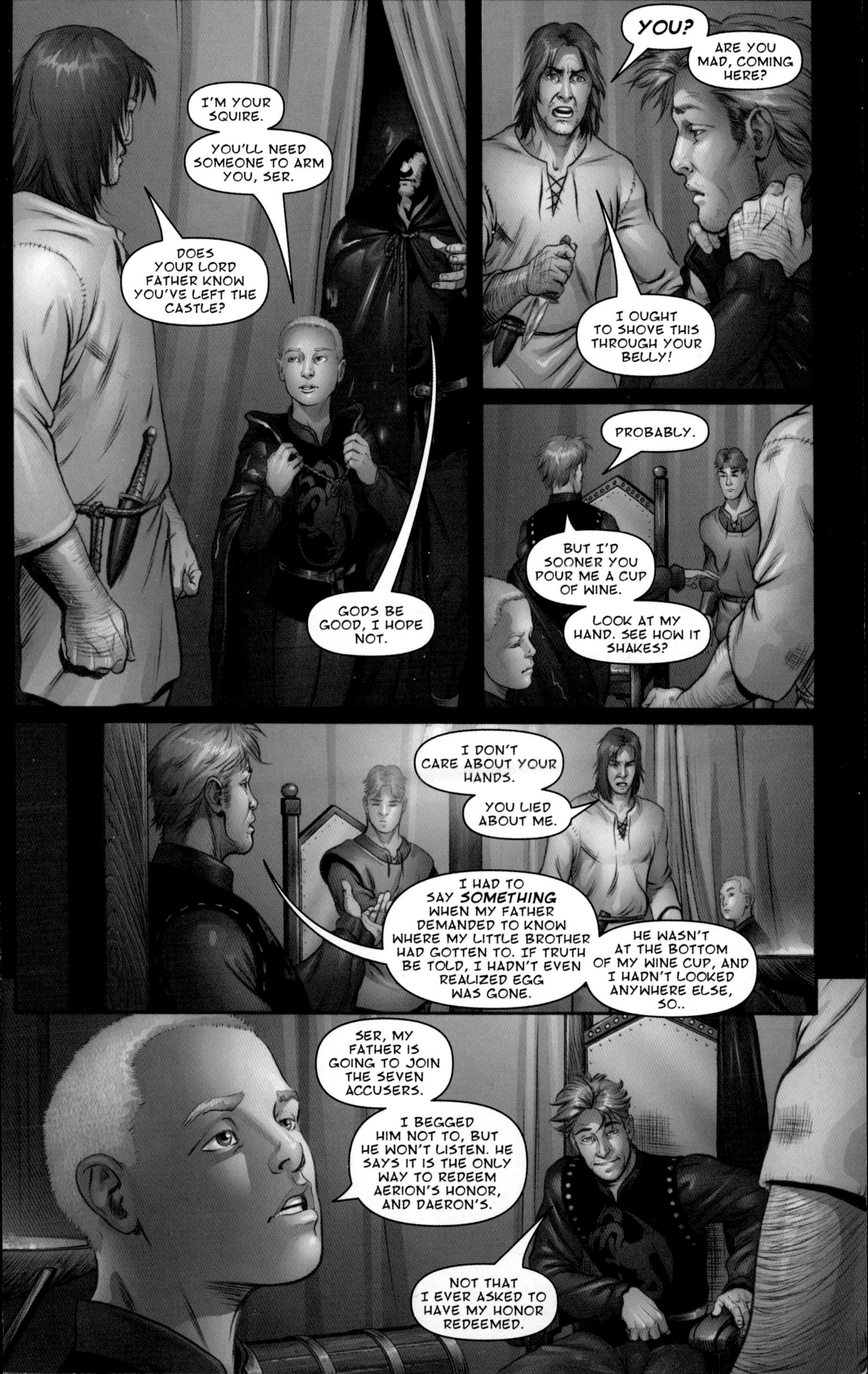

DOES YOUR LORD FATHER KNOW YOU'VE LEFT THE CASTLE?
I'M YOUR SQUIRE.
YOU'LL NEED SOMEONE TO ARM YOU, SER.
GODS BE GOOD, I HOPE NOT.
YOU?
ARE YOU MAD, COMING HERE?
I OUGHT TO SHOVE THIS THROUGH YOUR BELLY!
PROBABLY.
BUT I'D SOONER YOU POUR ME A CUP OF WINE.
LOOK AT MY HAND. SEE HOW IT SHAKES?
I DON'T CARE ABOUT YOUR HANDS.
YOU LIED ABOUT ME.
I HAD TO SAY SOMETHING WHEN MY FATHER DEMANDED TO KNOW WHERE MY LITTLE BROTHER HAD GOTTEN TO. IF TRUTH BE TOLD, I HADN'T EVEN REALIZED EGG WAS GONE.
HE WASN'T AT THE BOTTOM OF MY WINE CUP, AND I HADN'T LOOKED ANYWHERE ELSE, SO..
SER, MY FATHER IS GOING TO JOIN THE SEVEN ACCUSERS.
I BEGGED HIM NOT TO, BUT HE WON'T LISTEN. HE SAYS IT IS THE ONLY WAY TO REDEEM AERION'S HONOR, AND DAERON'S.
NOT THAT I EVER ASKED TO HAVE MY HONOR REDEEMED.

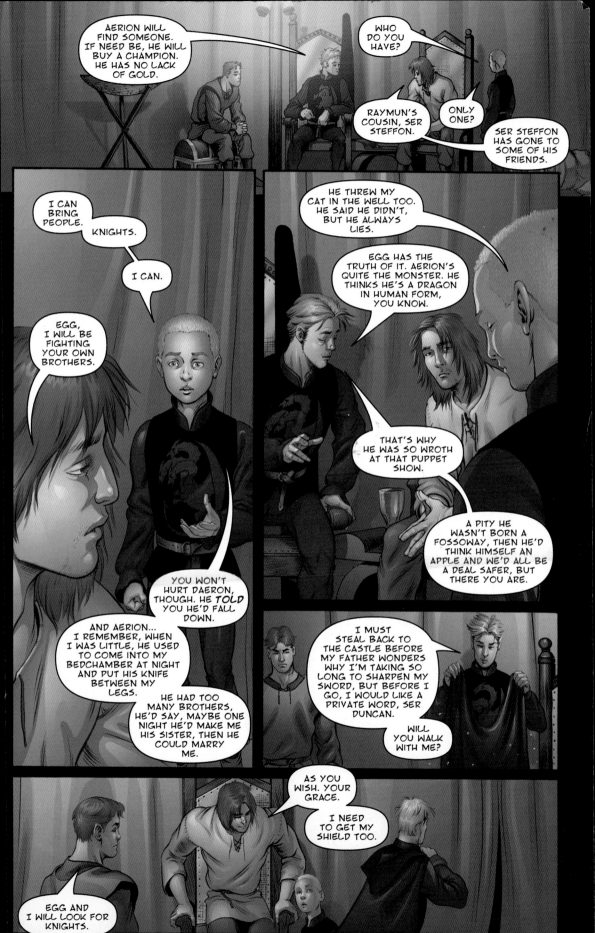

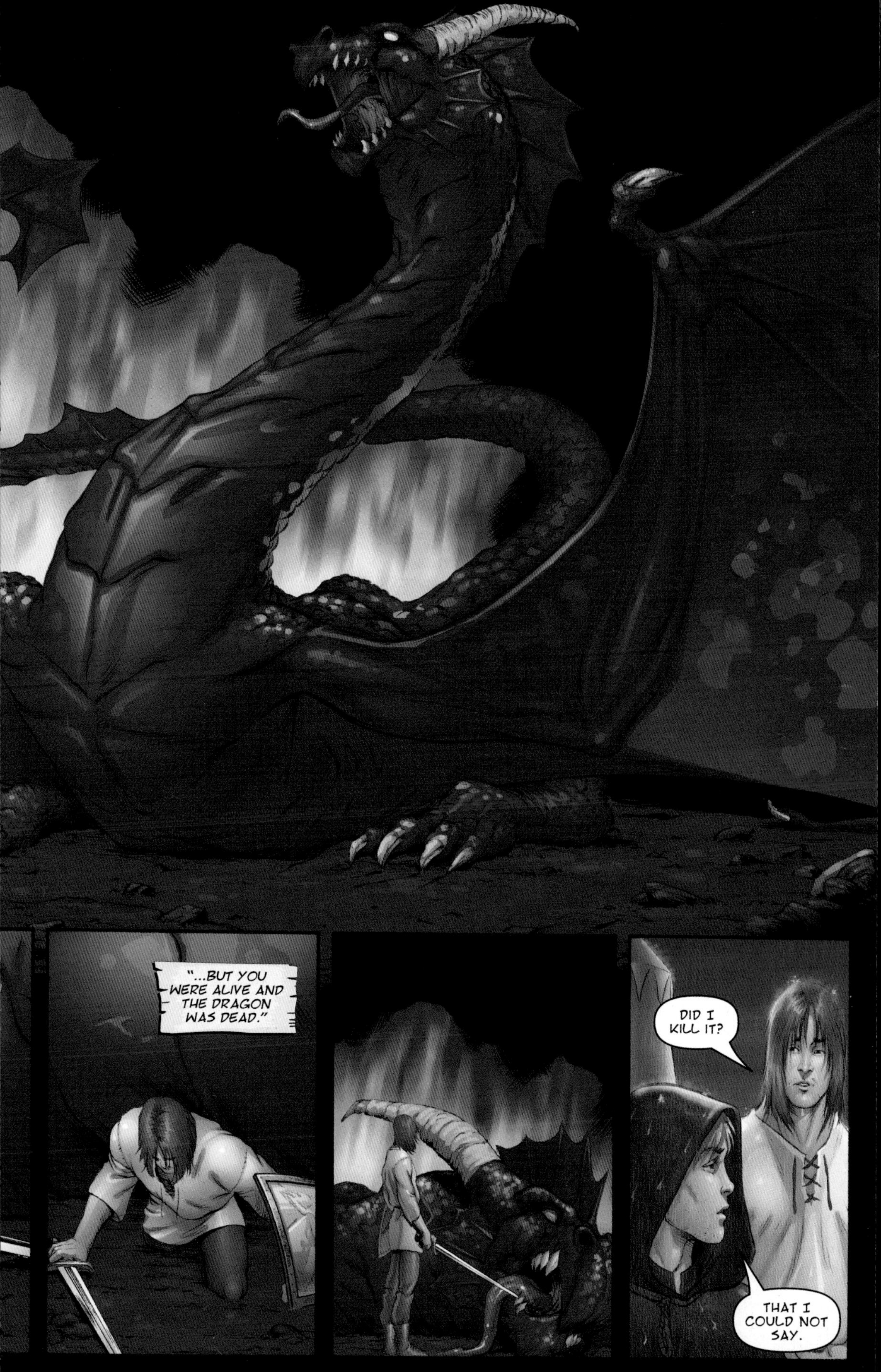
"...BUT YOU WERE ALIVE AND THE DRAGON WAS DEAD."
DID I KILL IT?
THAT I COULD NOT SAY.

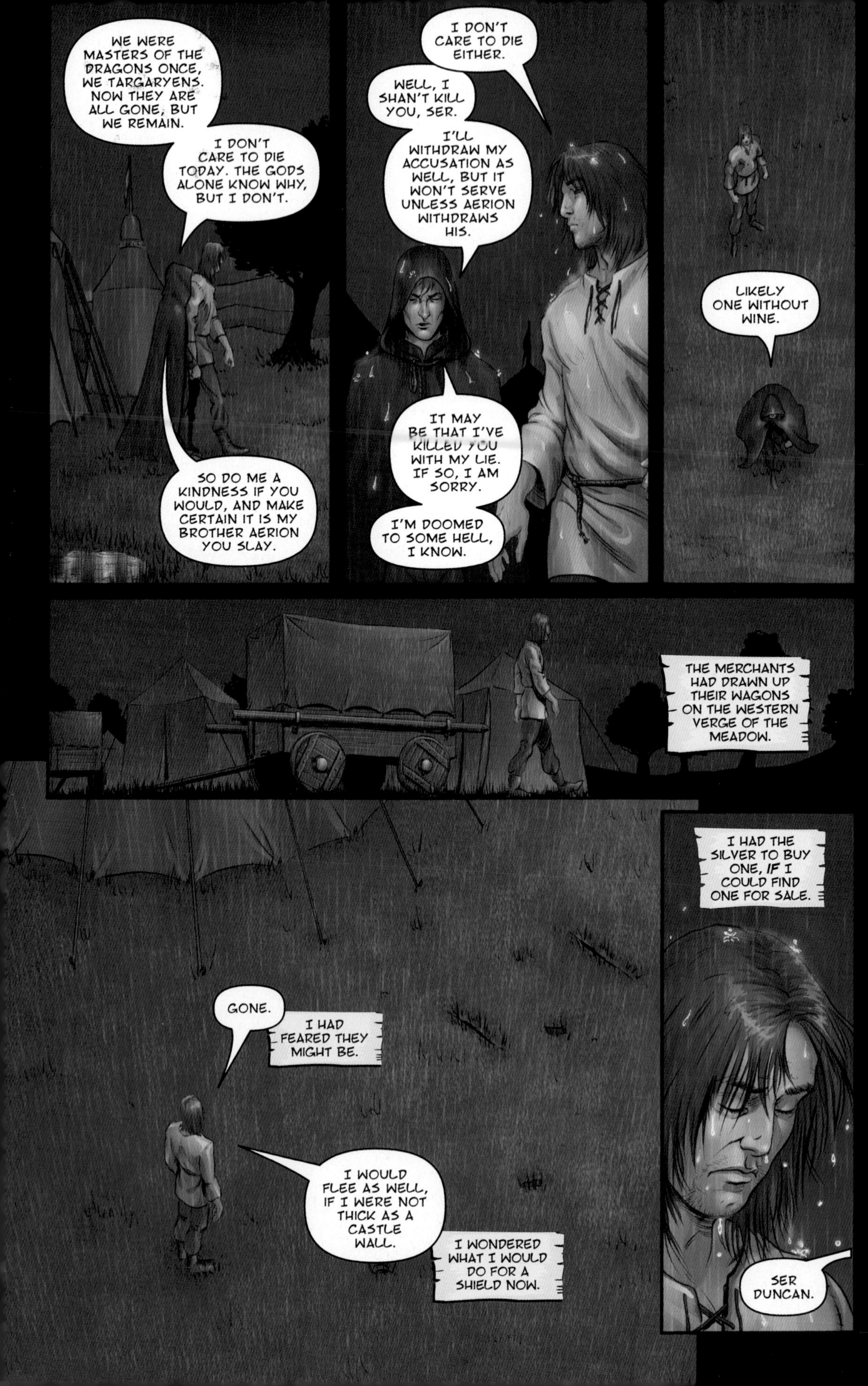
WE WERE MASTERS OF THE DRAGONS ONCE, WE TARGARYENS. NOW THEY ARE ALL GONE, BUT WE REMAIN.
I DON'T CARE TO DIE TODAY. THE GODS ALONE KNOW WHY, BUT I DON'T.
SO DO ME A KINDNESS IF YOU WOULD, AND MAKE CERTAIN IT IS MY BROTHER AERION YOU SLAY.
I DON'T CARE TO DIE EITHER.
WELL, I SHAN'T KILL YOU, SER.
I'LL WITHDRAW MY ACCUSATION AS WELL, BUT IT WON'T SERVE UNLESS AERION WITHDRAWS HIS.
IT MAY BE THAT I'VE KILLED YOU WITH MY LIE. IF SO, I AM SORRY.
I'M DOOMED TO SOME HELL, I KNOW.
LIKELY ONE WITHOUT WINE.
THE MERCHANTS HAD DRAWN UP THEIR WAGONS ON THE WESTERN VERGE OF THE MEADOW.
GONE.
I HAD FEARED THEY MIGHT BE.
I WOULD FLEE AS WELL, IF I WERE NOT THICK AS A CASTLE WALL.
I WONDERED WHAT I WOULD DO FOR A SHIELD NOW.
I HAD THE SILVER TO BUY ONE, IF I COULD FIND ONE FOR SALE.
SER DUNCAN.

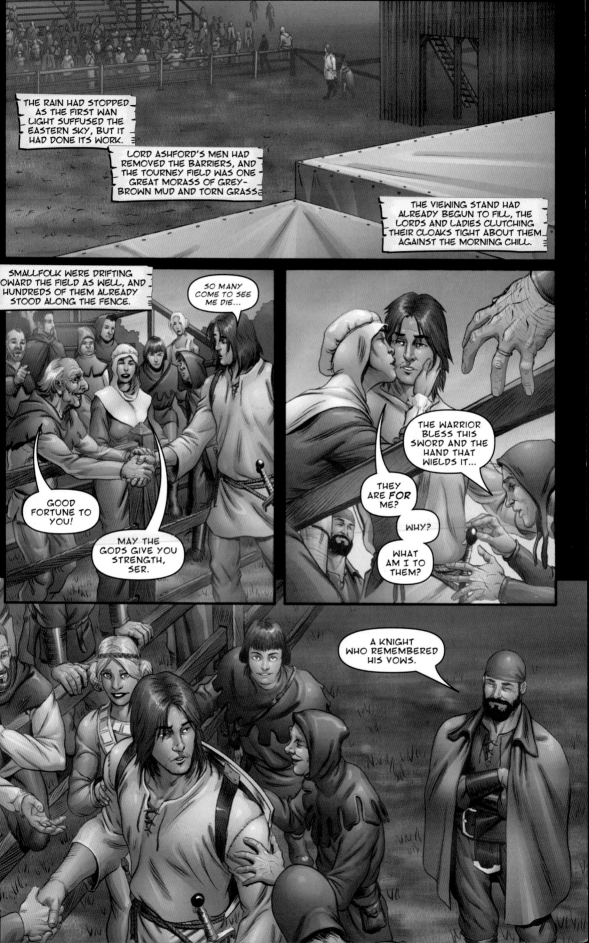

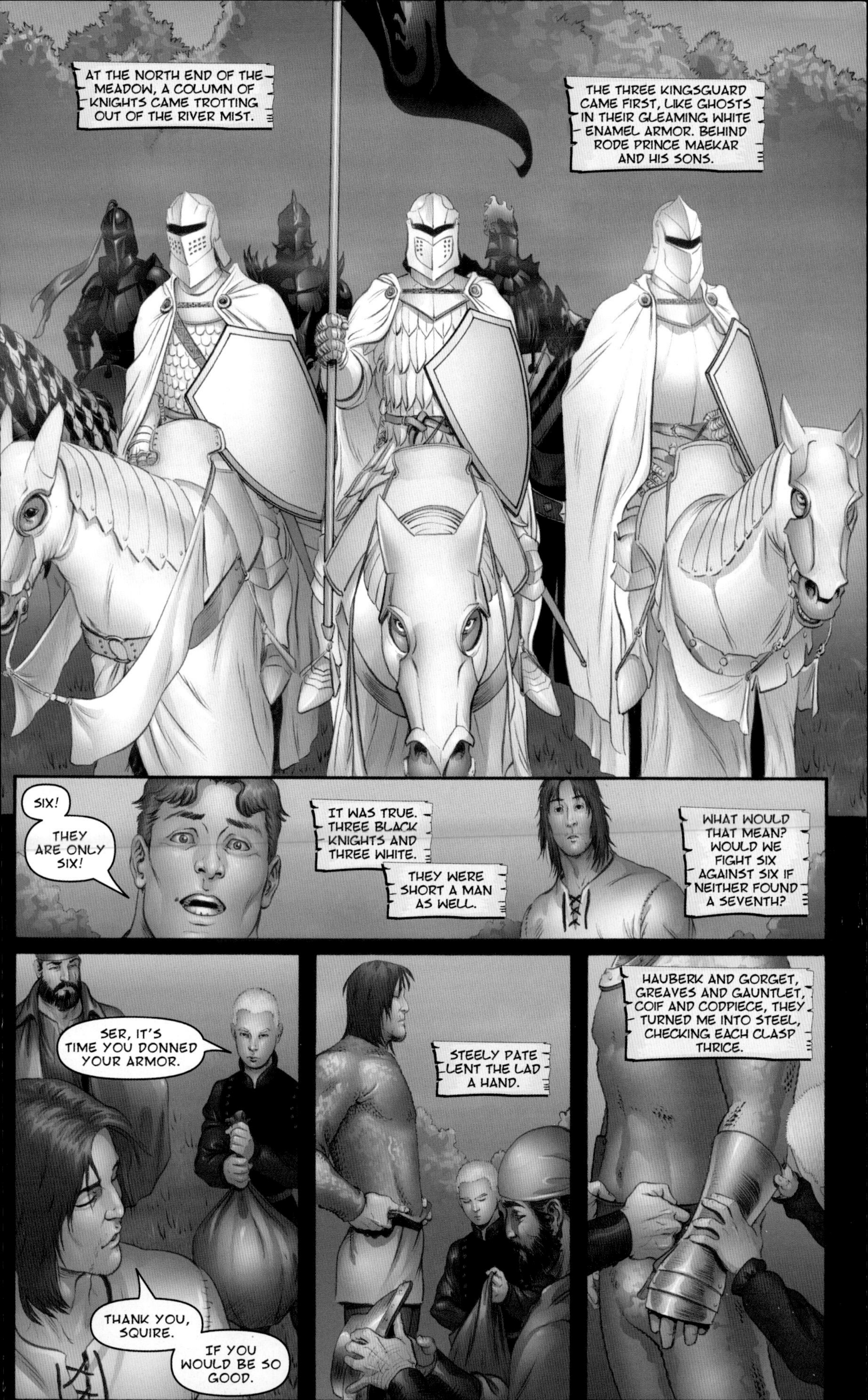
AT THE NORTH END OF THE MEADOW, A COLUMN OF KNIGHTS CAME TROTTING OUT OF THE RIVER MIST.
THE THREE KINGSGUARD CAME FIRST, LIKE GHOSTS IN THEIR GLEAMING WHITE ENAMEL ARMOR. BEHIND RODE PRINCE MAEKAR AND HIS SONS.
SIX!
THEY ARE ONLY SIX!
IT WAS TRUE. THREE BLACK KNIGHTS AND THREE WHITE.
THEY WERE SHORT A MAN AS WELL.
WHAT WOULD THAT MEAN? WOULD WE FIGHT SIX AGAINST SIX IF NEITHER FOUND A SEVENTH?
SER, IT'S TIME YOU DONNED YOUR ARMOR.
THANK YOU, SQUIRE.
IF YOU WOULD BE SO GOOD.
STEELY PATE LENT THE LAD A HAND.
HAUBERK AND GORGET, GREAVES AND GAUNTLET, COIF AND CODPIECE, THEY TURNED ME INTO STEEL, CHECKING EACH CLASP THRICE.

A DEEP EXPECTANT SILENCE FELL ACROSS ASHFORD MEADOW.

EIGHTY YARDS AWAY, AERION'S HORSE TRUMPETED WITH IMPATIENCE AND PAWED THE MUDDY GROUND.

THUNDER WAS VERY STILL BY COMPARISON; HE WAS AN OLDER HORSE, VETERAN OF HALF A HUNDRED FIGHTS, AND HE KNEW WHAT WAS EXPECTED OF HIM.

THE SIGHT OF MY ELM TREE AND SHOOTING STAR GAVE ME HEART.

IT MUST BE I WHO PUTS IT IN SER DUNCAN'S HAND.

MAY THE GODS BE WITH YOU, SER.

"OAK AND IRON, GUARD ME WELL, OR ELSE I'M DEAD AND DOOMED TO HELL."

YOUR LANCE...

NO!

TO EITHER SIDE, MY COMPANIONS TOOK UP THEIR OWN LANCES AND SPREAD OUT IN A LONG LINE...

...BUT THE NARROW EYESLIT OF THE GREATHELM LIMITED MY VISION TO WHAT WAS DIRECTLY AHEAD.

THE VIEWING STAND WAS GONE, AND LIKEWISE THE SMALLFOLK CROWDING THE FENCE--

--THERE WAS ONLY THE MUDDY FIELD, THE PALE BLOWING MIST, AND THE PRINCELING ON HIS CHARGER WITH FLAMES ON HIS HELM AND A DRAGON ON HIS SHIELD.

I WATCHED HIS SQUIRE HAND HIM A WAR LANCE -- AERION MEANT TO PUT THAT THROUGH MY HEART.

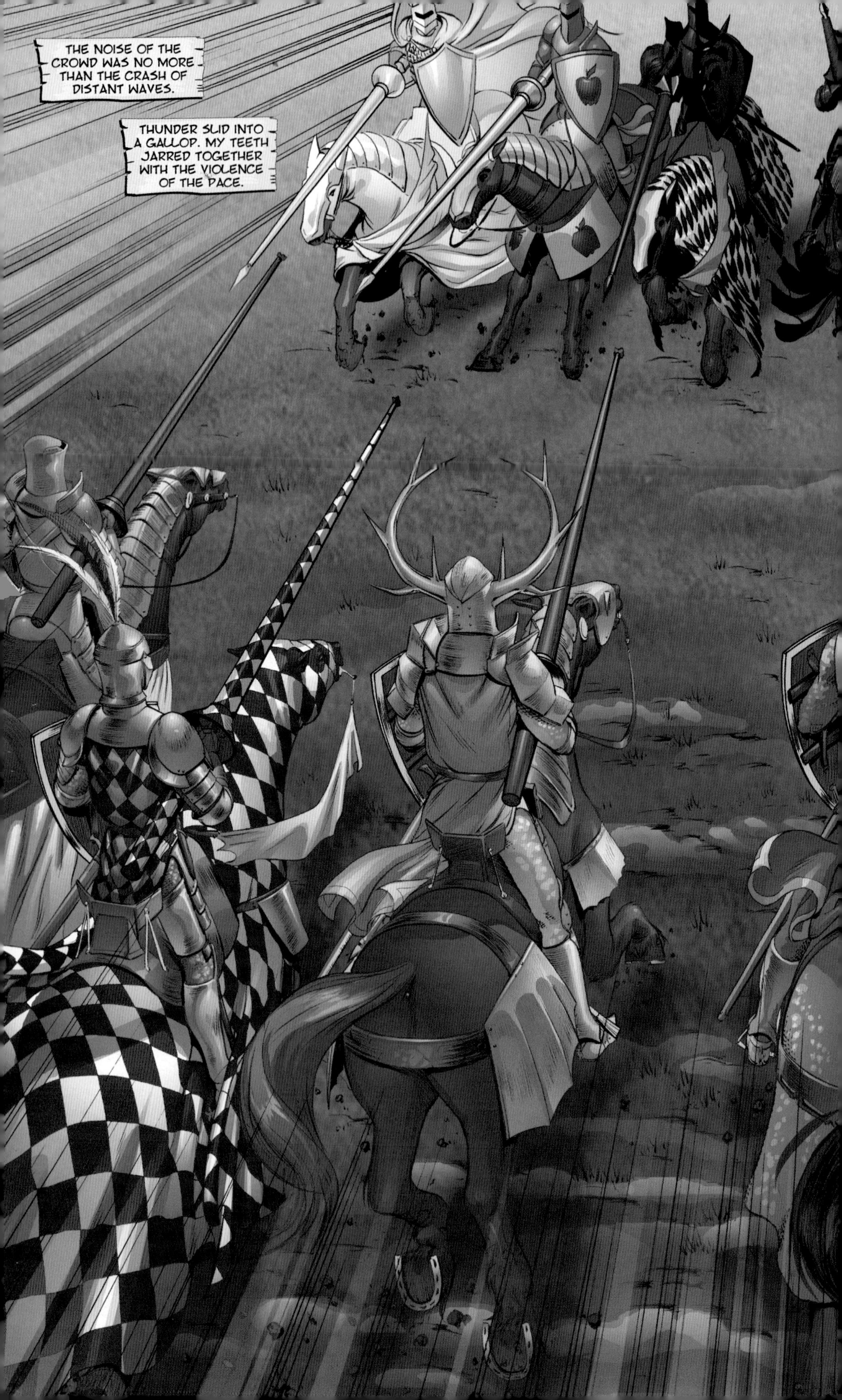
THE NOISE OF THE CROWD WAS NO MORE THAN THE CRASH OF DISTANT WAVES.
THUNDER SLID INTO A GALLOP. MY TEETH JARRED TOGETHER WITH THE VIOLENCE OF THE PACE.

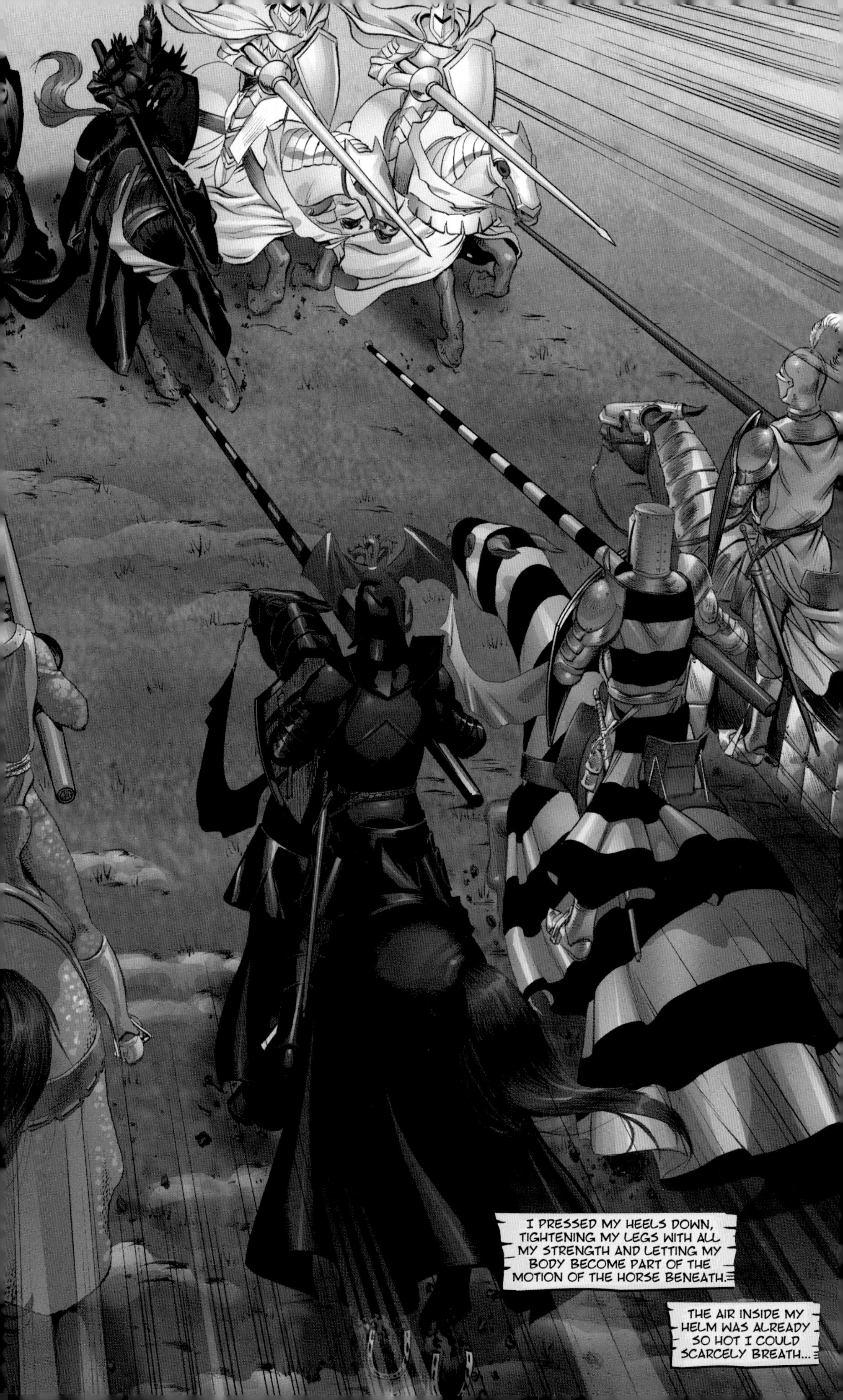
I PRESSED MY HEELS DOWN, TIGHTENING MY LEGS WITH ALL MY STRENGTH AND LETTING MY BODY BECOME PART OF THE MOTION OF THE HORSE BENEATH.
THE AIR INSIDE MY HELM WAS ALREADY SO HOT I COULD SCARCELY BREATH...

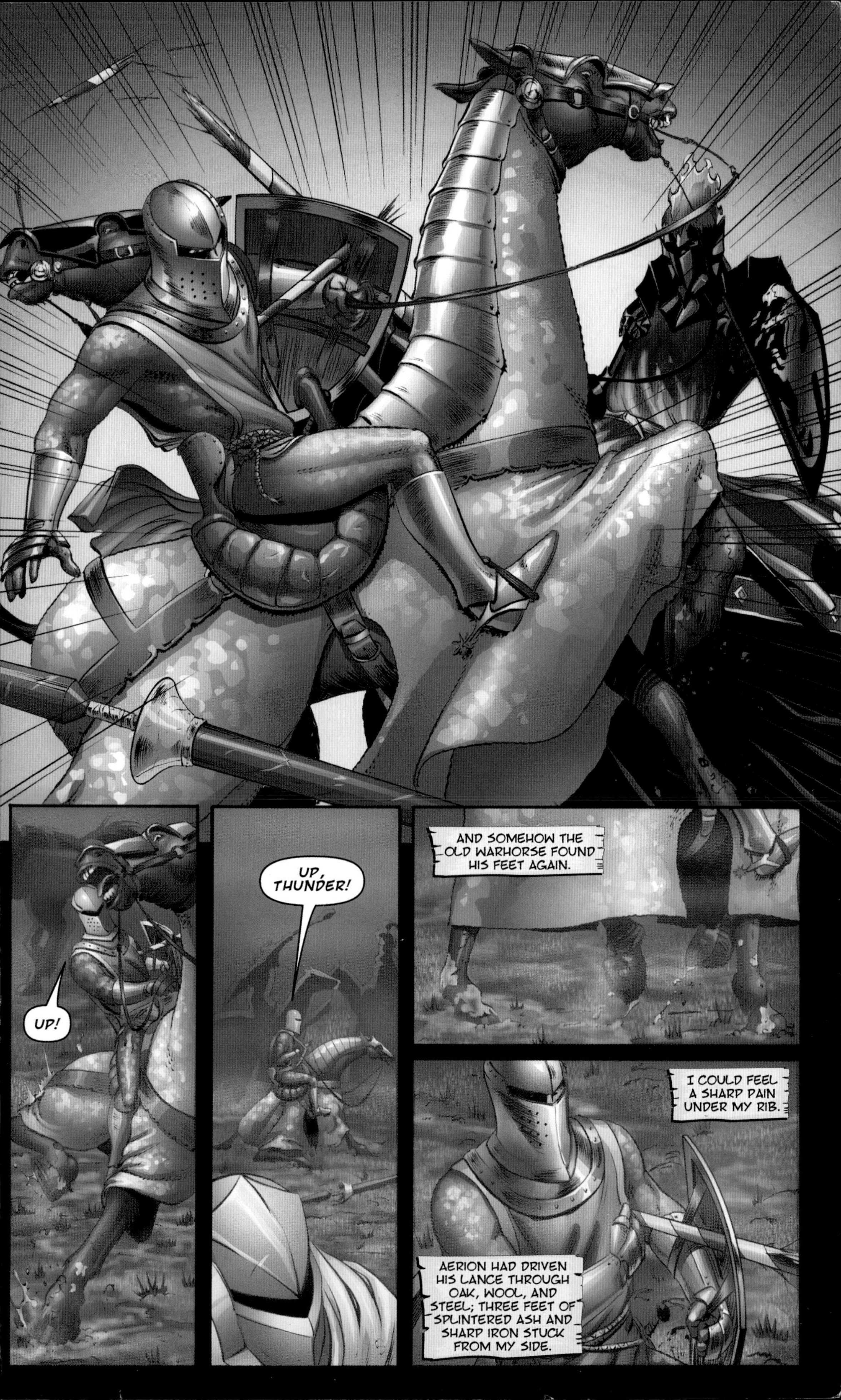
UP!
UP, THUNDER!
AND SOMEHOW THE OLD WARHORSE FOUND HIS FEET AGAIN.
I COULD FEEL A SHARP PAIN UNDER MY RIB.
AERION HAD DRIVEN HIS LANCE THROUGH OAK, WOOL, AND STEEL; THREE FEET OF SPLINTERED ASH AND SHARP IRON STUCK FROM MY SIDE.

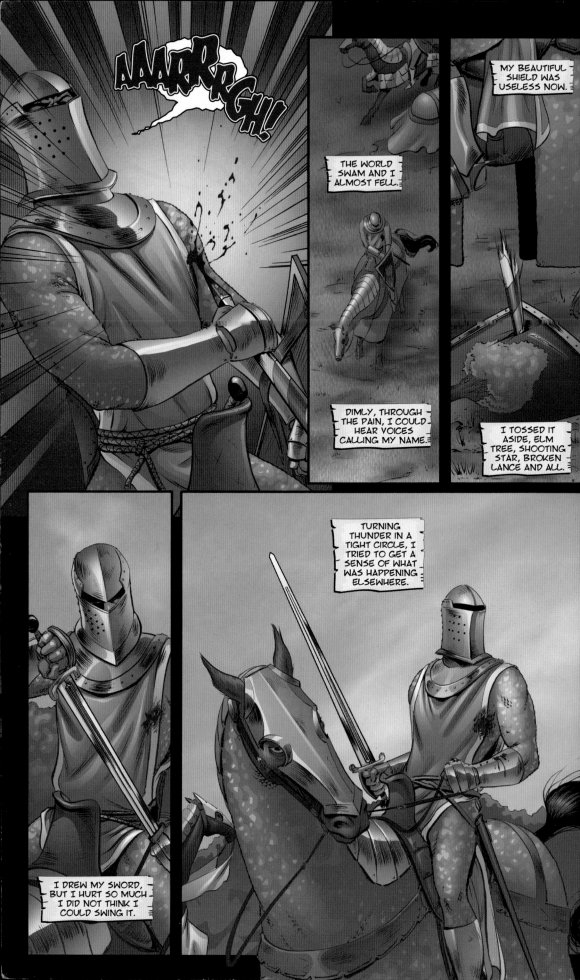

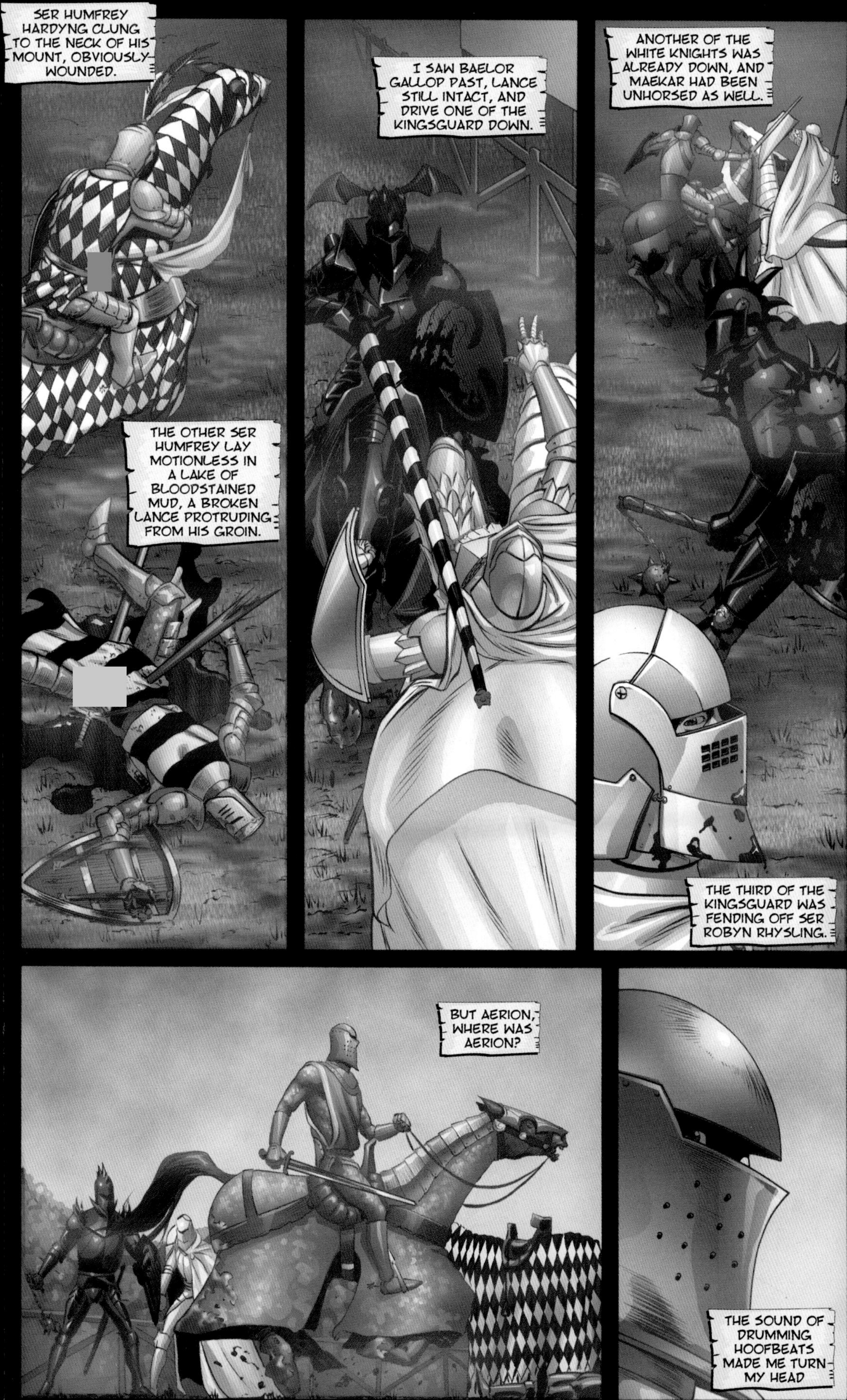
SER HUMFREY HARDYNG CLUNG TO THE NECK OF HIS MOUNT, OBVIOUSLY WOUNDED.
THE OTHER SER HUMFREY LAY MOTIONLESS IN A LAKE OF BLOODSTAINED MUD, A BROKEN LANCE PROTRUDING FROM HIS GROIN.
I SAW BAELOR GALLOP PAST, LANCE STILL INTACT, AND DRIVE ONE OF THE KINGSGUARD DOWN.
ANOTHER OF THE WHITE KNIGHTS WAS ALREADY DOWN, AND MAEKAR HAD BEEN UNHORSED AS WELL.
THE THIRD OF THE KINGSGUARD WAS FENDING OFF SER ROBYN RHYSLING.
BUT AERION, WHERE WAS AERION?
THE SOUND OF DRUMMING HOOFBEATS MADE ME TURN MY HEAD

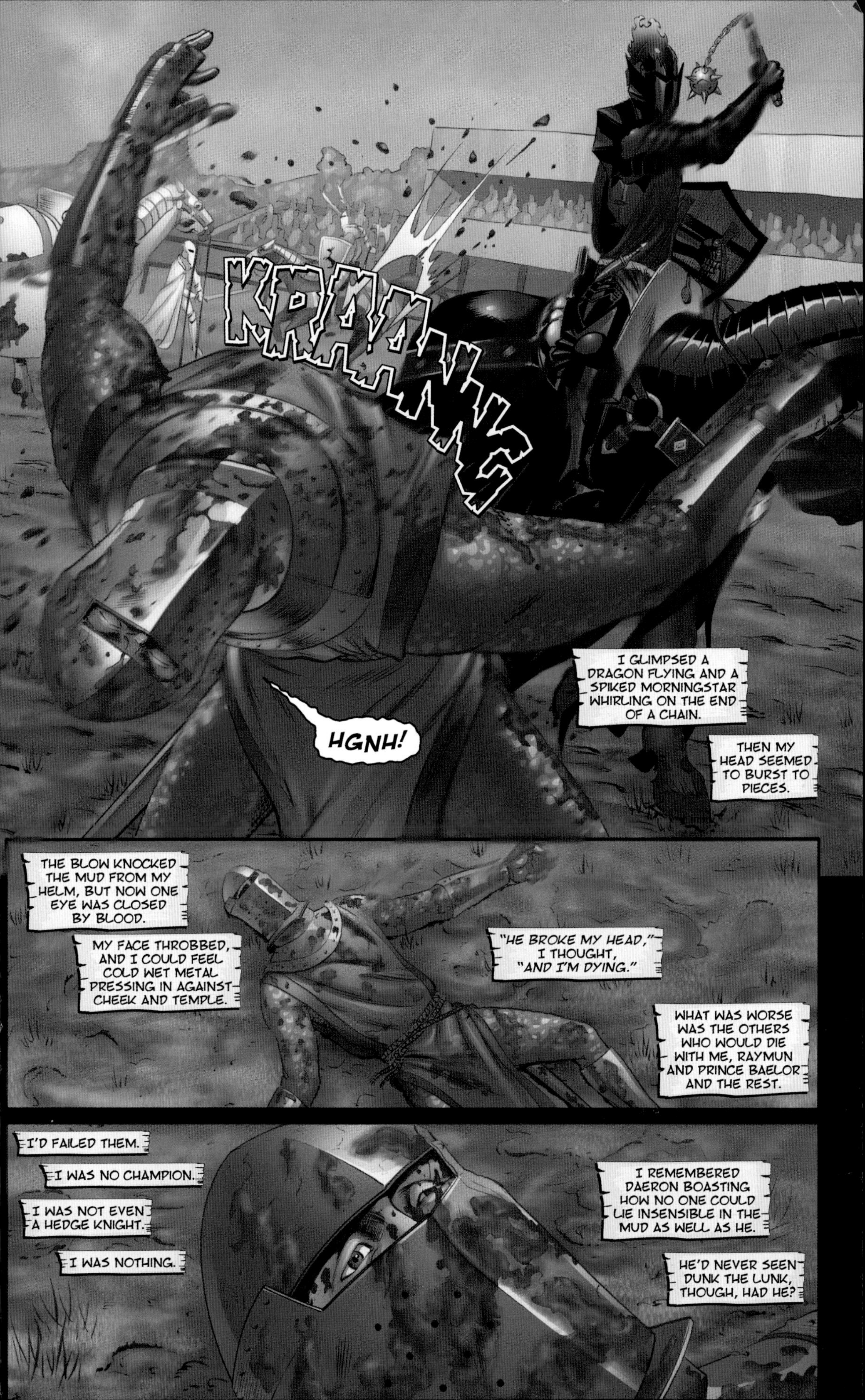
KRAAANG
I GLIMPSED A DRAGON FLYING AND A SPIKED MORNINGSTAR WHIRLING ON THE END OF A CHAIN.
HGNH!
THEN MY HEAD SEEMED TO BURST TO PIECES.
THE BLOW KNOCKED THE MUD FROM MY HELM, BUT NOW ONE EYE WAS CLOSED BY BLOOD.
MY FACE THROBBED, AND I COULD FEEL COLD WET METAL PRESSING IN AGAINST CHEEK AND TEMPLE.
"HE BROKE MY HEAD," I THOUGHT, "AND I'M DYING."
WHAT WAS WORSE WAS THE OTHERS WHO WOULD DIE WITH ME, RAYMUN AND PRINCE BAELOR AND THE REST.
I'D FAILED THEM.
I WAS NO CHAMPION.
I WAS NOT EVEN A HEDGE KNIGHT.
I WAS NOTHING.
I REMEMBERED DAERON BOASTING HOW NO ONE COULD LIE INSENSIBLE IN THE MUD AS WELL AS HE.
HE'D NEVER SEEN DUNK THE LUNK, THOUGH, HAD HE?

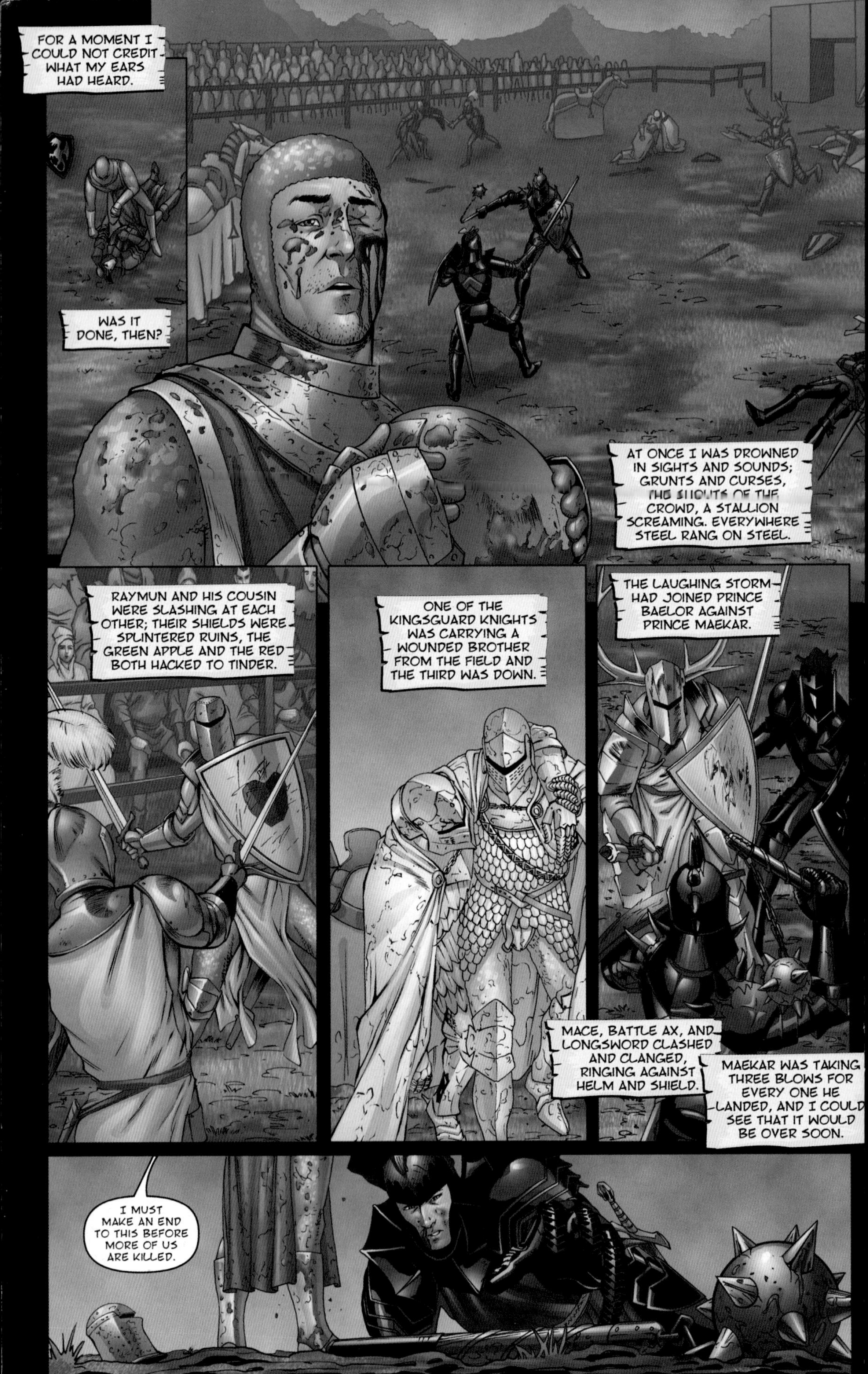
FOR A MOMENT I COULD NOT CREDIT WHAT MY EARS HAD HEARD.
WAS IT DONE, THEN?
AT ONCE I WAS DROWNED IN SIGHTS AND SOUNDS; GRUNTS AND CURSES, THE SHOUTS OF THE CROWD, A STALLION SCREAMING. EVERYWHERE STEEL RANG ON STEEL.
RAYMUN AND HIS COUSIN WERE SLASHING AT EACH OTHER; THEIR SHIELDS WERE SPLINTERED RUINS, THE GREEN APPLE AND THE RED BOTH HACKED TO TINDER.
ONE OF THE KINGSGUARD KNIGHTS WAS CARRYING A WOUNDED BROTHER FROM THE FIELD AND THE THIRD WAS DOWN.
THE LAUGHING STORM HAD JOINED PRINCE BAELOR AGAINST PRINCE MAEKAR.
MACE, BATTLE AX, AND LONGSWORD CLASHED AND CLANGED, RINGING AGAINST HELM AND SHIELD.
MAEKAR WAS TAKING THREE BLOWS FOR EVERY ONE HE LANDED, AND I COULD SEE THAT IT WOULD BE OVER SOON.
I MUST MAKE AN END TO THIS BEFORE MORE OF US ARE KILLED.

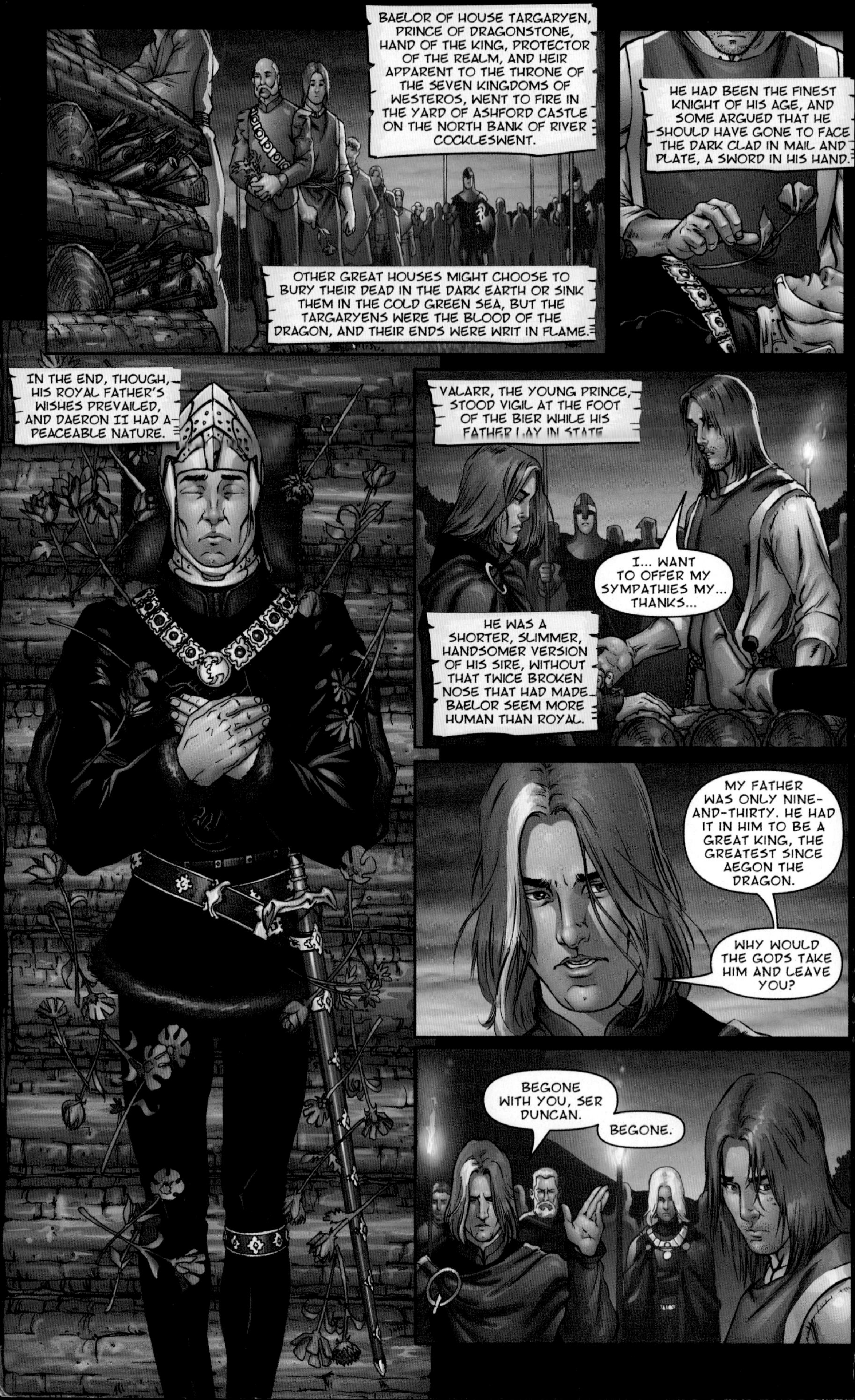
BAELOR OF HOUSE TARGARYEN, PRINCE OF DRAGONSTONE, HAND OF THE KING, PROTECTOR OF THE REALM, AND HEIR APPARENT TO THE THRONE OF THE SEVEN KINGDOMS OF WESTEROS, WENT TO FIRE IN THE YARD OF ASHFORD CASTLE ON THE NORTH BANK OF RIVER COCKLESWENT.
OTHER GREAT HOUSES MIGHT CHOOSE TO BURY THEIR DEAD IN THE DARK EARTH OR SINK THEM IN THE COLD GREEN SEA, BUT THE TARGARYENS WERE THE BLOOD OF THE DRAGON, AND THEIR ENDS WERE WRIT IN FLAME.
HE HAD BEEN THE FINEST KNIGHT OF HIS AGE, AND SOME ARGUED THAT HE SHOULD HAVE GONE TO FACE THE DARK CLAD IN MAIL AND PLATE, A SWORD IN HIS HAND.
IN THE END, THOUGH, HIS ROYAL FATHER'S WISHES PREVAILED, AND DAERON II HAD A PEACEABLE NATURE.
VALARR, THE YOUNG PRINCE, STOOD VIGIL AT THE FOOT OF THE BIER WHILE HIS FATHER LAY IN STATE
I... WANT TO OFFER MY SYMPATHIES MY... THANKS...
HE WAS A SHORTER, SLIMMER, HANDSOMER VERSION OF HIS SIRE, WITHOUT THAT TWICE BROKEN NOSE THAT HAD MADE BAELOR SEEM MORE HUMAN THAN ROYAL.
MY FATHER WAS ONLY NINE-AND-THIRTY. HE HAD IT IN HIM TO BE A GREAT KING, THE GREATEST SINCE AEGON THE DRAGON.
WHY WOULD THE GODS TAKE HIM AND LEAVE YOU?
BEGONE WITH YOU, SER DUNCAN.
BEGONE.

# Roll of Arms

## Champions, Challengers, and Other Competitors in the Passage at Arms at Ashford Meadow on the Cockleswhent in the Two Hundred and Ninth Year Since Aegon's Conquest

SPECIAL THANKS TO
WWW.WESTEROS.ORG

DESIGNED BY
BILL TORTOLINI

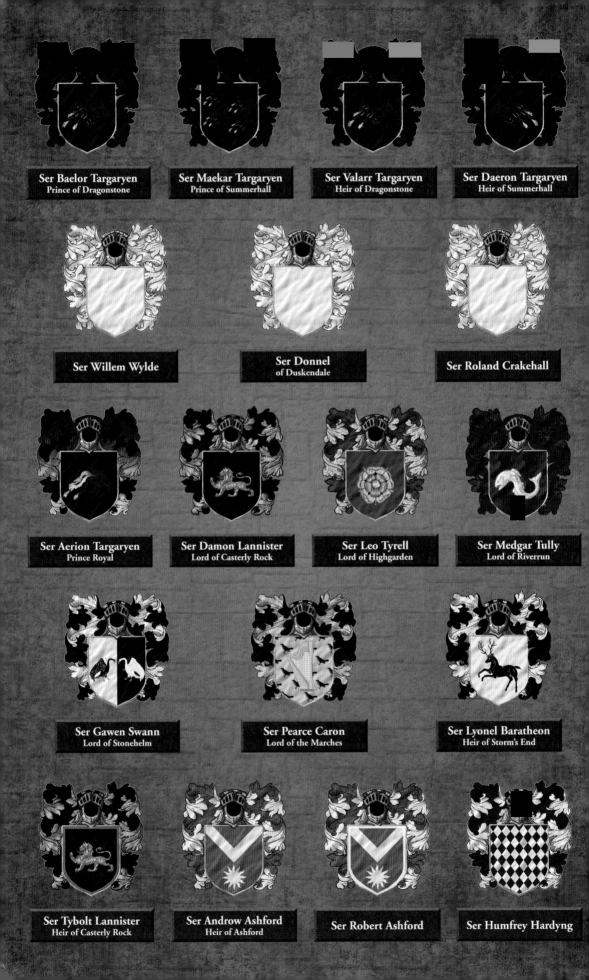

**Ser Baelor Targaryen**
Prince of Dragonstone

**Ser Maekar Targaryen**
Prince of Summerhall

**Ser Valarr Targaryen**
Heir of Dragonstone

**Ser Daeron Targaryen**
Heir of Summerhall

**Ser Willem Wylde**

**Ser Donnel**
of Duskendale

**Ser Roland Crakehall**

**Ser Aerion Targaryen**
Prince Royal

**Ser Damon Lannister**
Lord of Casterly Rock

**Ser Leo Tyrell**
Lord of Highgarden

**Ser Medgar Tully**
Lord of Riverrun

**Ser Gawen Swann**
Lord of Stonehelm

**Ser Pearce Caron**
Lord of the Marches

**Ser Lyonel Baratheon**
Heir of Storm's End

**Ser Tybolt Lannister**
Heir of Casterly Rock

**Ser Androw Ashford**
Heir of Ashford

**Ser Robert Ashford**

**Ser Humfrey Hardyng**

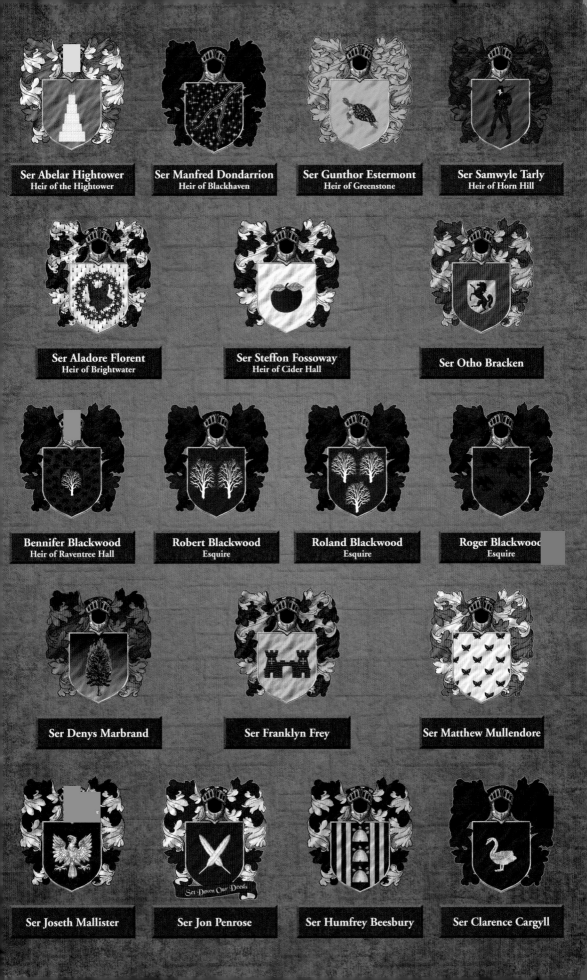

**Ser Abelar Hightower**
Heir of the Hightower

**Ser Manfred Dondarrion**
Heir of Blackhaven

**Ser Gunthor Estermont**
Heir of Greenstone

**Ser Samwyle Tarly**
Heir of Horn Hill

**Ser Aladore Florent**
Heir of Brightwater

**Ser Steffon Fossoway**
Heir of Cider Hall

**Ser Otho Bracken**

**Bennifer Blackwood**
Heir of Raventree Hall

**Robert Blackwood**
Esquire

**Roland Blackwood**
Esquire

**Roger Blackwood**
Esquire

**Ser Denys Marbrand**

**Ser Franklyn Frey**

**Ser Matthew Mullendore**

**Ser Joseth Mallister**

**Ser Jon Penrose**

Set Down Our Deeds

**Ser Humfrey Beesbury**

**Ser Clarence Cargyll**

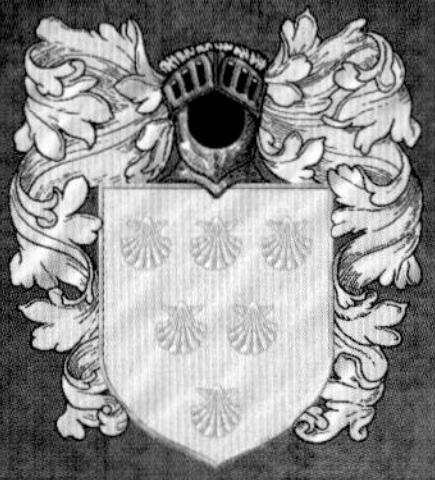

Ser Ormond Westerling

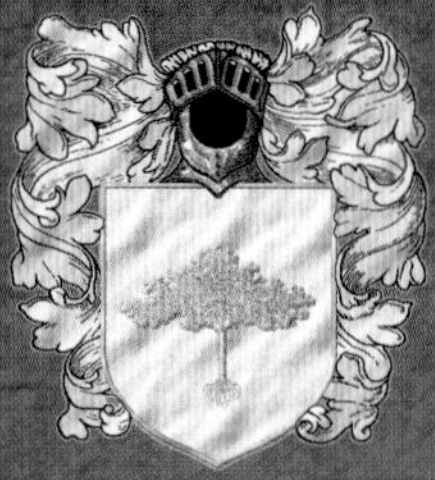

Ser Nyles Rowan

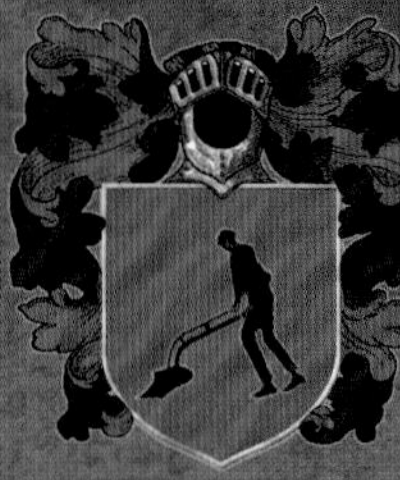

Ser Desmond Darry

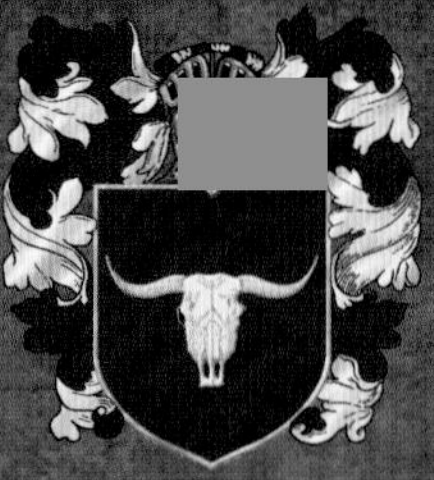

Ser Humphrey Bulwer

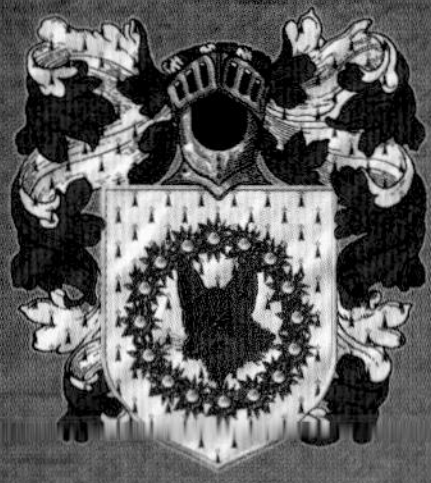

Ser Jon Florent

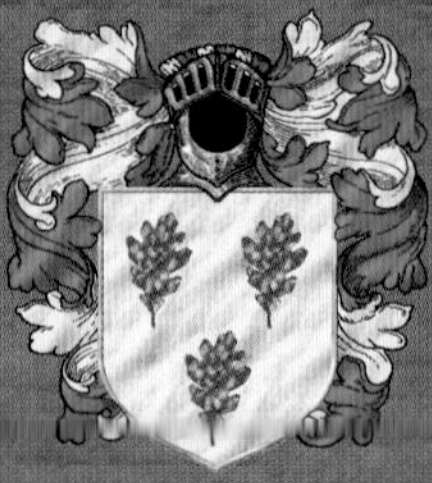

Ser Gwayne Oakheart

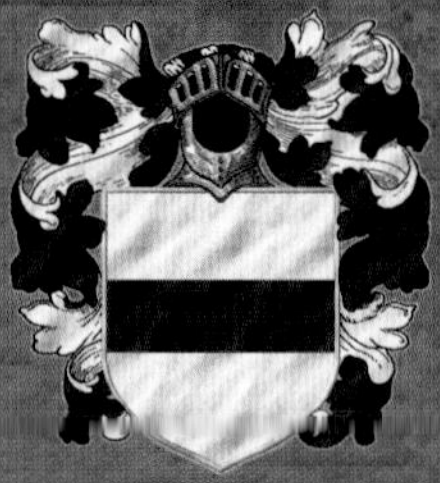

Ser Elwood Blackbar

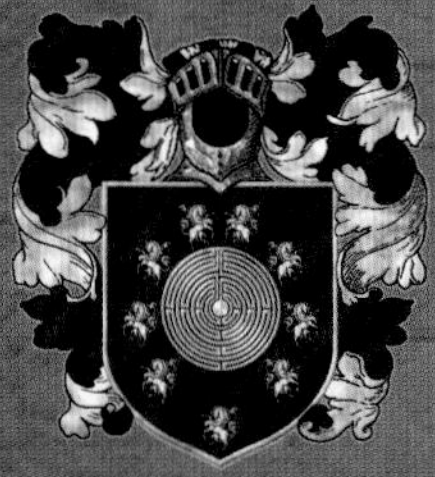

Ser Corwin Rogers

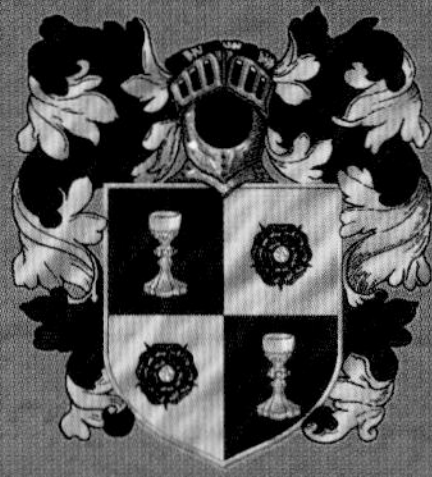

Ser Tommen Costayne

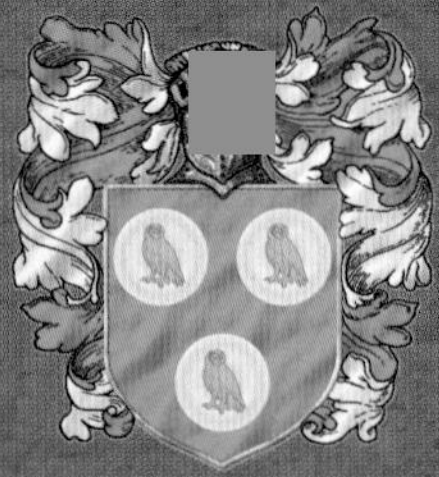

Ser Alyn Garner

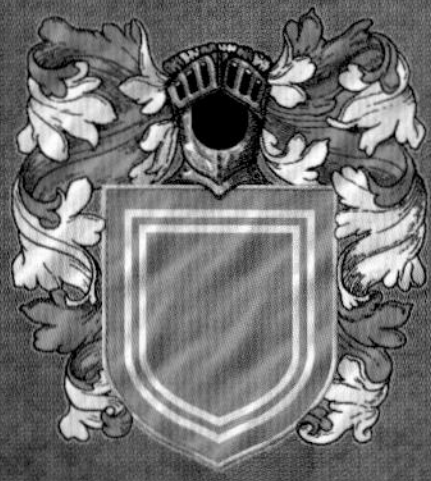

Ser Myles Greenfield

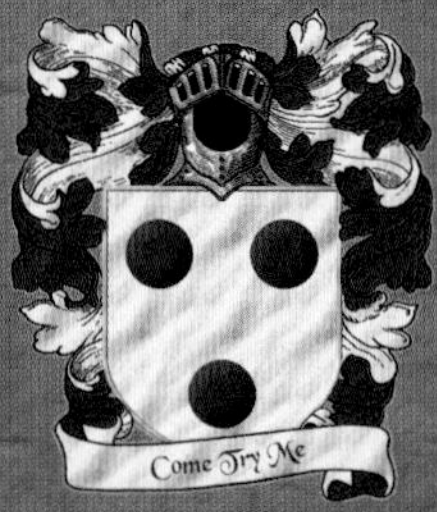
Come Try Me

Ser Petyr Plumm

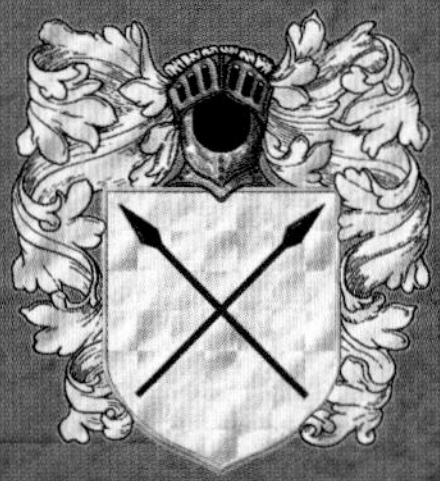

Ser Walder Stackspear

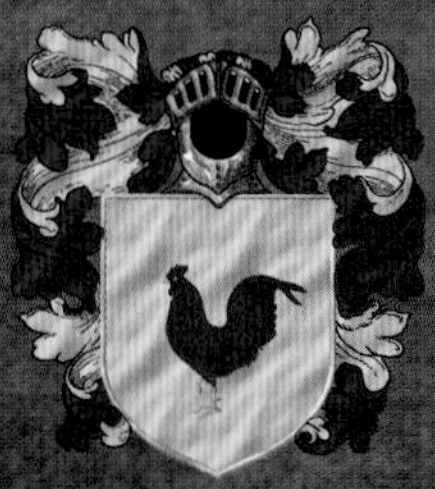

Ser Harrold Swyft

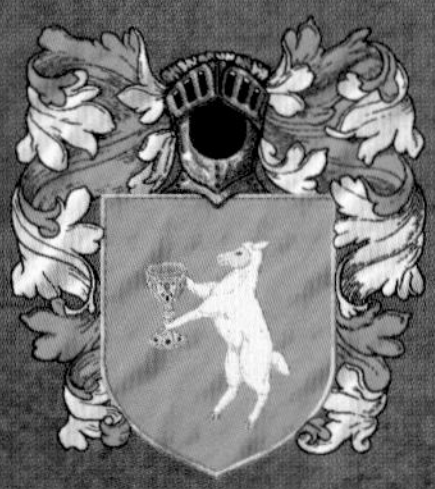

Ser Samwell Stokeworth

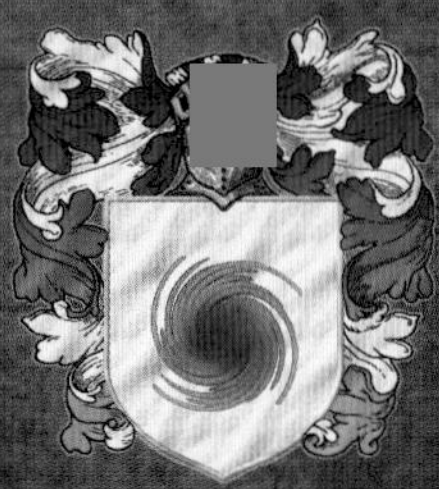

Ser Criston Wylde

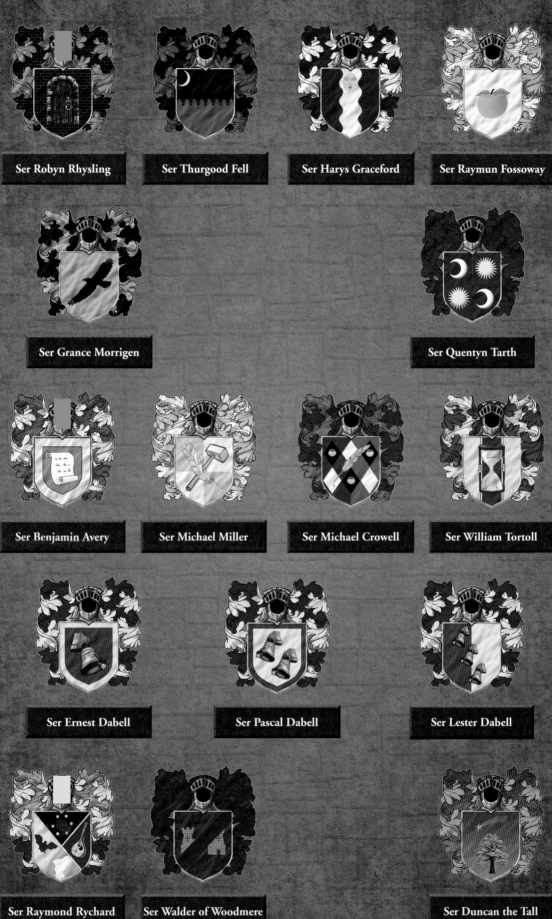

Ser Robyn Rhysling

Ser Thurgood Fell

Ser Harys Graceford

Ser Raymun Fossoway

Ser Grance Morrigen

Ser Quentyn Tarth

Ser Benjamin Avery

Ser Michael Miller

Ser Michael Crowell

Ser William Tortoll

Ser Ernest Dabell

Ser Pascal Dabell

Ser Lester Dabell

Ser Raymond Rychard

Ser Walder of Woodmere

Ser Duncan the Tall

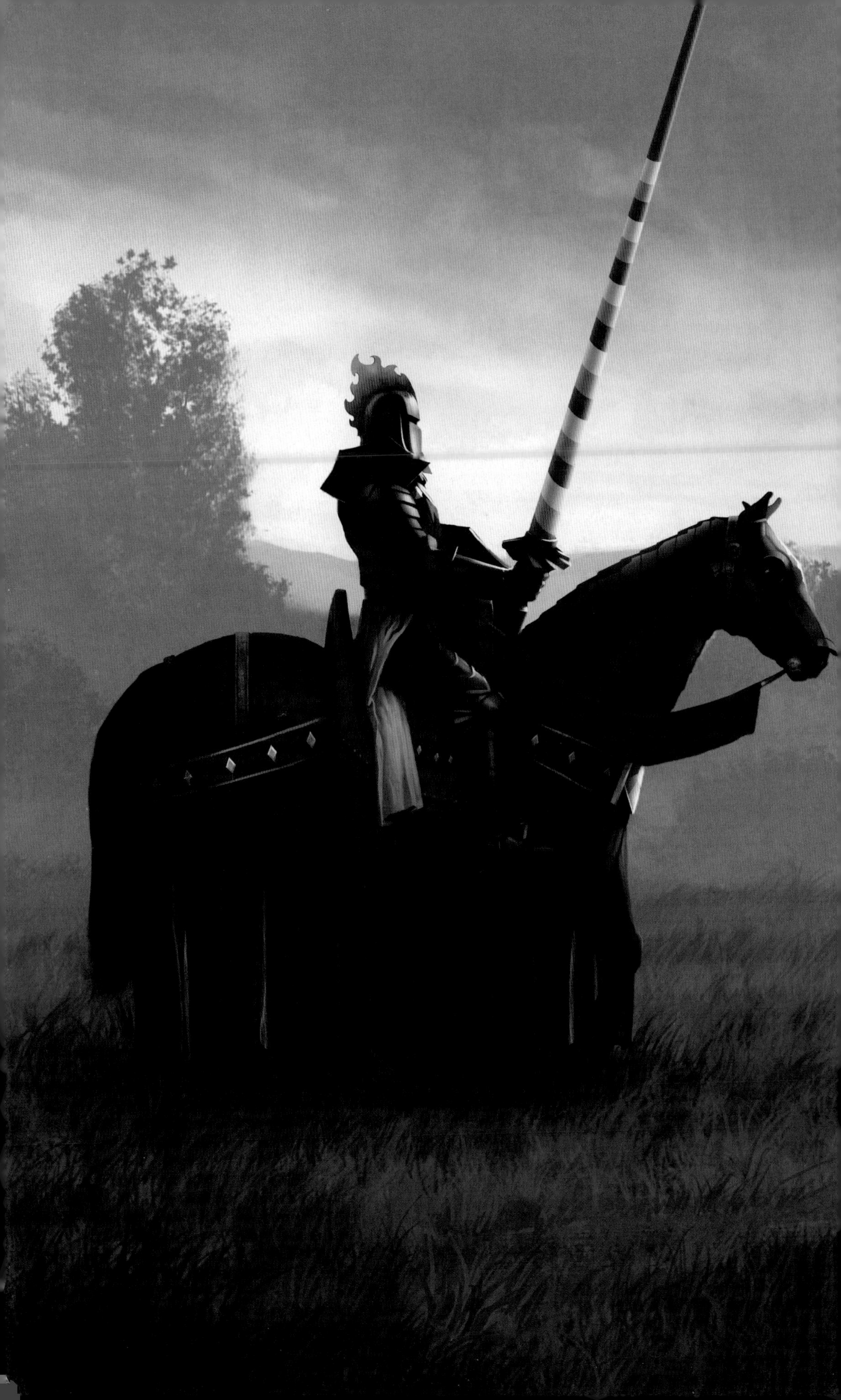

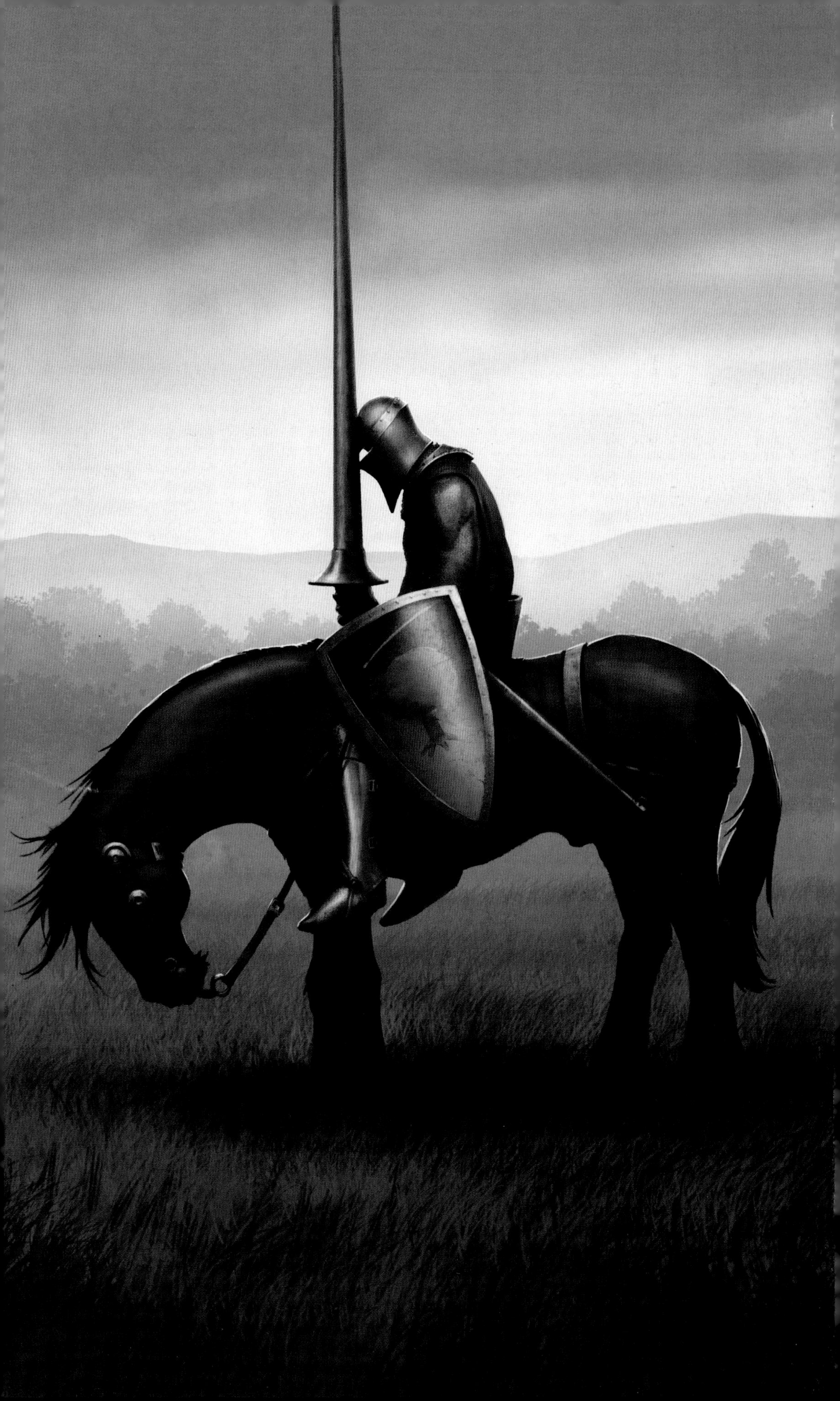

For Dad

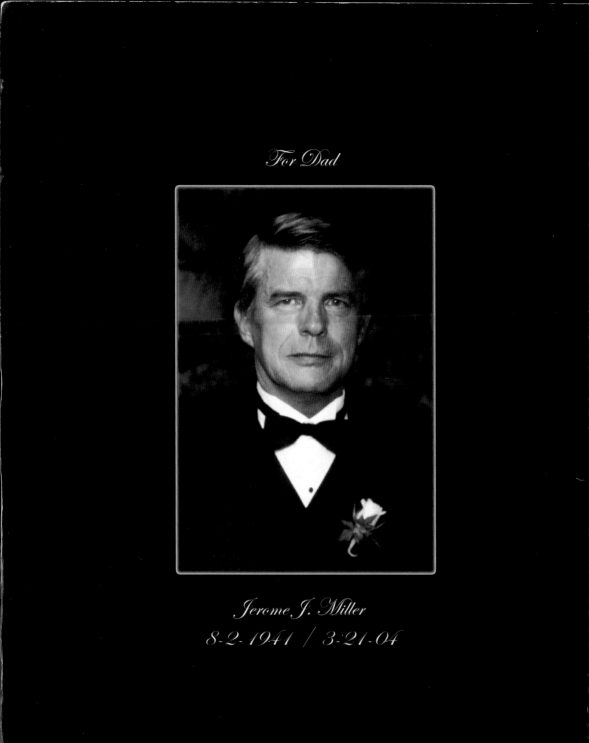

Jerome J. Miller

8-2-1941 / 3-21-04

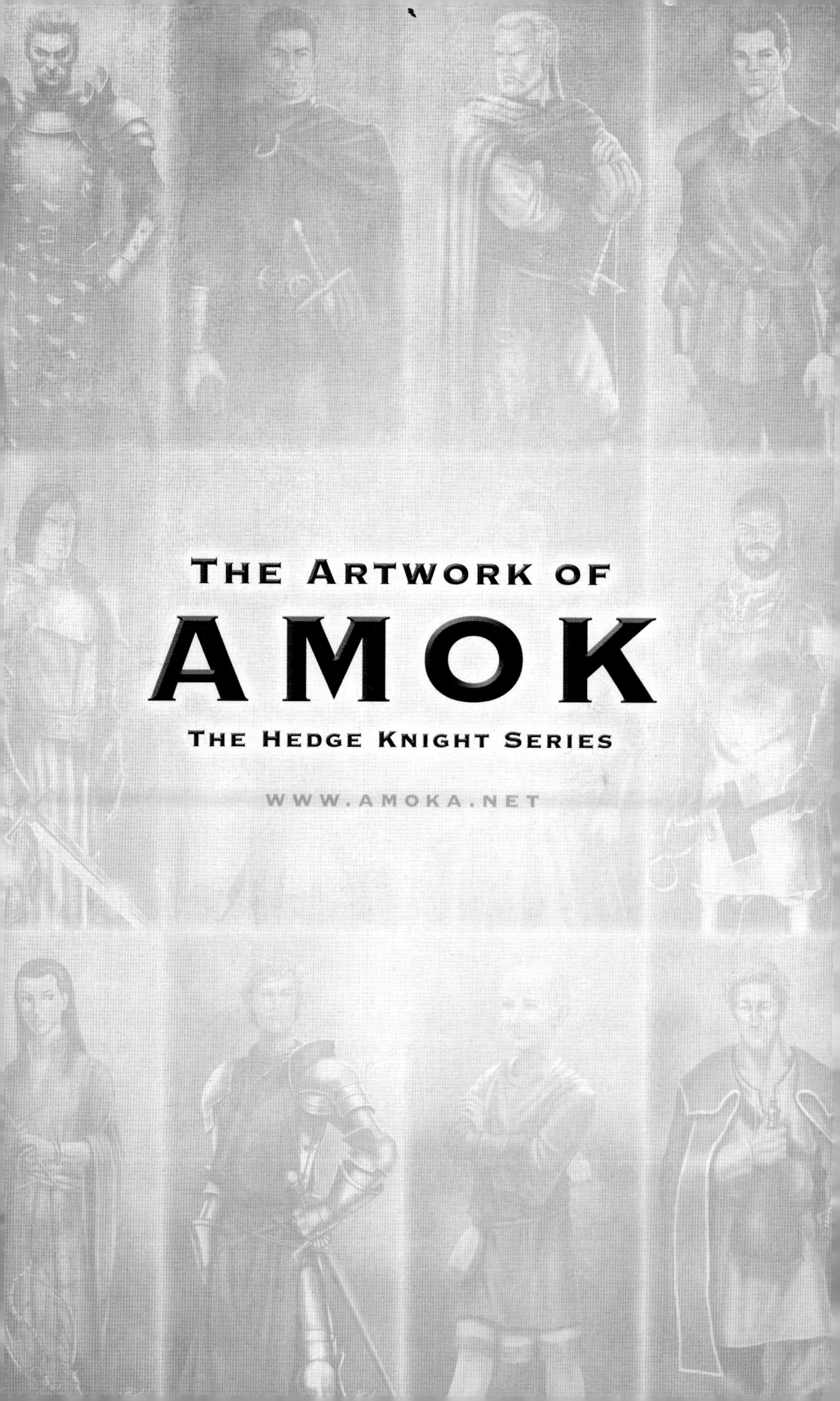
THE ARTWORK OF
AMOK
THE HEDGE KNIGHT SERIES
WWW.AMOKA.NET

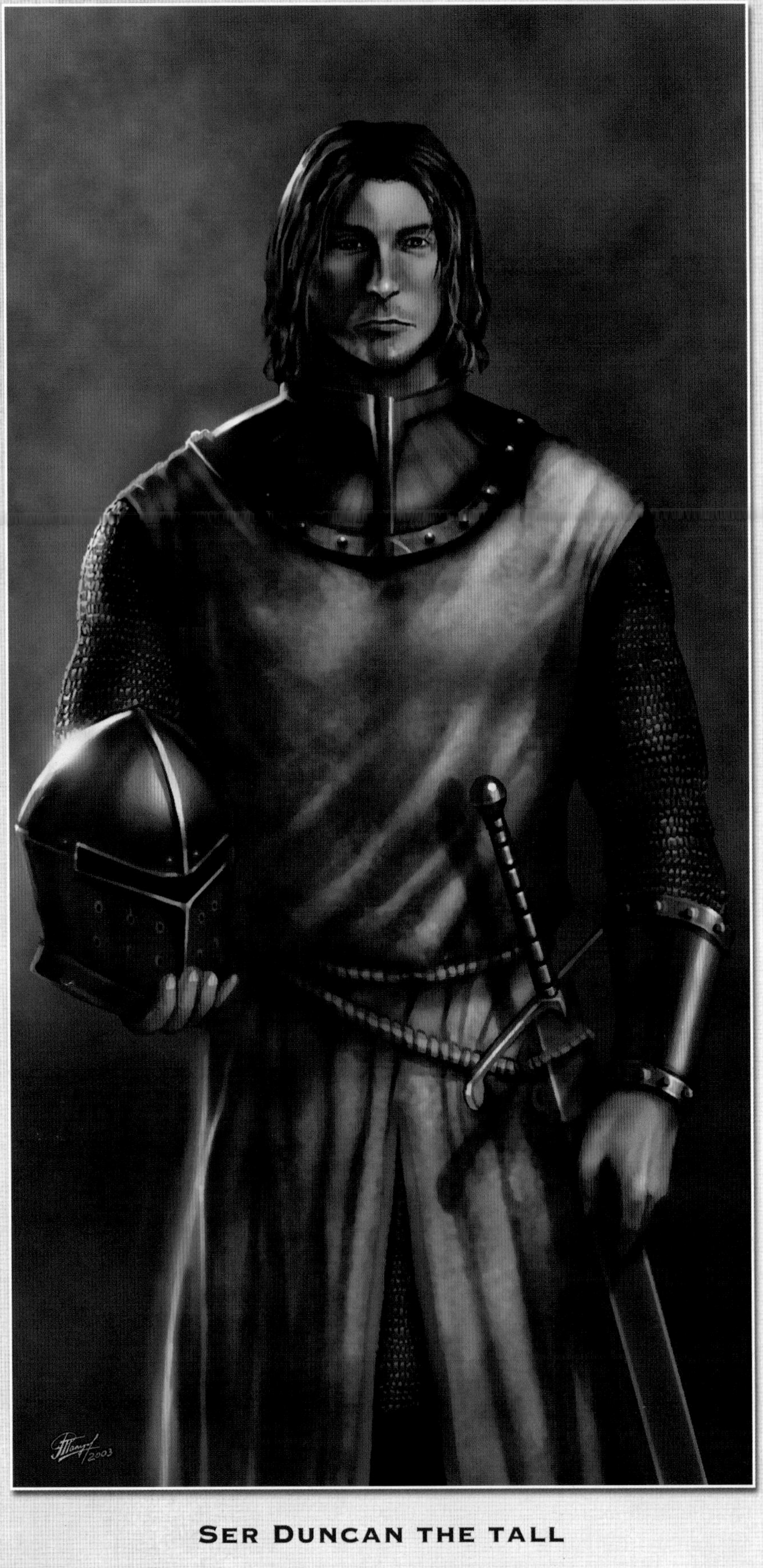

**Ser Duncan the Tall**

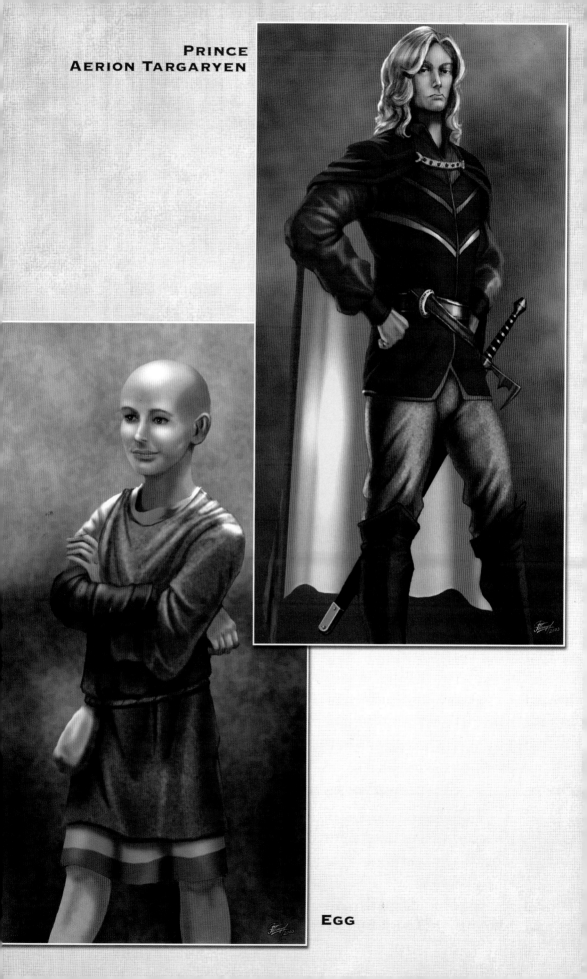

Prince Aerion Targaryen

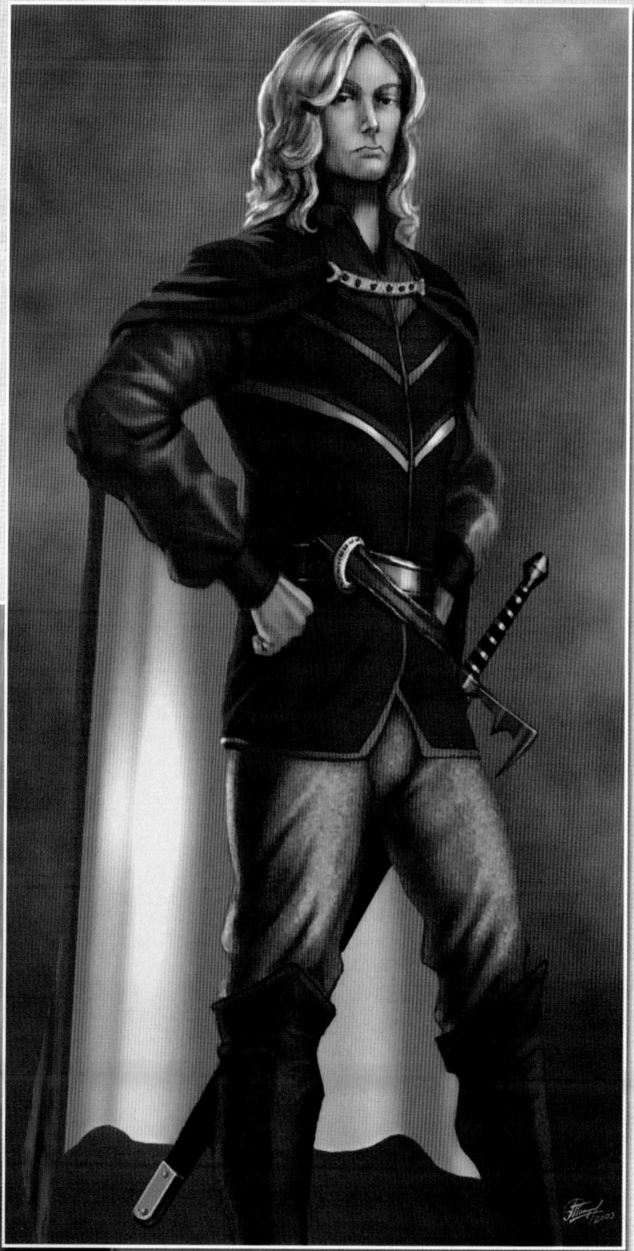

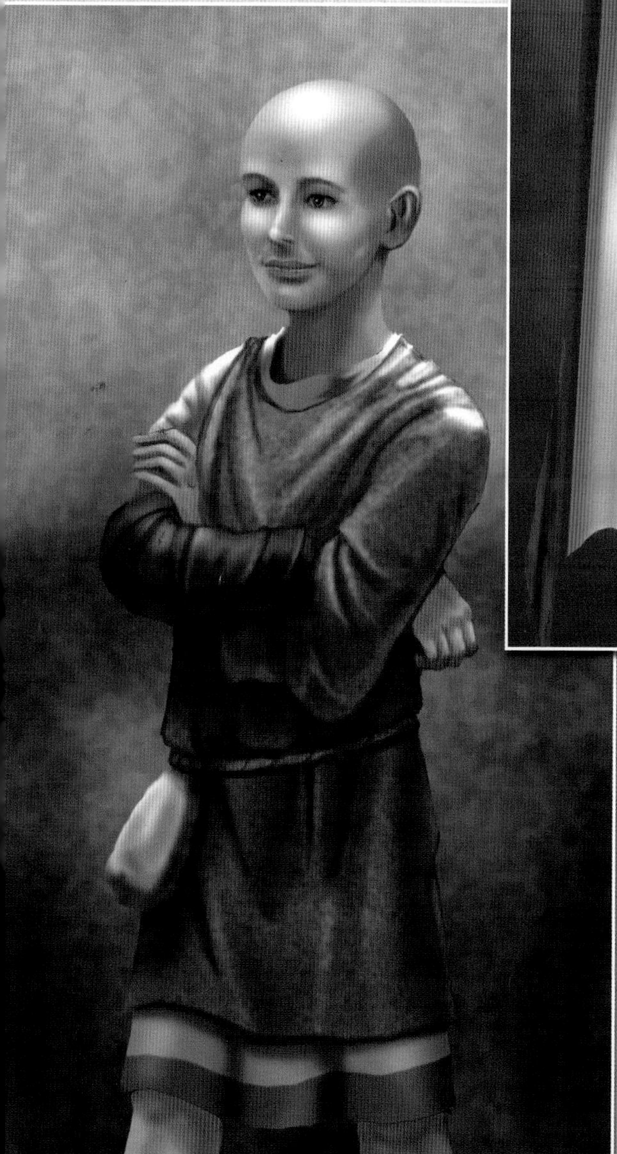

Egg

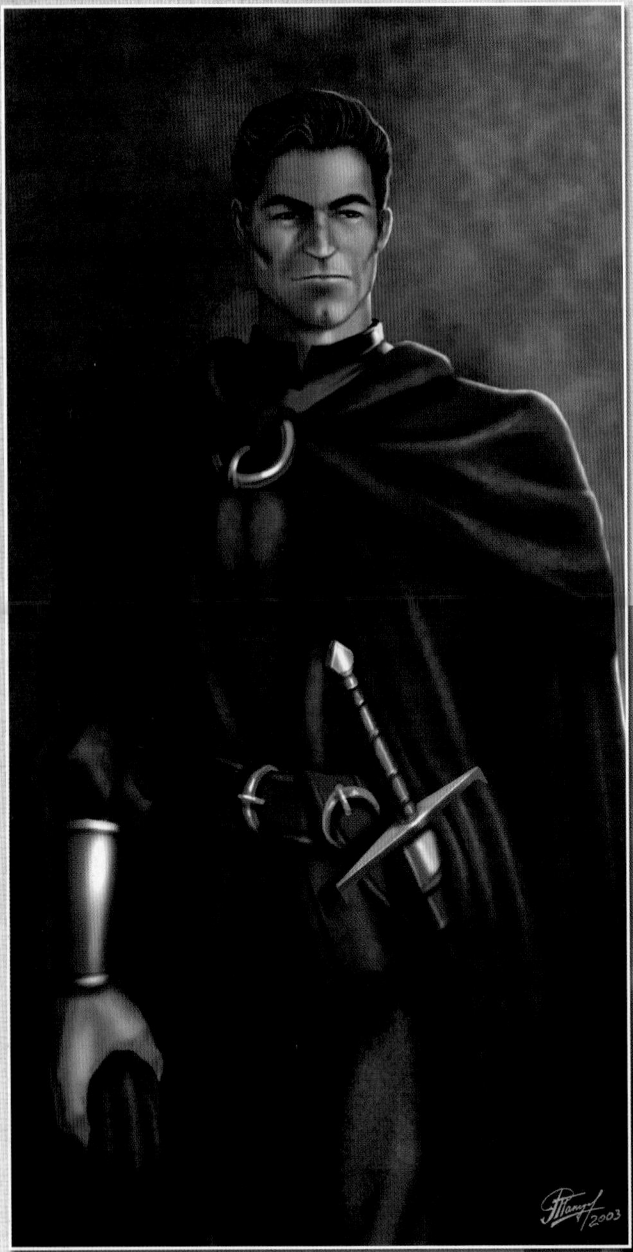

**Prince**
**Baelor Targaryen**

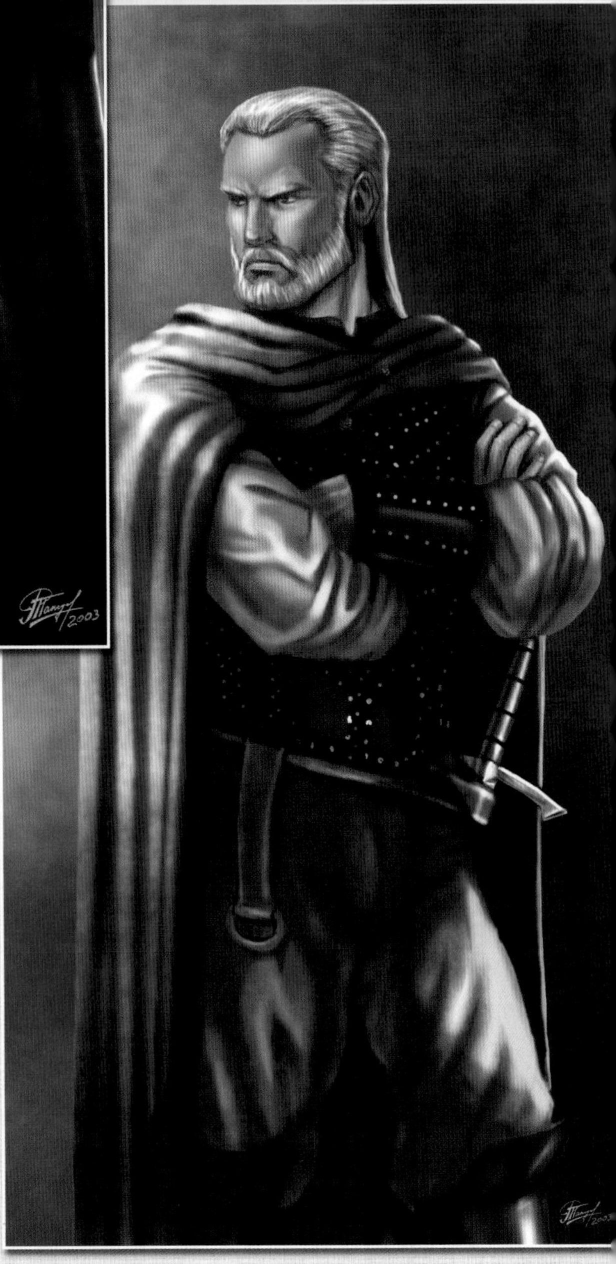

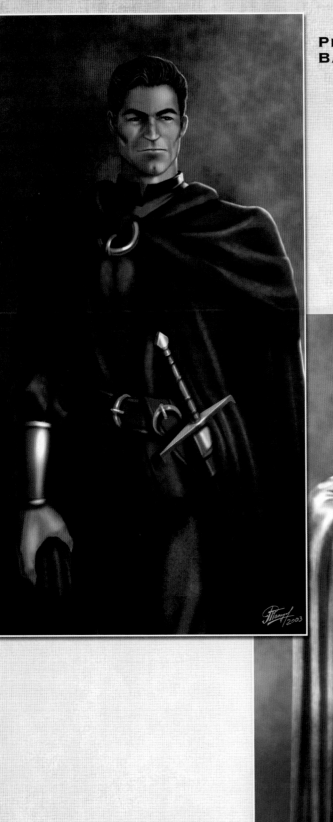

**Prince**
**Maekar Targaryen**

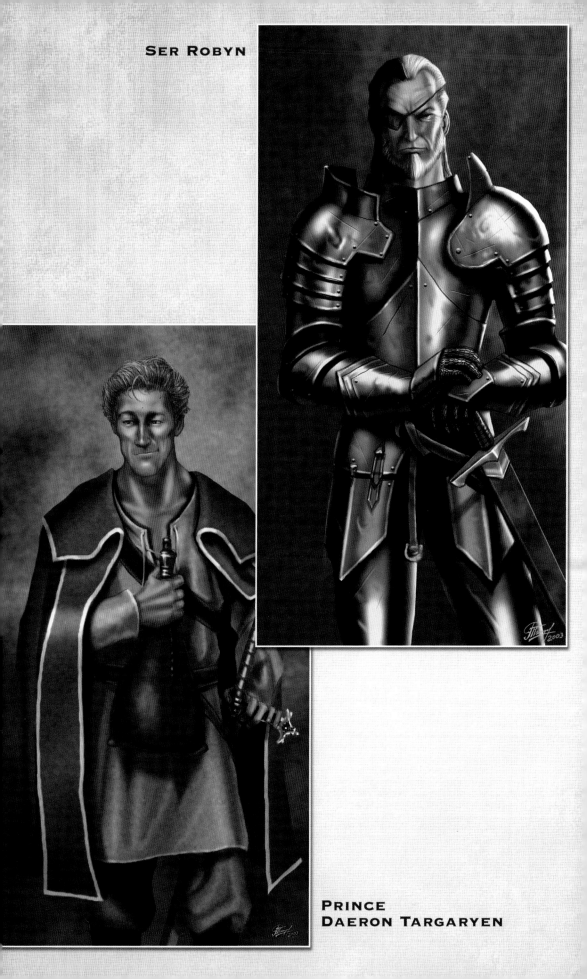

Ser Robyn

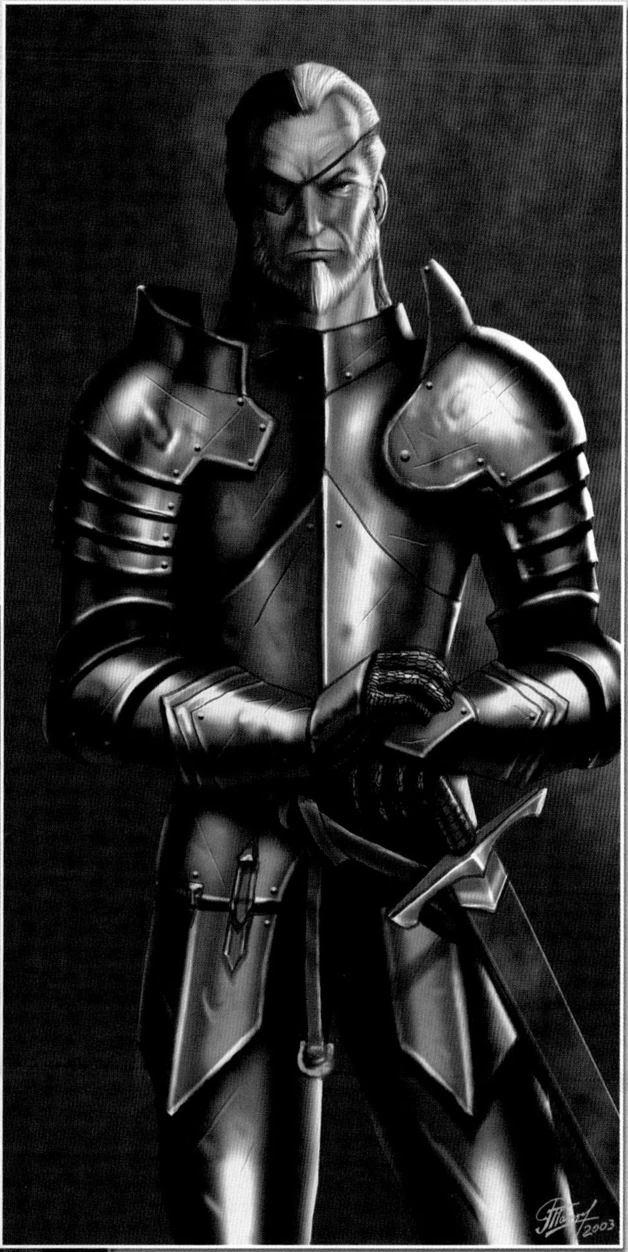

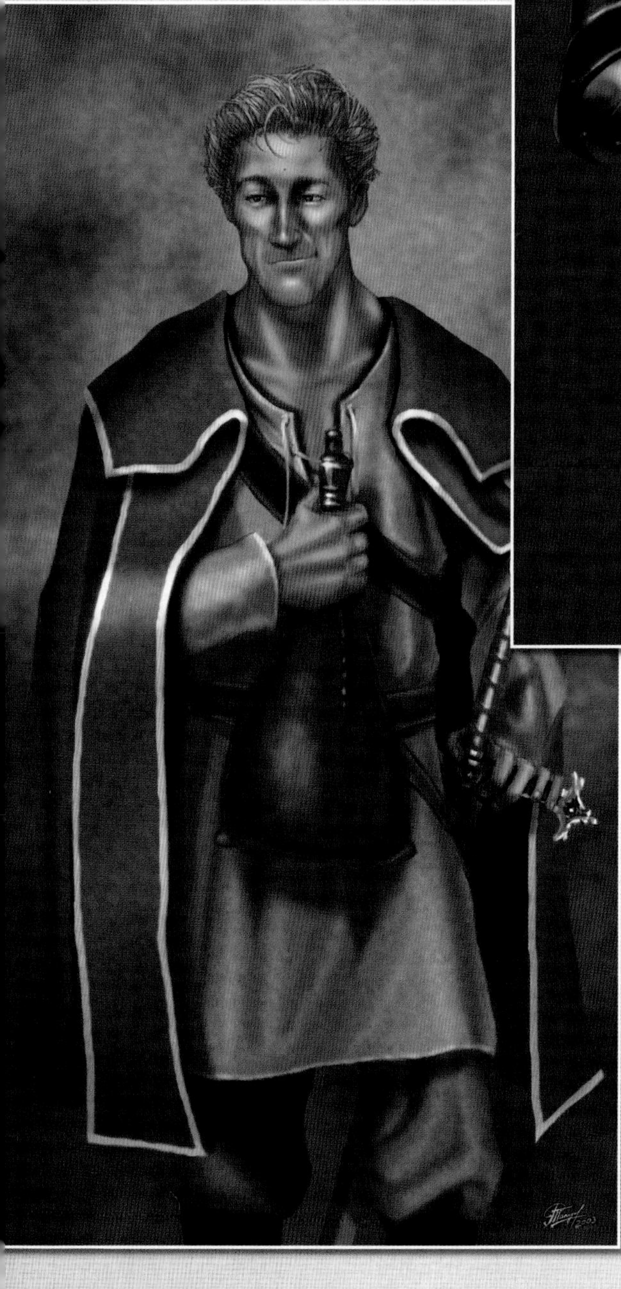

Prince
Daeron Targaryen

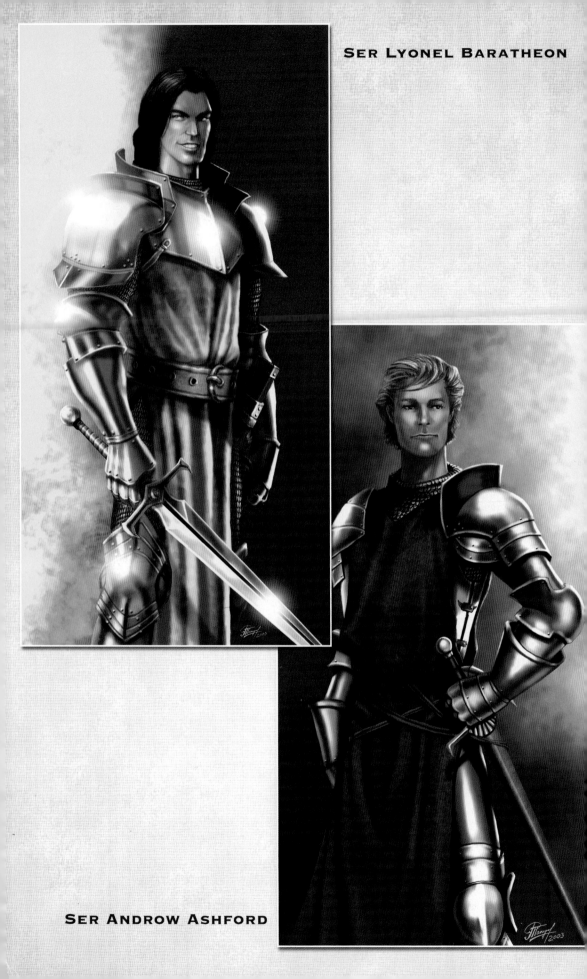

## Ser Lyonel Baratheon

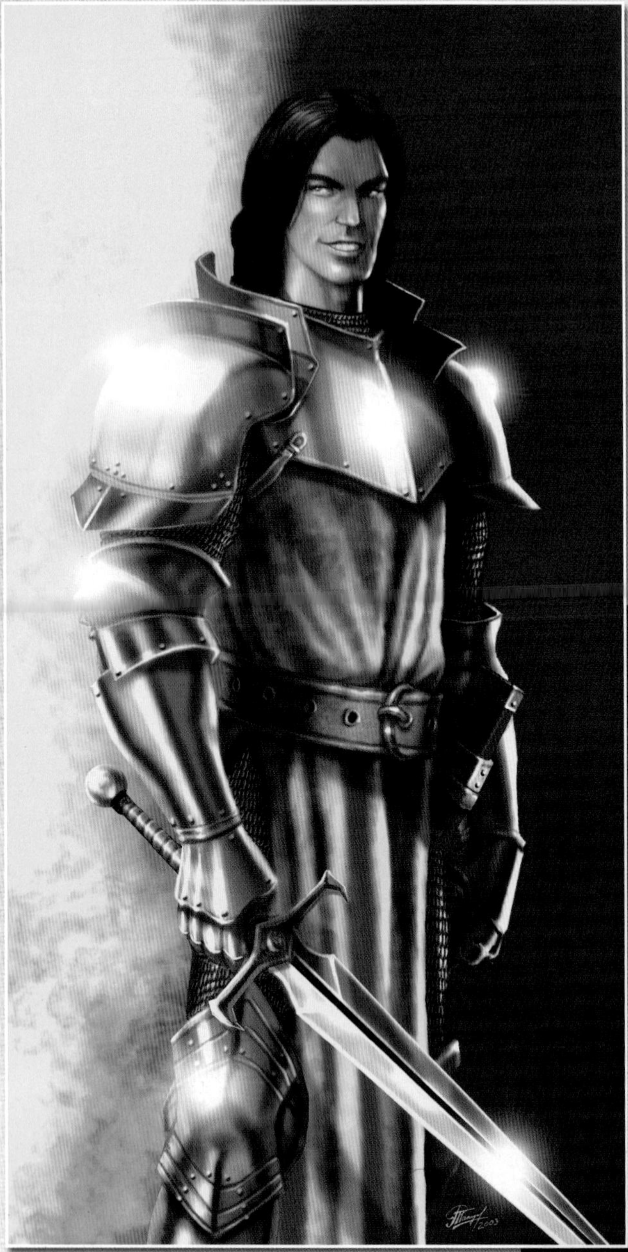

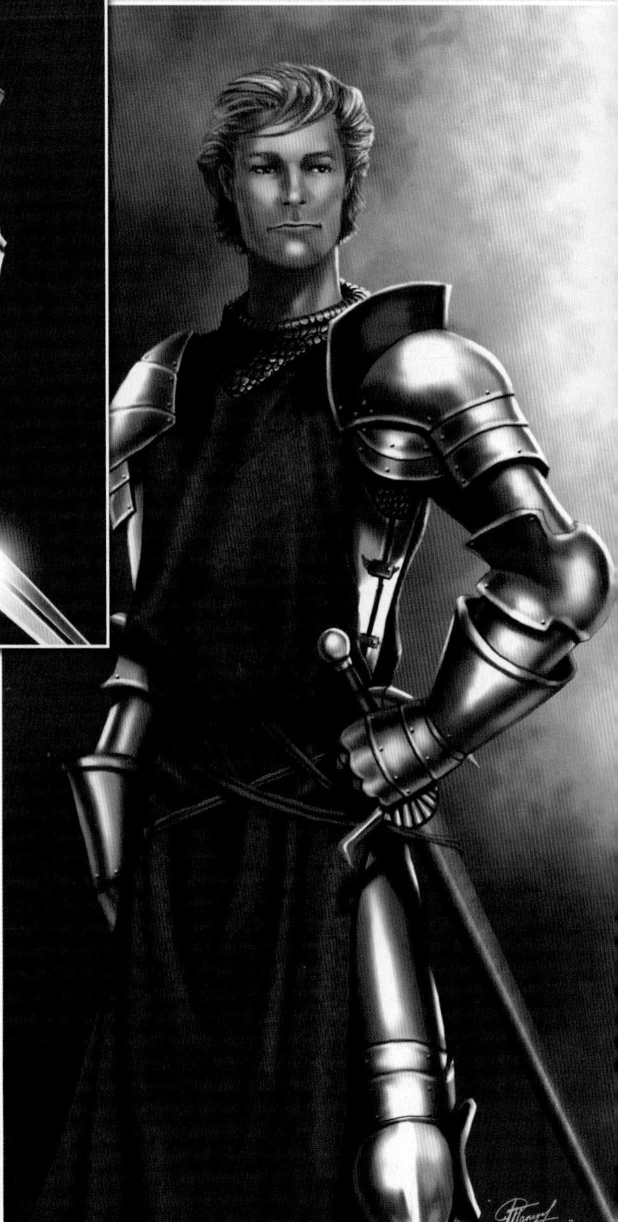

## Ser Androw Ashford

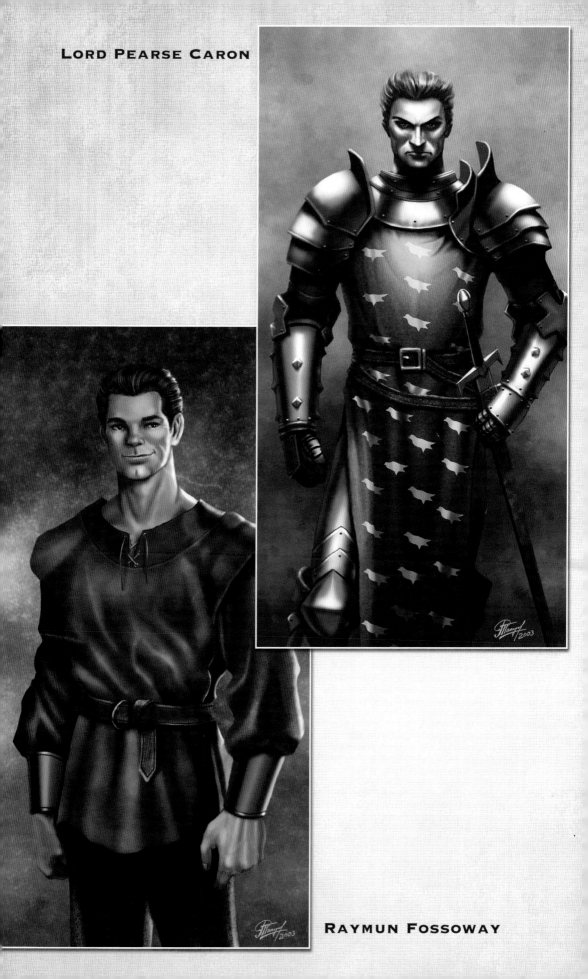

LORD PEARSE CARON

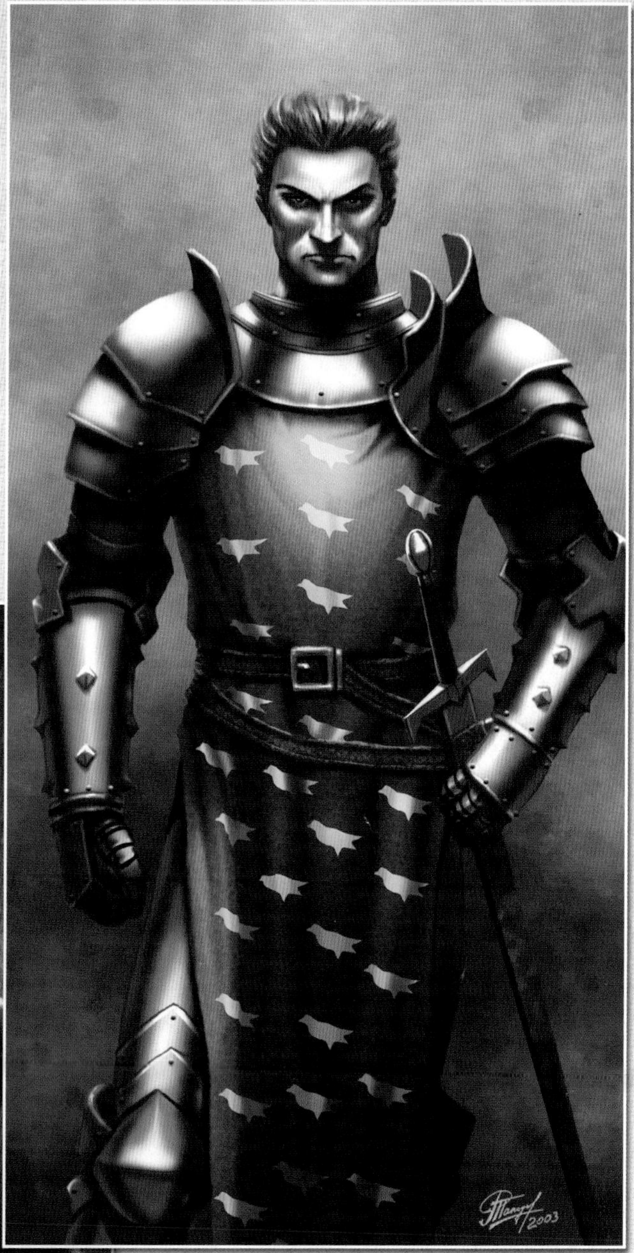

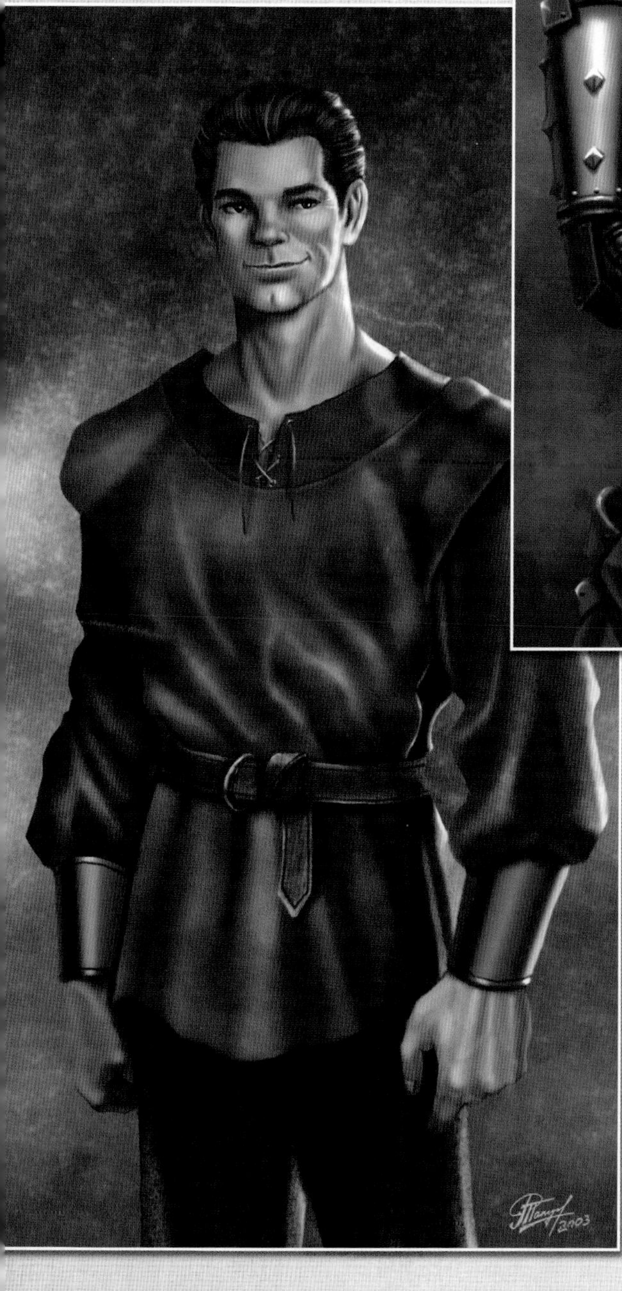

RAYMUN FOSSOWAY

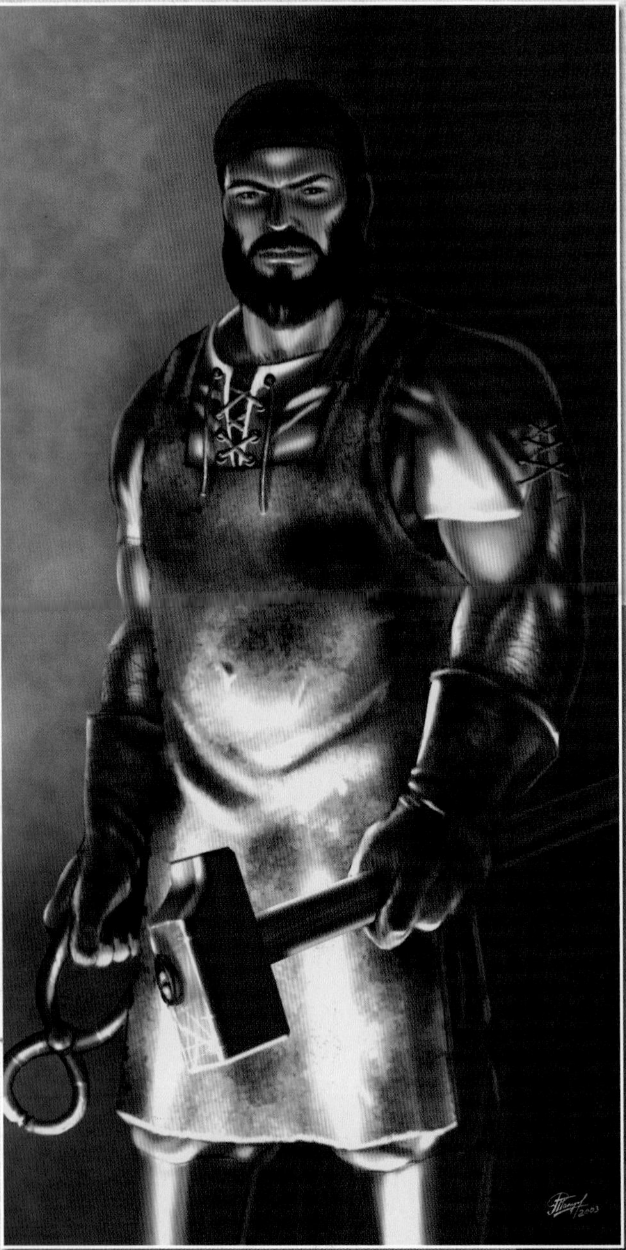

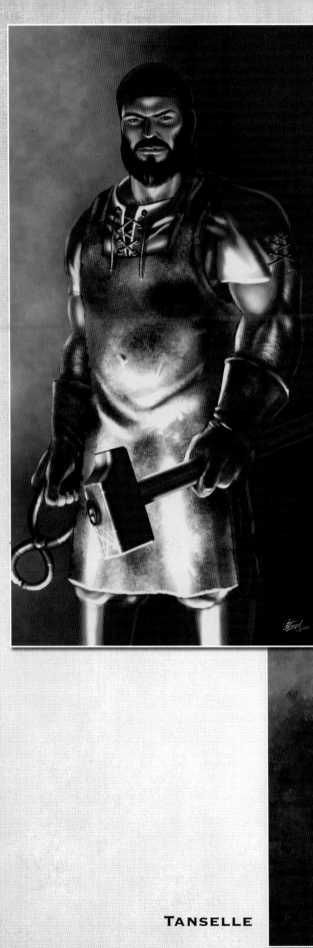

**STEELY PATE**

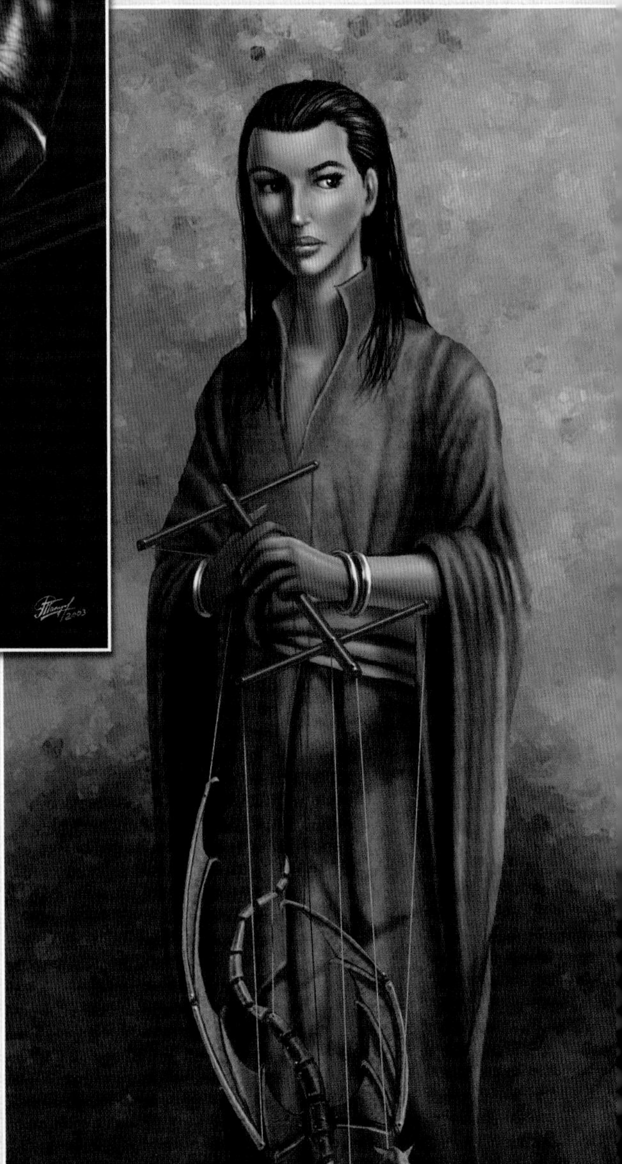

**TANSELLE**

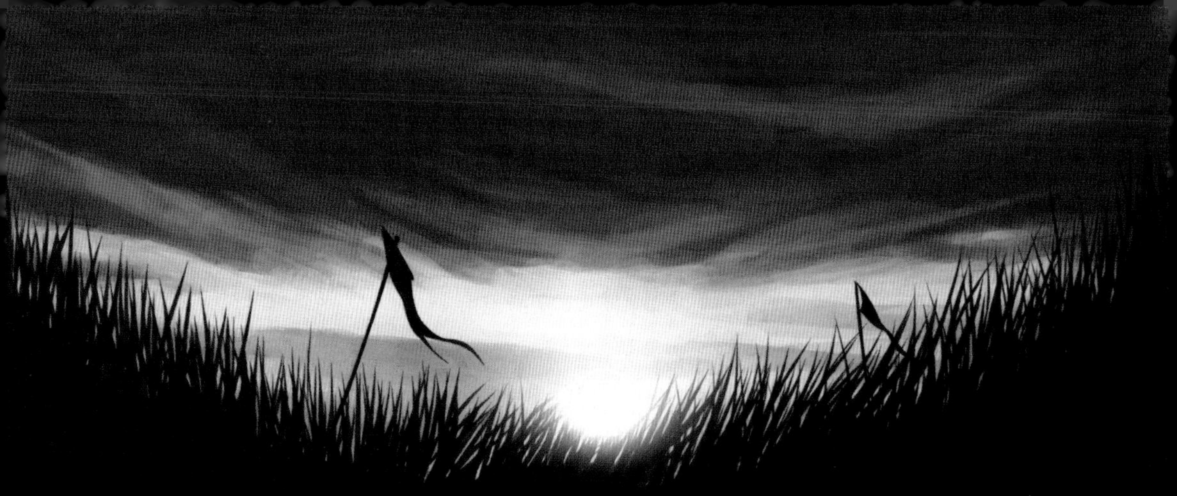

# George RR Martinås
# Battle on Redgrass Field

(FROM THE SWORN SWORD)

**A TALE OF THE SEVEN KINGDOMS**
**by GEORGE R. R. MARTIN**

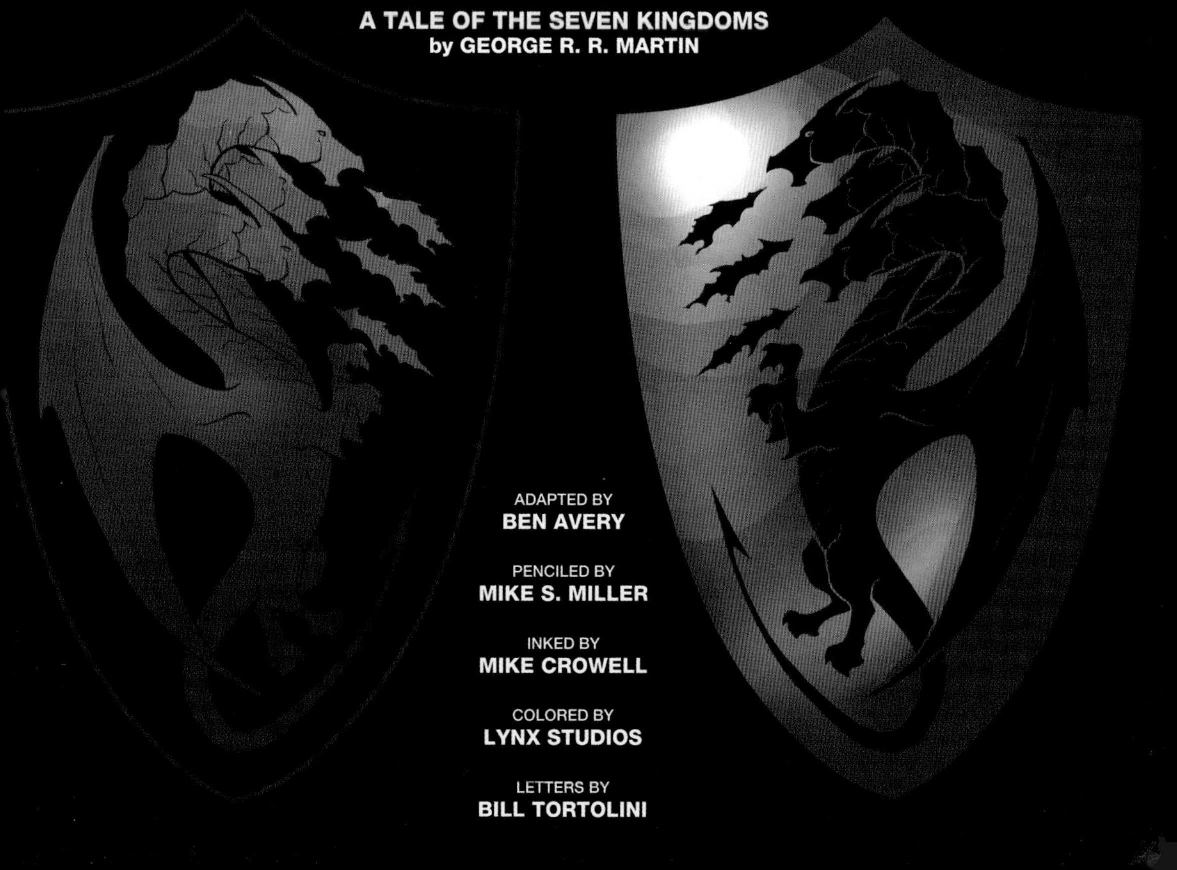

ADAPTED BY
**BEN AVERY**

PENCILED BY
**MIKE S. MILLER**

INKED BY
**MIKE CROWELL**

COLORED BY
**LYNX STUDIOS**

LETTERS BY
**BILL TORTOLINI**

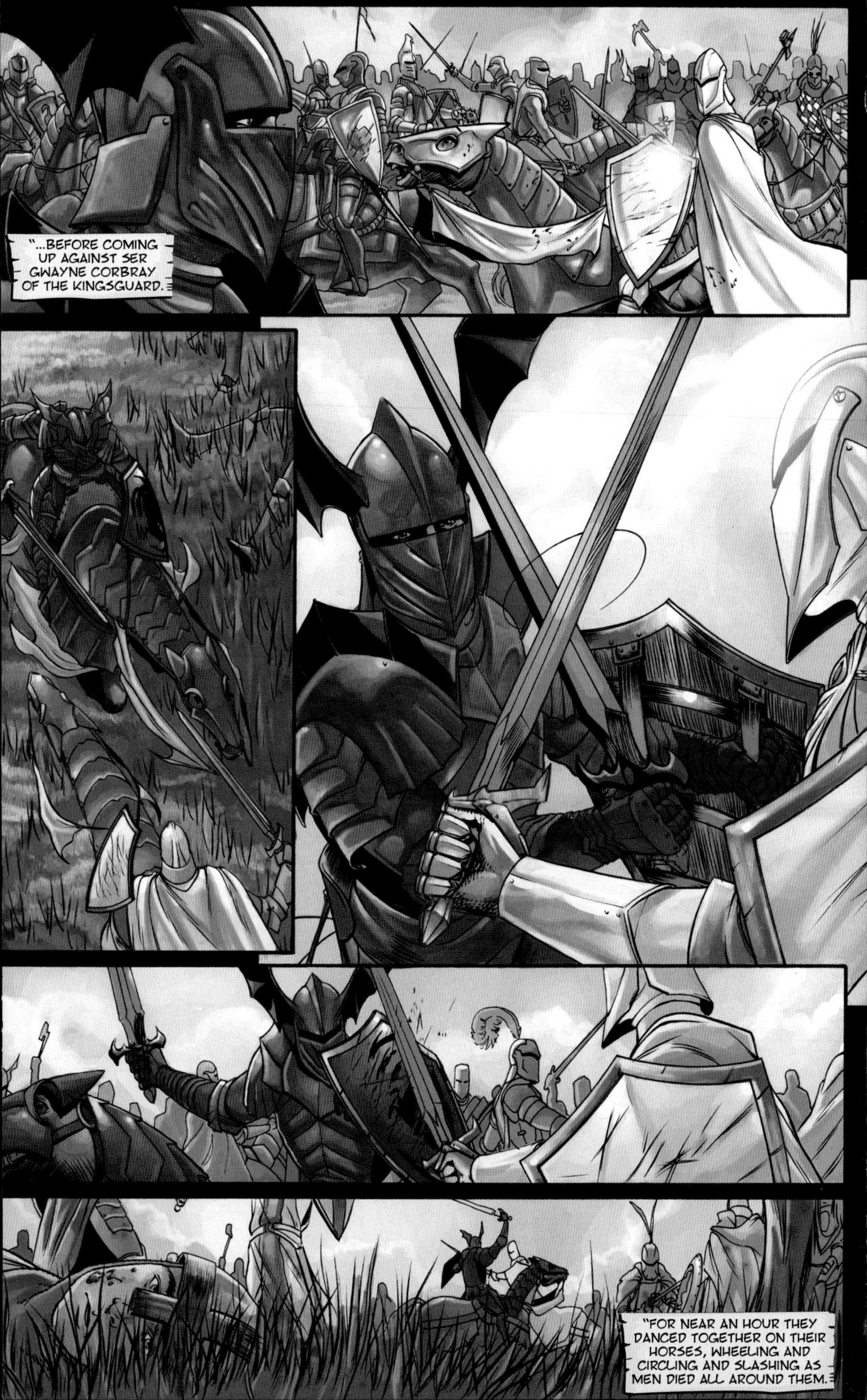
"...BEFORE COMING UP AGAINST SER GWAYNE CORBRAY OF THE KINGSGUARD.
"FOR NEAR AN HOUR THEY DANCED TOGETHER ON THEIR HORSES, WHEELING AND CIRCLING AND SLASHING AS MEN DIED ALL AROUND THEM.

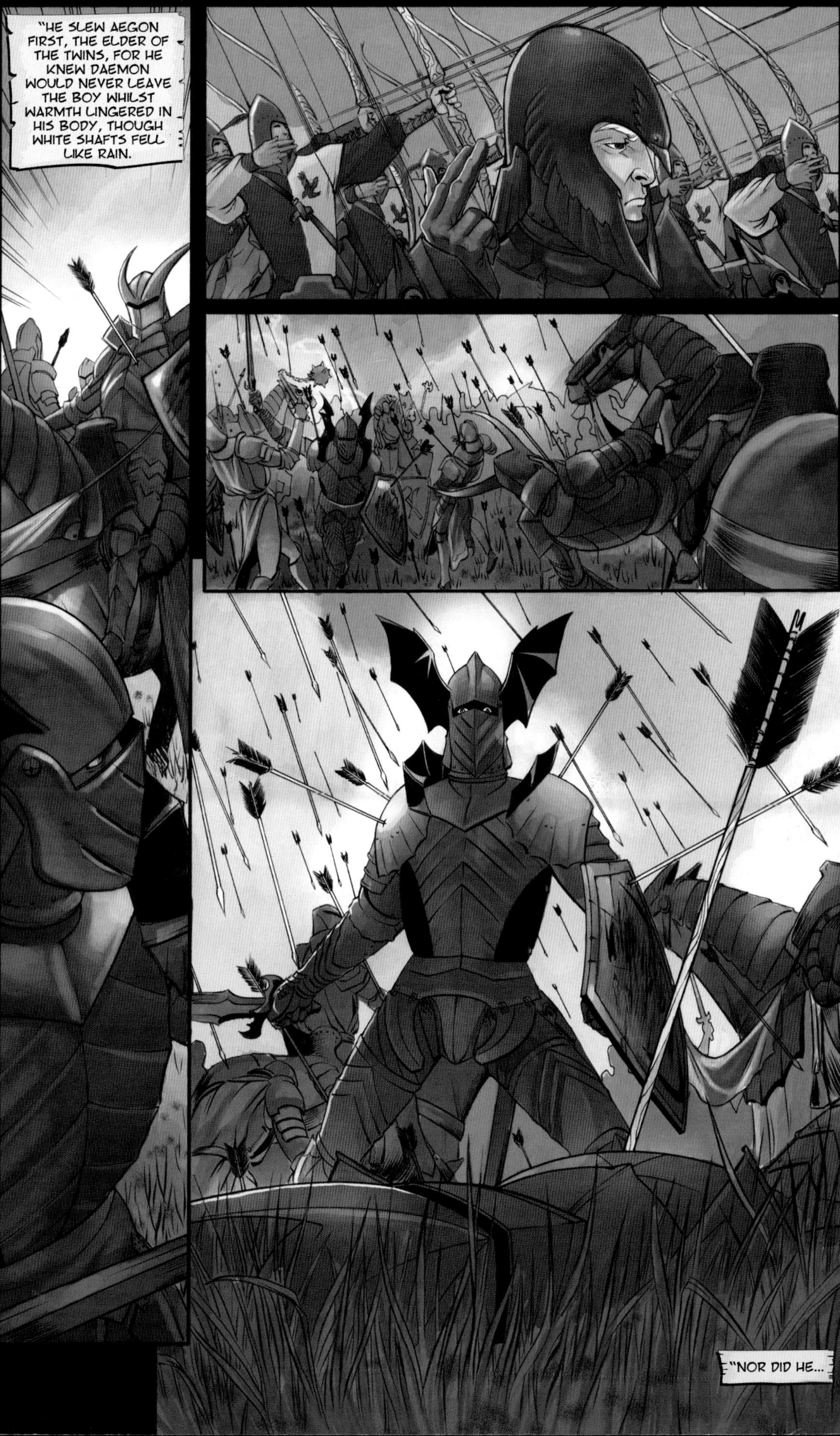
"HE SLEW AEGON FIRST, THE ELDER OF THE TWINS, FOR HE KNEW DAEMON WOULD NEVER LEAVE THE BOY WHILST WARMTH LINGERED IN HIS BODY, THOUGH WHITE SHAFTS FELL LIKE RAIN.
"NOR DID HE...

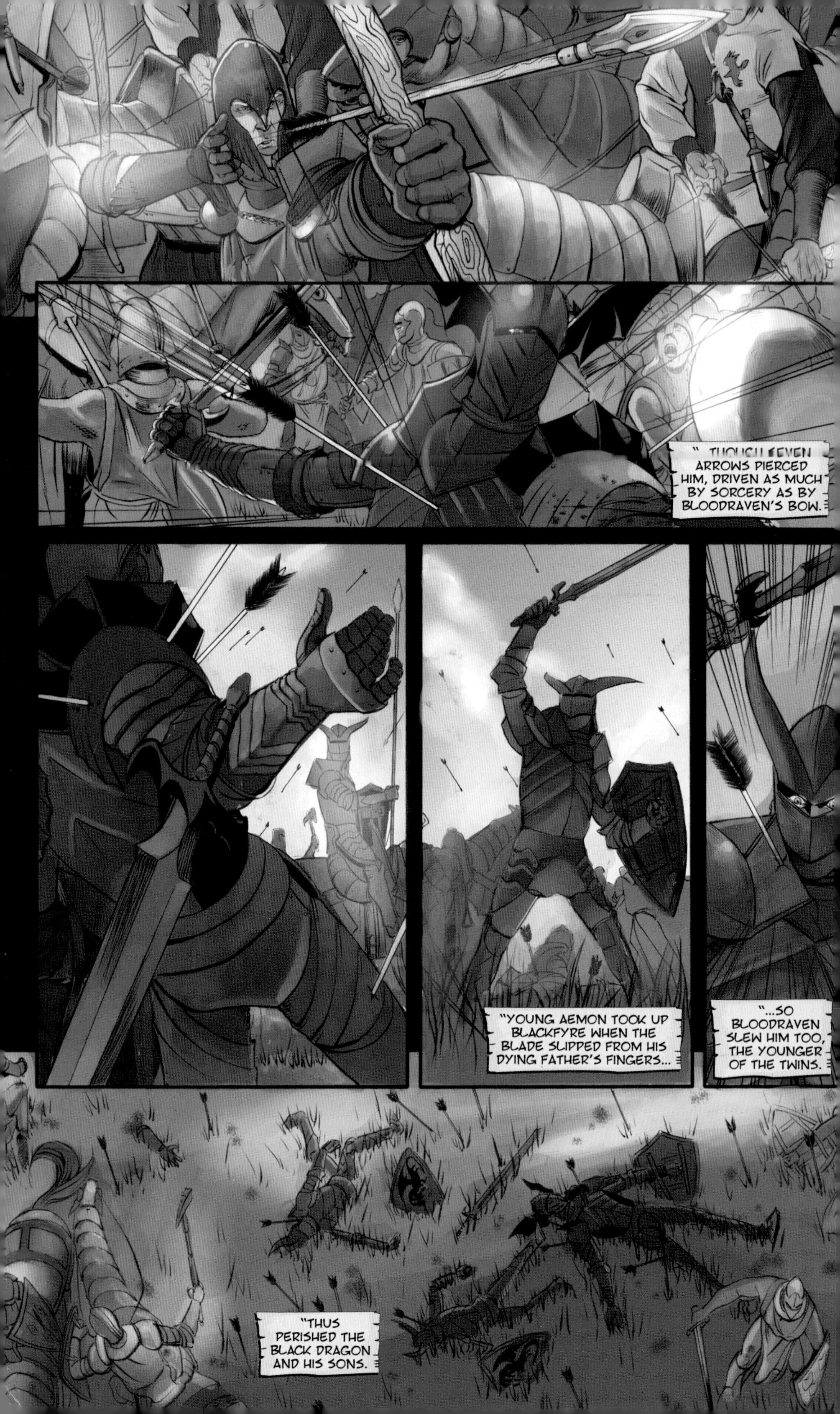
"THOUGH SEVEN
ARROWS PIERCED
HIM, DRIVEN AS MUCH
BY SORCERY AS BY
BLOODRAVEN'S BOW.
"YOUNG AEMON TOOK UP BLACKFYRE WHEN THE BLADE SLIPPED FROM HIS DYING FATHER'S FINGERS...
"...SO BLOODRAVEN SLEW HIM TOO, THE YOUNGER OF THE TWINS.
"THUS PERISHED THE BLACK DRAGON AND HIS SONS.

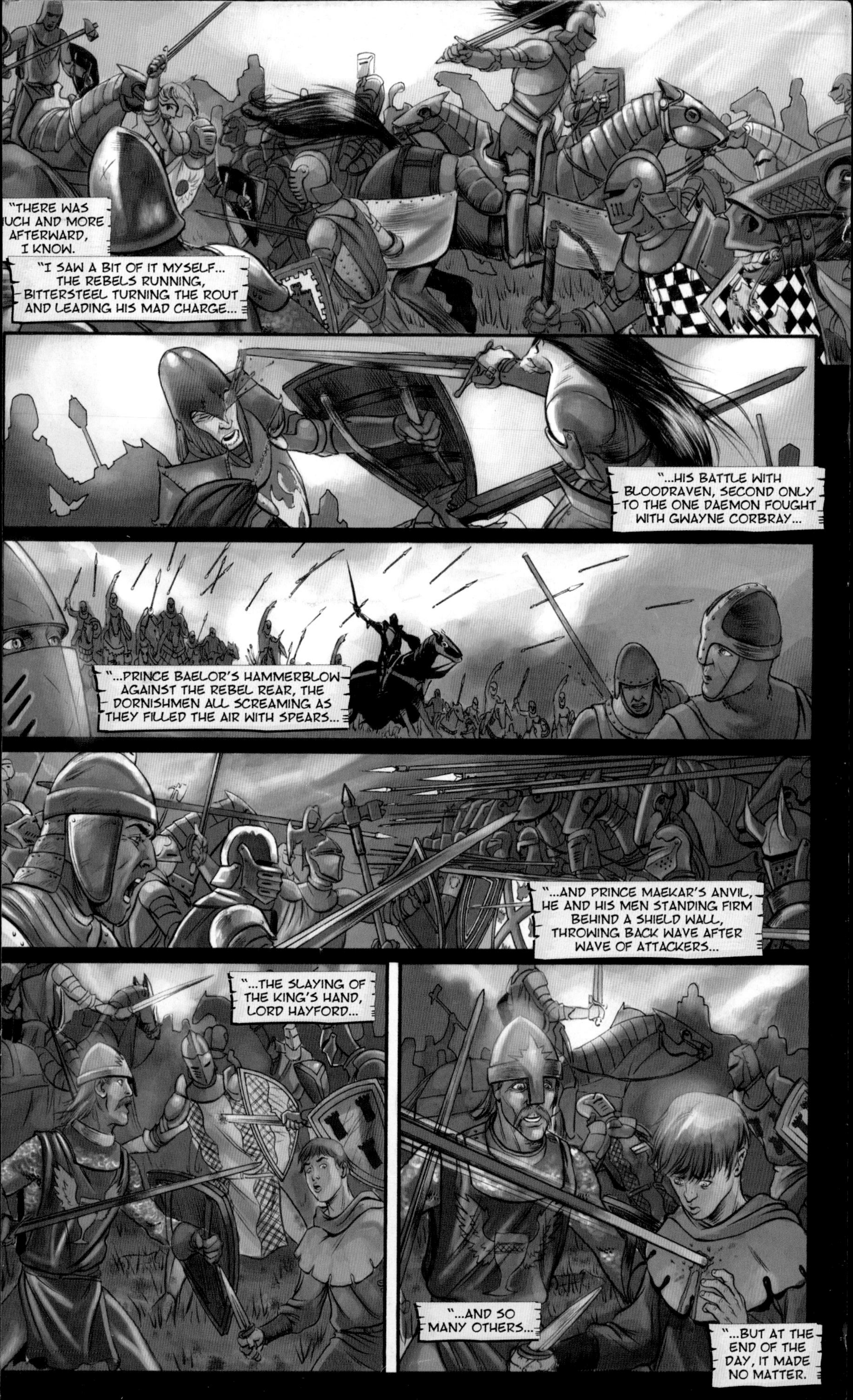
"THERE WAS
MUCH AND MORE
AFTERWARD,
I KNOW.
"I SAW A BIT OF IT MYSELF... THE REBELS RUNNING, BITTERSTEEL TURNING THE ROUT AND LEADING HIS MAD CHARGE...
"...HIS BATTLE WITH BLOODRAVEN, SECOND ONLY TO THE ONE DAEMON FOUGHT WITH GWAYNE CORBRAY...
"...PRINCE BAELOR'S HAMMERBLOW AGAINST THE REBEL REAR, THE DORNISHMEN ALL SCREAMING AS THEY FILLED THE AIR WITH SPEARS...
"...AND PRINCE MAEKAR'S ANVIL, HE AND HIS MEN STANDING FIRM BEHIND A SHIELD WALL, THROWING BACK WAVE AFTER WAVE OF ATTACKERS...
"...THE SLAYING OF THE KING'S HAND, LORD HAYFORD...
"...AND SO MANY OTHERS...
"...BUT AT THE END OF THE DAY, IT MADE NO MATTER.

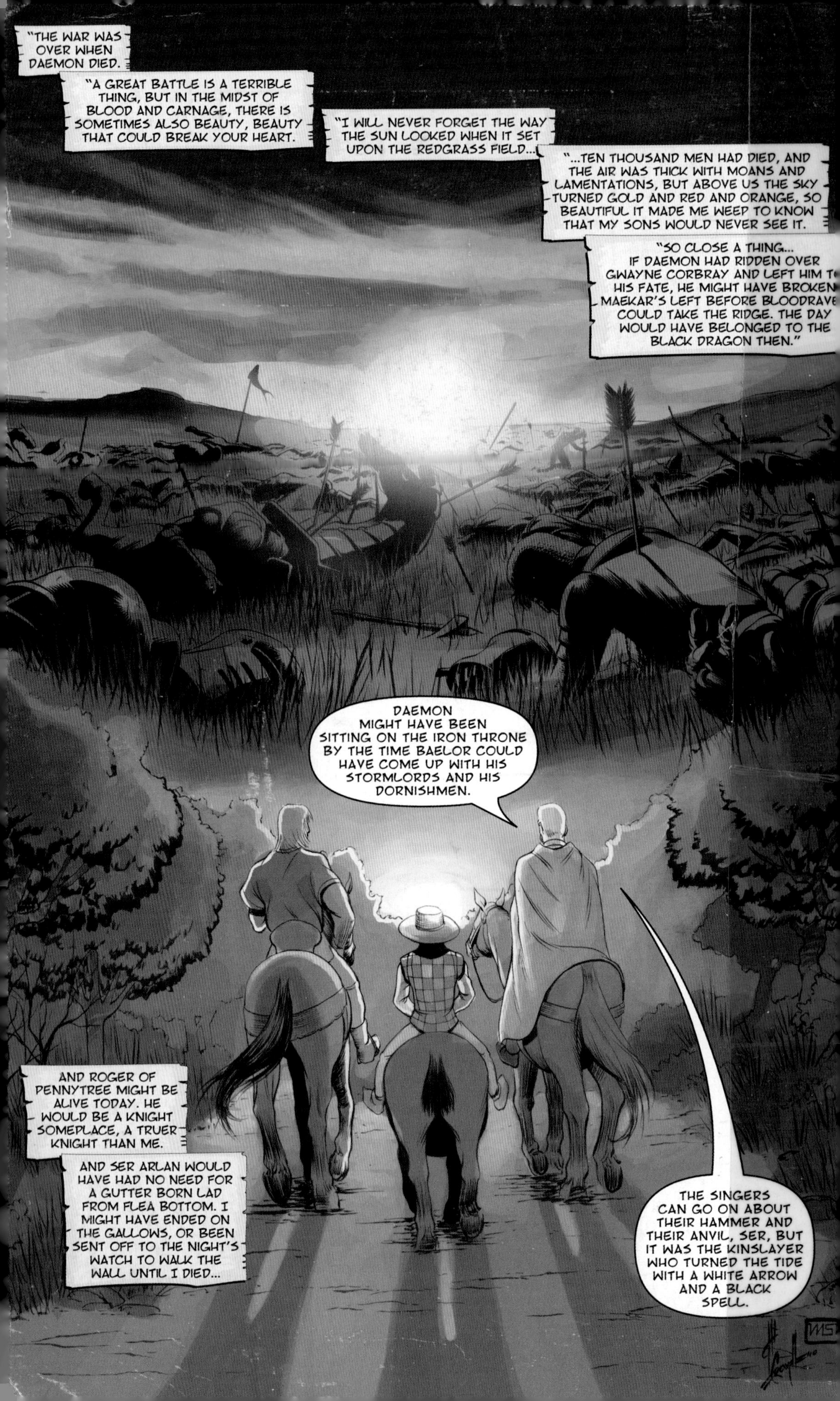
"THE WAR WAS OVER WHEN DAEMON DIED.
"A GREAT BATTLE IS A TERRIBLE THING, BUT IN THE MIDST OF BLOOD AND CARNAGE, THERE IS SOMETIMES ALSO BEAUTY, BEAUTY THAT COULD BREAK YOUR HEART.
"I WILL NEVER FORGET THE WAY THE SUN LOOKED WHEN IT SET UPON THE REDGRASS FIELD...
"...TEN THOUSAND MEN HAD DIED, AND THE AIR WAS THICK WITH MOANS AND LAMENTATIONS, BUT ABOVE US THE SKY TURNED GOLD AND RED AND ORANGE, SO BEAUTIFUL IT MADE ME WEEP TO KNOW THAT MY SONS WOULD NEVER SEE IT.
"SO CLOSE A THING... IF DAEMON HAD RIDDEN OVER GWAYNE CORBRAY AND LEFT HIM TO HIS FATE, HE MIGHT HAVE BROKEN MAEKAR'S LEFT BEFORE BLOODRAVEN COULD TAKE THE RIDGE. THE DAY WOULD HAVE BELONGED TO THE BLACK DRAGON THEN."
DAEMON MIGHT HAVE BEEN SITTING ON THE IRON THRONE BY THE TIME BAELOR COULD HAVE COME UP WITH HIS STORMLORDS AND HIS DORNISHMEN.
AND ROGER OF PENNYTREE MIGHT BE ALIVE TODAY. HE WOULD BE A KNIGHT SOMEPLACE, A TRUER KNIGHT THAN ME.
AND SER ARLAN WOULD HAVE HAD NO NEED FOR A GUTTER BORN LAD FROM FLEA BOTTOM. I MIGHT HAVE ENDED ON THE GALLOWS, OR BEEN SENT OFF TO THE NIGHT'S WATCH TO WALK THE WALL UNTIL I DIED...
THE SINGERS CAN GO ON ABOUT THEIR HAMMER AND THEIR ANVIL, SER, BUT IT WAS THE KINSLAYER WHO TURNED THE TIDE WITH A WHITE ARROW AND A BLACK SPELL.
MS